Mixed Signals

ALSO BY KATHRYN SIKKINK:

Ideas and Institutions: Developmentalism in Brazil and Argentina (1991)

Activists beyond Borders: Advocacy Networks in International Politics
　　(coauthor, 1998)

The Power of Human Rights: International Norms and Domestic Change
　　(coeditor, 1999)

Restructuring World Politics: Transnational Social Movements, Networks, and Norms
　　(coeditor, 2002)

MIXED SIGNALS

U.S. Human Rights Policy and Latin America

KATHRYN SIKKINK

A CENTURY FOUNDATION BOOK

Cornell University Press

Ithaca and London

Copyright © 2004 by The Century Foundation, Inc.

First published 2004 by Cornell University Press

Printed in the United States of America

Library of Congress Cataloging-in-Publication Data

Sikkink, Kathryn, 1955–
    Mixed messages : U.S. human rights policy and Latin America /
Kathryn Sikkink.
        p. cm.
    Includes bibliographical references and index.
    ISBN 0-8014-4270-2 (cloth : alk. paper)
    1. Human rights–Latin America.   2. Civil rights–Latin America.
3. Democracy–Latin America.   4. Latin America–Relations–
United States.   5. United States–Relations–Latin America.   I. Title.
JC599.L3S55 2004
323'.098–dc22   2004007159

Cornell University Press strives to use environmentally responsible suppliers
and materials to the fullest extent possible in the publishing of its books.
Such materials include vegetable-based, low-VOC inks and acid-free papers
that are recycled, totally chlorine-free, or partly composed of nonwood fibers.
For further information, visit our website at www.cornellpress.cornell.edu.

Cloth printing   10 9 8 7 6 5 4 3 2 1

For my sons, Daniel and Matthew Sikkink Johnson, with love

Contents

Foreword

Our nation is founded on bedrock beliefs in individual freedom and individual rights. In the early days of the Republic, of course, many basic rights, including the right to vote, were limited to white male property owners. But over more than two centuries, our concept of and support for human rights has broadened both at home and, increasingly, abroad. The effort to expand and defend these rights continues to this day. The story of the progress we have made, however, is not a straightforward tale of constant improvement but rather one that more often involves two steps forward, one step back.

The historical unevenness of America's commitment to rights may be especially relevant today when the nation is a prime target for terrorists and our willingness to maintain and extend human, civil, and legal rights is being tested in new ways. In fact, when the history of the current "American Era" is written, we can only hope that if anything is remembered as truly exceptional about our nation it will be our abiding commitment to basic human rights in the face of extraordinary dangers.

The Century Foundation has long believed in the importance of examining events beyond America's borders. During World War II, the Twentieth Century Fund, as we were then named, under the leadership of Evans Clark, joined many other nongovernmental organizations in activities aimed at promoting human rights and establishing the United Nations. After the war, we supported research and writing on economic, social, and political conditions in many countries across the globe.

Our interest in other nations did not begin to focus on human rights issues and policies aimed at dealing with them until later. Starting in the late 1980s, we backed research that resulted in books looking at the role of the United Nations, such as Rosemary Righter's *Utopia Lost: The United Nations and World Order;* reports examining related issues, such as Alan Dowty's *Closed Borders: The Contemporary Assault on Freedom of Movement;* explorations of our nation's attempts to deal with the problems inherent in achieving more humanitarian societies, such as Howard J. Wiarda's *The Democratic Revolution in Latin America* and Tony Smith's *America's Mission: The United States and the Worldwide Struggle for Democracy in the Twentieth Century;* and studies of the problems created by ethnic conflict, such as David Callahan's *Unwinnable Wars: American Power and Ethnic Conflict,* as well as a series of reports on preventive action that could ease conflicts between groups, which culminated in Barnett Rubin's *Blood on the Doorstep: The Politics of Preventive Action.* We also set up a distinguished international task force to examine what steps needed to be taken to ensure adherence to the international rule of law in situations such as that in Bosnia; the result of that effort was the publication of *Making Justice Work: The Report of the Task Force on Apprehending Indicted War Criminals.*

This volume extends the tradition of our support for work on these issues. Kathryn Sikkink, a professor of political science at the University of Minnesota, traces the modern history of human rights, especially as it emerged from the determination among many people to make a better world after World War II. She reports extensively on the place of human rights concerns during the construction of the United Nations. While she provides a knowledgeable global perspective on U.S. policy and human rights, a considerable portion of the book is focused on her specialty, U.S. relations with Latin America. In the second part of the book, for example, she demonstrates how intellectual rigor can be brought to the task—often seen as highly subjective—of evaluating the success or failure of human rights policies. Her case studies of several Central and South American nations also provide specific examples of how this analytical approach can be useful in practice.

Sikkink has spent much of her career examining these issues, and her understanding and insight are apparent in this book. She tells the epic tale of the emergence of human rights issues in Washington policy circles especially well, reciting battles lost and won along the way to the modern status of rights as a critical part of U.S. foreign policy. This history would be known to every schoolchild if we paid as much attention to the struggles for human rights in the hemisphere as we did to the wars and other violent campaigns conducted over the same time span. There are heroes (and villains) aplenty in this story, some immediately recognizable, such as Eleanor Roosevelt, and others probably known only to specialists, such as Hernan Santa Cruz of Chile and Donald Fraser, a leader in Congress and then in the executive branch.

In the current era, as Sikkink's analysis makes clear, while human rights have a powerful legitimacy in international affairs, U.S. administrations frequently have chosen courses of action with troubling implications. She documents, for example, the recent history of U.S. rejection of international treaties "with teeth." In other words, while her book is generally replete with great successes for human rights advocates, it also makes clear how much more needs to be done.

Kathryn Sikkink's topic is at the heart of one of America's self-proclaimed goals for itself. And, her book should provoke self-appraisal that is especially necessary as we struggle with the threat of terrorism. We need to recognize that it may be among the most dangerous self-delusions to believe that one's own people are somehow above human failings. We are all too human. And, we need to be brave, most of all, in addressing our own shortcomings. In the long run, we shall certainly be a stronger people for having, even under pressure, sustained the courage of our convictions.

On behalf of the Trustees of The Century Foundation, I commend Kathryn Sikkink for bringing her lifetime of knowledge and commitment to this important topic.

RICHARD C. LEONE, PRESIDENT
The Century Foundation
May 2004

PREFACE

The U.S. ambassador was worried. He feared that the government in the country where he was posted was not receiving a strong disapproval signal from Washington for its human rights violations. The foreign minister had just returned from an official visit to Washington, where he had met with the vice president and other high-level officials. The vice president had urged the foreign minister to "diminish the terrorist problem quickly." The U.S. secretary of state had told him, however, that "if the terrorist problem was over by December or January," he believed "serious problems could be avoided in the U.S." But U.S. officials had failed to stress human rights or the rule of law in their discussions about winning the war on terrorism. The foreign minister was euphoric. After his successful visit he now believed that there would be no confrontation between the two countries over human rights.

Is this Pakistan, or Colombia, or Israel in 2004? No, we are talking about Argentina in 1976. Admiral Cesar Guzzetti, the foreign minister, traveled to Washington in October of that year to seek support from the United States at a time when agents of the Argentine state were kidnapping and "disappearing" political opponents. For the previous six months Robert Hill, the U.S. ambassador, had been trying to raise human rights concerns with the Argentine military junta. He had assured the Argentine government that human rights issues were of real concern to the U.S. government. He protested cases of disappearances and death. But, Hill noted in a cable to Washington, "Guzzetti went to the U.S. fully expecting to hear some strong, firm, direct warning of his government's human rights practices. Rather than that, he has returned in a state of jubilation convinced that there is no real problem with the U.S. government over this issue."[1]

This is just one example of many where the U.S. government has given mixed signals about its commitment to promoting human rights and the rule of law as part of foreign policy. Those mixed signals were most frequent in situations of civil war, guerrilla movements, or acts of terrorism. Latin American military governments often interpreted these cues as green lights to fight terrorism without concern for human rights or the rule of law.

The problem of terrorism did not begin with the 2001 attacks on the World Trade Center. Latin American militaries have long used the language of a "war on terrorism" to describe their struggles against domestic guerrilla movements. U.S. counterinsurgency policy in the late twentieth century addressed these unconventional wars. The excesses and mistakes of counterinsurgency wars taught us some lessons. The most important: a war on terrorism fought without regard to the rule of law can lead to massive violations of human rights. States, in responding to guerrilla actions, engaged in what has been called state terrorism. They imprisoned, tortured, and killed thousands of their own citizens. If we in the United States forget this history and its relevance to our current struggles, we run the risk of once again being complicit with repression.

We learned some other lessons. The only long-term solution to the problem of terrorism is one that promotes democracy, human rights, and the rule of law. This is not naïve idealism. It describes a painful process that most of Latin America has passed through in the last three decades. Most of these countries now have functioning democracies and are building the rule of law. The message that Ambassador Hill gave to the Argentine military in 1976 is as relevant to the war against terrorism today as it was to the "dirty war" then.

Hill said to Guzzetti that "We fully understand that Argentina is involved in an all-out struggle against subversion. There are, however, some norms which can never be put aside by governments dedicated to the rule of law. Respect for human rights is one of them." Hill urged the Argentine government to make a statement "deploring terrorism of any kind, whether from left or right, and reaffirming the government's resolve to enforce law and respect human rights."[2]

When Guzzetti met in New York with Henry Kissinger, then secretary of state, he heard a different message. Guzzetti told Kissinger, "Our struggle has had very good results in the last four months. The terrorist organizations have been dismantled." Kissinger replied, "Look, our basic attitude is that we would like you to succeed. I have an old-fashioned view that friends ought to be supported. What is not understood in the United States is that you have a civil war. We read about human rights problems but not the context. The quicker you succeed the better. The human rights problem is a growing one. . . . We want a stable situation. We won't cause you unnecessary difficulties. If you can finish before Congress gets back, the better."[3]

These high-level diplomatic meetings are important for the cues that officials convey about the central meaning of U.S. policy. Argentine officials took away very clear cues from their conversations with Kissinger and Vice President Rockefeller in 1976. Their impression was that the U.S. government's "overriding concern was not with human rights but rather that the government of Argentina 'get it over quickly.'"[4] Kissinger and Rockefeller essentially gave Guzzetti a green light for repression. At the time Kissinger had this conversation, Argentine armed forces were engaged in some of the most extreme repression of the dirty war.

Other cues were possible. Ambassador Hill tried to send them but was overruled by his superiors. When President Carter came into office in 1977, his administration sent fairly consistent high-level cues that the U.S. government cared about human rights and that the tenor of U.S.–Argentine relations would depend on the human rights situation. Such cues were not limited to Democratic administrations. Officials in the Reagan administration sent clear cues to Chile in 1989 that they supported a yes vote in the plebiscite that would end Pinochet's term in office. The first Bush administration finally sent a clear cue to El Salvador that it supported a negotiated resolution to the civil war, one that guaranteed protection of human rights. Broadly speaking, these policies were successful examples of U.S. support for human rights and the rule of law in societies that faced civil wars or armed guerrillas.

In some ways, the research for this book began when, as an undergraduate exchange student from the University of Minnesota, I arrived in Montevideo, Uruguay, in April 1976. Uruguay had been under increasingly authoritarian rule since 1973, and by 1976 the regime's human rights violations had started to draw international attention. Shortly before I left for Uruguay, Amnesty International had launched its first ever "country campaign" targeting Uruguay— a tactic that would become a staple of its later work. As part of the campaign, Amnesty published a report on Uruguay, prompting the *New York Times* to run an editorial entitled "Uruguay: Torture Chamber of the Americas." In Uruguay, I came to understand the human rights situation through the lives of Uruguayans I met. Some of my friends and acquaintances at the university had been imprisoned and tortured. Fear pervaded their lives. Everyone knew someone in prison.

While in Montevideo, I interviewed staff people at the U.S. embassy. The 1976 election campaign was well under way, and challenger Jimmy Carter had started to use human rights language to criticize the foreign policies of President Ford and Secretary of State Kissinger. I was curious about what people in the embassy in Uruguay were saying about human rights. Only one of the embassy staff people I interviewed admitted that they thought the Amnesty International report was accurate. The others told me that their boss, Ambassador Ernest Siracusa, assured them that the report was highly misleading. Siracusa was quoted in the *Washington Post* of April 21, 1976, saying that the Amnesty International report of "massive arrests" was "grossly exaggerated."

Talking to these foreign service officers about their jobs, I realized that their attitudes about human rights had been influenced by their ambassador, their job descriptions, and the general ethos of the foreign service. They were doing their jobs, and that meant following the ambassador's instructions and talking to people in the Uruguayan government. In preparation for my trip, I had read Philip Agee's book *Inside the Company,* an exposé by a former CIA official that included a detailed description of his work in Uruguay. Agee describes sitting in the central police station in Montevideo and listening to a person being tortured in another room.[5] Some people inside the U.S. embassy had extensive contacts with the Uruguayan military and were complicit with their practices. But many others were basically well-meaning people, trying to do their jobs and, if possible, to move ahead in the foreign service to more interesting placements. Their ability to make sense of the situation in Uruguay was constrained by a foreign service that did not consider human rights an appropriate topic for foreign policy.

Years later, I interviewed Lawrence Pezzullo, who served as President Jimmy Carter's ambassador to Uruguay. Pezzullo arrived at the embassy shortly after I left Uruguay in 1977. "It really was shocking. We had an embassy in Uruguay that was an apologist for the Uruguayan government. . . . They knew nothing. . . . You've got to sift out fact from fiction. An embassy can find out things if you want to. Once you find them out you can stand your ground. We had no factual evidence at the embassy. . . . How many in prison? In what conditions? Who does it? Who tortures? Where? Who gives instructions?"[6] In 1965, CIA officer Agee had been able to learn who the Uruguayan police tortured, where, and who gave the instructions. But apparently he did not report this information to his ambassador or to other employees at the embassy.[7] We need to ask not only what the embassy knew, but *who* in the embassy knew about human rights violations.

Ambassador Pezzullo suggested that the first ingredient of good policy is good information. "How can we make policy about political prisoners if we don't even have an idea of how many there are?" Pezzullo asked his staff. Around the same time, a State Department official echoed Pezzullo's concerns in a meeting in Washington, D.C. "It is a sad day for American diplomacy and for the American foreign service when the reporting from the Methodist church in Uruguay is more accurate than from our embassy in Montevideo."[8] Under Pezzullo, the embassy determined that there were over four thousand political prisoners, and the staff began to work on getting them released.[9] But much more important than the issue of good information was Ambassador Pezzullo's new way of thinking about foreign policy in Uruguay. He used a human rights framework that directed him to ask different questions and give different cues. This human rights framework to U.S. foreign policy had its beginnings in the U.S. Congress in the mid-1970s.

One morning in early 1976 I opened one of Uruguay's heavily censored newspapers. To my surprise, I found a full transcript of a hearing on human rights in Uruguay held in the U.S. House of Representatives under the leadership of Donald Fraser, the representative of my home district in Minneapolis. The Uruguayan newspapers during the dictatorship never published anything about human rights violations. What was going on? I bought another newspaper. The same transcript was there—more than a full page spread. Every newspaper carried the same. I was mystified. The transcript was the talk of the town. No one understood why it had been published. One rumor said that the U.S. embassy had insisted it be published; my interviews with embassy staff convinced me this wasn't the case. Others guessed that the Uruguayan military ordered the transcript to be published, because they hoped that the discussion of Uruguay in the halls of the U.S. Congress would outrage nationalist sentiment.[10] But at least in my circles the transcript provoked disbelief rather than backlash. People had come to expect the United States to support authoritarianism, and yet here was a part of the U.S. government condemning human rights violations by the Uruguayan military. In September 1976, the U.S. Congress voted to discontinue military aid to Uruguay on human rights grounds, demonstrating that it could put its words into action in this case.

Twenty-five years after my stay in Uruguay, I arrived in Guatemala City to conduct research on human rights. Once again, I had read the reports of domestic and international human rights organizations before I arrived. One of the most detailed reports was the annual State Department country report, which provided an exhaustive summary of the human rights situation in Guatemala. I arrived at a U.S. embassy that looked like the one in Uruguay, concrete and boxy, with tight security regulations. Inside the embassy, however, the situation was different. I could now address my questions to a human rights officer, Jason Donovan.[11] Within five minutes I learned he had contacts with members of all the human rights organizations where I had been interviewing. He provided names and phone numbers for other people I had hoped to reach. He picked up the phone and arranged for me to meet with a judge I wanted to interview. Donovan was one of a new breed who had entered the foreign service after the Cold War. He had his opinions about the quality and reliability of different human rights organizations, but he didn't question the purpose of integrating human rights issues in U.S. foreign policy. That day, he was helping arrange for the U.S. ambassador, Prudence Bushnell, to meet with Guatemalan judges. The trial for the murder of Bishop Gerardi was beginning, with members of the Presidential Guard as defendants. The house of one of the young judges had been bombed just the day before the trial opened. The meeting of ambassadors from the United States and Europe with the judges was designed to underscore their support for an independent judiciary.

Still, the ambiguity of U.S. policy hadn't disappeared. Within this very embassy a few years earlier, U.S. officials had told Jennifer Harbury that they had no knowledge of her husband, guerrilla leader Efrain Bamaca, all the while knowing that he was being held and probably tortured by Guatemala security forces on the CIA payroll. As in Uruguay in the 1960s, the Bamaca case revealed that in the early 1990s the CIA was continuing to pay for information that it knew was being extracted through torture. To protect their sources, the CIA misled family members and the public about their practices.[12] U.S. officials continued to give contradictory cues on the issue of human rights.

These contradictions grew from an identity conflict at the heart of U.S. policy toward Latin America during this period. There was no one U.S. policy, no single vision of who or what the United States was and what it stood for. Nowhere was this conflict more evident than in U.S. policy toward Latin America. Since the 1950s, intense anticommunism had informed all aspects of U.S. policy in the region. This anticommunism was often justified by referring to the abysmal human rights practices of communist regimes. But by the 1970s, anticommunism led the United States to support, arm, and train authoritarian regimes that carried out massive human rights abuses against their citizens. In principle, anticommunism could be made compatible with a commitment to human rights, but U.S. policy makers in Latin America had come to accept as an article of faith that anticommunism required strong support for authoritarian military regimes.

Human rights policy offered a different policy framework. When it was consistently implemented, the United States switched from contributing to authoritarianism to joining coalitions in favor of democracy. In some cases, U.S. human rights policy helped get political prisoners out of jail, in others it saved lives. Overall, this transformation has led to less violence and less conflict in the region. It has improved the image of the United States in the western hemisphere, and it has generated positive support among the U.S. public for a foreign policy that includes a human rights agenda.

Some of this seems to have been forgotten in the wake of the terror attacks of September 11, 2001. A human rights framework helps us see September 11 as a crime against humanity. The victims of this crime are entitled not only to our deepest sympathy but also to justice, either in our courts or in an international tribunal. A vigorous campaign is necessary to investigate the crimes of September 11, to bring the perpetrators to justice and to prevent future crimes of this nature. Coordinated international campaigns to track down the criminals, stop their sources of finance and weapons, and break their networks are essential. But a human rights framework requires vigilance: the struggle against terrorism must not be used to justify human rights violations in this country or abroad. Yet in speech after speech, policy makers in the Bush administration subordinate all other foreign policy goals to the struggle against terrorism.

For someone familiar with the history of U.S.–Latin American relations, the new rhetoric of the war on terrorism sounds hauntingly familiar. Authoritarian governments in Latin America have justified their human rights abuses in the name of fighting terrorism. Yet those governments adopted state terror to fight guerrilla insurgencies. They used the very instruments of their opponents, and in the process they fed the spiral of violence rather than ended it. Some aspects of U.S. policy after 9/11 repeat these mistakes. The United States is using the imperative of a war on terror to justify repressive practices, including prolonged detention without charges or access to lawyers, and torture and degrading treatment of prisoners, as in the case of the Abu Ghraib prison in Iraq. We need constantly to stress the importance of fighting terrorism while respecting human rights and the rule of law.

In the late 1970s, virtually all Latin American countries had repressive authoritarian regimes. Now, despite continuing human rights problems, almost all are democratic. By the 1980s and early 1990s, Latin America benefited from a dynamic and democratic civil society, a commitment to human rights by a wide range of regional actors, and regional human rights institutions and mechanisms in the inter-American system. Latin American countries are playing new leadership roles in global politics. U.S. human rights policy toward the region has been one small but important piece of this transformation.

Human rights policy represented a dramatic and unexpected policy change. This change wasn't predestined or obvious. It was the result of a struggle over the heart of U.S. policy that took place in the 1970s through the early 1990s. It involved the intense efforts of individuals and groups who worked for decades, both in Latin America and in the United States, to build a policy with greater respect for human rights and international law.

Some see human rights policy as yet another naïve, flawed campaign to impose U.S. values on the world. But human rights policy is different, I believe, because it grew out of a more genuinely multilateral impulse after 1945 in which the United States took leadership but was not the sole instigator. Many other countries helped build multilateral human rights institutions in the postwar period, during which the United States, consumed by the crusade of the Cold War, was often absent. When the U.S. Congress rediscovered human rights in the early to mid-1970s, it could draw on these international norms and institutions rather than project U.S. power and values unilaterally. Because U.S. human rights policy now draws on this broader international normative and legal consensus, it has a better chance of success.

Human rights is not just a doctrine governing a small subarea of foreign policy—it is an overarching policy paradigm on a par with containment, anticommunism, or antiterrorism. This book takes human rights doctrine seriously as one of the most important shifts in U.S. policy since the advent of containment. It traces the origins and authors of human rights policy and then evaluates the successes and limitations of that policy in Latin America, where it has been implemented most fully and over the longest period of time.

After his release from prison, Jacobo Timerman, an Argentine editor who had been clandestinely imprisoned by the Argentine military regime, was asked what difference U.S. human rights policy made. His reply: "America gets impatient with human rights, restless. You don't see the accomplishment. Do you expect to change a government with a policy? No, if you want to change a government you have to send in the Marines. What a human rights policy does is save lives. And Jimmy Carter's policy did. How many? I don't know. Two thousand? Is that enough? But the policy is even more important to you than to us. It builds up a democratic consciousness in the United States."[13]

Timerman recognized that U.S. human rights policy not only affects lives abroad, it is also essential for defining and redefining our identity in the United States—who we are as a people and what we stand for.

Acknowledgments

It seems especially appropriate that The Century Foundation supported the writing of this book because it was among the groups that during the Second World War publicized the idea of internationally protected human rights. The Century Foundation, then called The Twentieth Century Fund and represented by Evans Clark, was present at the main meetings of nongovernmental organizations to discuss war aims and postwar organization, and signed key letters and telegrams urging support for human rights and the founding of the United Nations. The efforts of The Twentieth Century Fund exemplify the numerous actions of individuals and NGOs that contributed to the decisions to include human rights provisions in the Charter of the United Nations and to draft a Universal Declaration of Human Rights. The language of the Universal Declaration of Human Rights, in turn, provided the starting point for U.S. human rights policy in the 1970s. I am deeply grateful to Michelle Miller-Adams, previously at The Century Foundation, who first envisioned and encouraged this book, and to Greg Anrig, who saw it through to its completion.

Because I have been working on this book for such a long time, my intellectual debts are immense. The inspiration for this book and the development of ideas that inform it came from chapters I wrote on different aspects of human rights policy toward Latin America for edited volumes and special issue projects. In particular I thank my various coauthors, editors, and coeditors for their feedback and support: Lisa Martin, Ellen Lutz, Hans Peter Schmitz,

Thomas Risse, Margaret Keck, Martha Finnemore, Stephen Ropp, Robert Putnam, Peter Evans, Harold Jacobson, Robert Keohane, Judith Goldstein, Lawrence Whitehead, Elizabeth Jelin, and Manuel Antonio Garreton.

My husband, Douglas Johnson, has been a constant source of inspiration, information, and support. I have learned more from him over the years than I can express. I give special thanks to my colleague David Samuels, who read an entire draft and gave me excellent comments. Without the intellectual and moral support of my dear friend and colleague Sally Kenney, I might not have ever finished this book. My colleague Daniel Kelliher gave me terrific advice on how to improve the preface and the introduction. The extraordinary group of human rights intellectuals and activists in Minneapolis, including David Weissbrodt, Barbara Frey, Cheryl Thomas, and Donald Fraser, provided feedback, information, and the general intellectual atmosphere where human rights scholarship can thrive. I have benefited greatly from the research assistance of talented students, including Ann Towns, Petrice Flowers, Mayra Gomez, Helen Kinsella, Jonneke Koomen, Ben Faltesek, and Douglas Olson.

For insights and assistance of various kinds, I also thank Cynthia Arnson, William Leogrande, Darren Hawkins, Martin Kifer, Carlos Osorio, Thomas Carothers, Jo-Marie Griesgraber, Margaret Levi, Jamie Mayerfeld, Robert Pastor, Lars Schoultz, Beth Simmons, Catalina Smulovitz, and Carlos Acuña. I presented chapters or pieces of chapters to panels at meetings of the International Studies Association; to the Political Science Department of the University of Washington; to a workshop at the Woodrow Wilson Center in Washington, D.C.; to the case-study group at the Center for Women and Public Policy of the Hubert Humphrey Center for Public Affairs at the University of Minnesota; and to a class on human rights law at the University of Minnesota Law School. I benefited greatly from the comments and encouragement of participants in each of these places.

I have learned much from the many people I have interviewed and from friends and colleagues in Latin America. Although I include only a fraction of those interviews in this book, all helped inform my perspective. In particular, I thank F. Allen "Tex" Harris, Marie-Claire Acosta, Patricia Valdez, Juan Mendez, Luis Moreno Ocampo, Emilio Mignone, Angela and Federico Westerkamp, and Rodolfo Stavenhagen.

This book is dedicated to my sons, Daniel and Matthew Sikkink Johnson, with love. It is written in the hope that when they are old enough to read and understand this volume, the motto *Nunca más* (Never again) will have become a reality throughout the Americas.

K. S.

MINNEAPOLIS, MINNESOTA

PART ONE

The Origins of Human Rights Policies

CHAPTER ONE

Introduction to the Origins of Human Rights Policies

Human rights issues permeate international relations today. Human rights have been called "the dominant moral vocabulary of foreign affairs" and "the single most magnetic political idea of the contemporary time."[1] Yet we are also in a period when human rights are increasingly imperiled. Major episodes of human rights violations, such as those in the former Yugoslavia and in Rwanda, coexist with significant improvements in human rights in other regions, especially in Latin America and Eastern Europe. After the attacks of September 11, 2001, some commentators questioned whether the "human rights era" had come and gone.[2] The question recognizes the prominence that human rights vocabulary and policy had gained since the end of the Cold War. How can we explain the rise of the human rights era? Are the reports of its demise premature?

Until recently, many policy makers thought that human rights was a "moral" concern that was not an appropriate part of foreign policy. At congressional hearings on U.S. policy in Brazil in 1971, the U.S. ambassador to Brazil approvingly quoted President Nixon, saying, "We hope that governments will evolve toward constitutional procedures but it is not our mission to try to provide, except by example, the answer to such questions to other sovereign nations. We deal with governments as they are."[3] At the same hearings one of the harshest congressional critics of U.S. policy in Latin America, Senator Frank Church, affirmed this notion of nonintervention. "How Brazilians organize their own affairs and how they treat each other are not proper concerns of the U.S. Senate." But he went on to say, "How the various agencies of the U.S. Government conduct themselves in Brazil and how they react to events here, however, are proper concerns of all Americans."[4]

Yet by 1996, President Clinton could state that the "overarching objective" of U.S. policy in the western hemisphere "is to preserve and defend civilian-elected governments and strengthen democratic practices respectful of human rights."[5] At the same time, in the last twenty-five years of the twentieth century, regional norms on democracy and human rights became stronger and regional institutions to implement those norms became more effective. The countries of the Americas modified the Charter of the Organization of American States (OAS) to permit the organization to suspend a member country when democracy was overthrown by a coup. New norms helped the OAS address democratic crises in Guatemala, Haiti, Peru, Paraguay, and Venezuela.

In this book I examine this important shift in foreign policy in the second half of the twentieth century, and specifically between 1973 and 1993: the incorporation of human rights as an integral and legitimate part of foreign policy. Where did these ideas and policies come from, and what kind of impact have they had? In Part I, I explore the origins of human rights policies, and in Part II, I examine their effectiveness. In this chapter, I set out the main questions of the book: What is a human rights policy? Why do states adopt human rights policies? What are the origins of the international human rights norms and U.S. human rights policy? When, and under what conditions, can human rights policies be effective? This chapter answers the first question and provides a theoretical framework to answer the second. Chapters 2 and 3 provide a historical overview of human rights policies to answer the second and third questions. The remaining chapters address the fourth question through an examination of U.S. policy and specific cases in Latin America. So, if you are familiar with the origins of human rights policies and want to read about effectiveness, you should turn directly to Chapter 4, which provides a theoretical and historical introduction to Part II of this book.

What Is a Human Rights Foreign Policy?

Types of Human Rights Ideas

Human rights are ideas about how individuals are entitled to be treated merely by virtue of being human. Over time, these ideas have gained widespread acceptance as norms defining what is necessary for humans to thrive. Human rights aim both to protect humans from abuses and to provide them with the elements necessary for a life of dignity. Human rights are social constructions. You can't see or touch them. People invented human rights, and they exist only because people believe and act as if they exist. I say this not to trivialize rights but to underscore the power of ideas. Torture is all too real. We can see or touch the instruments of torture and some of the wounds they leave. But the belief that a person has a *right* not to be tortured is a powerful idea that people have constructed over the last two centuries. Nothing intrinsic in the human body gives us a right not to be tortured. It is only our shared belief that produces the right, and our shared work on behalf of that right is what makes the right effective. These constructions have the capacity to shape the social and political world. They have gripped the human imagination and exerted a powerful impact on world politics.

The idea that the state should respect the human rights of its citizens is an old one, dating back at least to the Declaration of Independence and the Bill of Rights in the United States and to the Declaration of the Rights of Man and Citizen in France. We can call this the idea of the "rights of citizens." Although the early advocates of rights believed in principle that people in all countries were entitled to human rights, in practice the documents they developed granted rights mainly to citizens. This book is about the much newer idea that human rights should be an integral part of foreign policy and international relations.[6] This *"global* human rights idea" gained ground only in the second half of the twentieth century. In principle, it means that we are concerned about human rights violations wherever they occur, and that borders are not barriers to the protection of rights. In practice, the idea is excruciatingly difficult to implement. The global human rights idea is a logical extension of the idea of the rights of citizens, and yet efforts to put the two ideas into practice are separated by almost two hundred years.

When Thomas Jefferson wrote that "all men are created equal" and that they are endowed with "certain inalienable rights," he did not put limits on who was entitled to those rights, in terms of race, sex, ethnicity, or citizenship. But in practice, there were many limits. Only men with property possessed most of those rights; women, slaves, and Native Americans were excluded, and few thought about protecting the rights of citizens in other countries. Even then, however, some visionaries thought borders didn't matter when talking about rights. The marquis de Lafayette and the Englishman Thomas Paine saw themselves as part of a transnational struggle for human rights.

In general, early partisans of rights struggled in their own countries but kept out of the politics of other countries. They recognized the limits imposed by sovereignty—the idea that it was nobody else's business what a ruler did within his own borders. There have been so many exceptions to this idea that one author has called it "organized hypocrisy."[7] Still, for the broad range of issues that today we call human rights, the general understanding before the mid-twentieth century was that these issues were not a matter of international concern.

World War II and the Holocaust revealed the great moral flaw and the resulting human tragedy of this arrangement. They also reinvigorated an older belief that governments engaged in appalling mistreatment of their own people were also more likely to be aggressive toward other countries. For these reasons, the idea that human rights concerns should be a matter of foreign policy and international relations gained force after World War II.

Yet a link remained between the two conceptions of citizen's rights and global human rights. In many countries, including the United States and many of the countries of Latin America, the earlier struggle for the rights of citizens had imprinted the idea of rights in the very identity of the nation. People understood that rights were an integral part of who they were as a country and what they stood for. This "rights identity" created responsiveness to ideas about rights in the international arena. When the newer idea of global human rights reappeared, it resonated strongly in countries where rights were historically seen as part of national identity.

Sovereignty and human rights concerns have long been seen to conflict with each other. And yet, in the last two decades, international human rights policies have been able to coexist successfully with the sovereign state. Why? A state is actually exercising its sovereignty when it signs human rights treaties. Only a recognized sovereign state can sign an international treaty. Puerto Rico or Palestine, for example, cannot sign a human rights treaty. But a human rights treaty may limit a state's freedom of action in its domestic affairs. Human rights treaties and agreements may essentially "invite" other countries to challenge sovereignty by intervening in how a government treats its own citizens.[8]

So, for example, when Augusto Pinochet's authoritarian government in Chile ratified the Torture Convention (Convention against Torture and Other Cruel, Inhuman or Degrading Treatment or Punishment), he surely didn't intend to invite other countries to hold him responsible for torture during his government. But when the British Law Lords considered whether Pinochet could be extradited to Spain to stand trial for human rights abuses in Chile, they decided the language of the convention was clear. The Torture Convention called for universal jurisdiction: a torturer or an agent of the state who ordered torture could be put on trial in any country for his crime. The Law Lords determined that Pinochet could be held accountable for acts of torture during his government in Chile after 1988, when he ratified the Torture Convention. Because Chile had ratified the treaty accepting universal jurisdiction, it could no longer be considered a violation of its sovereignty to hold it to the language of the treaty.

Most governments clearly recognize the implications of human rights policy for their sovereignty. This is a particularly important issue in Latin America, where national sovereignty has long been jealously guarded. So, for example, when the Inter-American Commission on Human Rights took up three Mexican cases of electoral irregularities in 1989–90, the Mexican government adopted a rigid position that a decision of a domestic electoral body "is not and cannot be subject to international jurisdiction." The Mexican government argued that if a "State agreed to submit itself to international jurisdiction with respect to the election of its political bodies, a State would cease to be sovereign," and thus any conclusion issued by the commission would constitute an act of intervention in the internal affairs of the Mexican state.[9]

The commission did not accept the argument of the Mexican government, which eventually reformed its electoral laws along the lines suggested by the commission. In retrospect, the Mexican government appeared to be overreacting, since it certainly didn't "cease to be sovereign." Yet the Mexican government's argument underscores how fundamental understandings of sovereignty were altered as a result of human rights doctrine and practice in the region.

The Mexican government had ratified a treaty, the American Convention on Human Rights, recognizing the competence of the Inter-American Commission of Human Rights. Because these international treaties or conventions are voluntarily agreed to as formal invitations to oversee domestic practices, they can't be seen as violations of sovereignty. Nevertheless, countries frequently complain that their sovereignty is violated when international organizations do what the state "invited" them to do when it ratified the treaty. Why governments would agree voluntarily to curtail some of their basic sovereign attributes is a curious question. Why states adopt human rights policies is the main question I'll try to answer in part 1 of this book.

Human Rights and State Identity

One key contribution of recent international relations theory is the notion that state identity fundamentally shapes state preferences and actions.[10] According to this argument, states don't adopt certain foreign policies just because it is in their interest. They adopt them because state officials believe they live in the kind of state that *should* adopt such policies. So, for example, the United States may promote democracy abroad because both citizens and state officials believe that we have a democratic identity, and that states with a democratic identity should promote democracy abroad. This doesn't mean that interests have nothing to do with policy, but it does mean that we often need to know what kind of identity a state has before we can gauge how it understands its interests.

State identity involves important understandings of self, of what a state is, of what it stands for. For example, the United States is the world's largest producer of soybeans, but this fact doesn't form part of our identity because we do not perceive it as an important part of who we are. Identity is also about self-understandings, not about objective truth, or how we are perceived by others.

Identity is often defined by differences. Citizens or leaders of states come to know or understand their state's identity by contrasting it with other states. Some theorists stress the centrality of "danger" and "threat" as ways of defining differences and establishing identities. "Discourses of danger . . . by virtue of telling us what to fear, have been able to fix who 'we' are."[11] We might call this a "negative" definition of identity: we know who we are by knowing what we are not and what we fear. This aspect of identity has come into play vividly since September 11, 2001. Many U.S. citizens and state officials define U.S. identity in relation to their fear of terrorism.

A more positive vision of identity stresses those aspects of nationhood in which leaders and the public either take "special pride" or view as "more or less unchangeable."[12] We know who we are by knowing what we are proud of (or what we can't change). U.S. leaders are proud of our democracy, and this pride forms part of our identity. These two understandings of identity—the identity of fear and the identity of pride—are two sides to a single coin, but the matter of emphasis is important. Theorists of the identity of fear believe that states must continue to find or manufacture threats to sustain themselves.[13] An identity of pride holds the possibility that state identity can exist without the constant invoking of danger.

We know that identity contributes to a human rights policy when a country's leaders justify the policy in terms of national pride, danger, or some mix of the two. Because the United States and most states in Latin America are civic communities, where the basis of citizenship is not religion, ethnicity, or blood but shared ideals or values, identity has been particularly important. U.S. identity stresses individual civil and political rights, equality of opportunity, anti-statism, and rule of law. These are belief systems or foundational myths, not empirical realities. Foreign policies congruent with this national identity will find more support among the population.[14] But U.S. foreign policies don't follow obviously or easily from these ideas about identity. Often very different foreign policies lay claim to the same identity and to the same foundational myths. Foreign policy debates are debates not only about what we should do abroad but about who we are as a people. Identity isn't a thing we can know and see, but despite its illusive quality, some leaders have been effective in invoking an understanding of U.S. identity that resonates broadly with American public opinion. Leaders promoting human rights policies have been particularly successful in invoking U.S. identity in support of their foreign policy goals.

The concept of state identity comes from recent debates in international relations theory, but it is very similar to older concepts that scholars and foreign policy makers have talked about for years. Debates over what some call the "heart" or "soul" of foreign policy are often debates over state identity and its role in foreign policy. Scholars sometimes refer to national character, national purpose, national impulse, political culture, self-image, or vision as an explanation for foreign policy.[15] These arguments about the role of self-image in foreign policy have been particularly important in explanations of U.S. foreign policy.[16] Since leaders may be divided on their beliefs about national character, foreign policy debates are often about which vision of national identity should prevail and how it should shape policy.[17] For example, in the United States, different understandings of U.S. identity have influenced the prolonged debate over whether to pursue foreign policy through multilateral or unilateral means.[18]

Beliefs and Human Rights

Beliefs about state identity are not the only ideas that are important for understanding human rights policy. Even policy makers and advocates who agree that human rights should be a part of foreign policy often differ as to what kinds of policies can most effectively address human rights abuses. So, for example, policy makers disagree about whether cutting foreign aid to a country leads to an improvement in human rights practices. Because these disagreements are about causes and effects, you can use evidence to evaluate them.[19] We shall do so in part 2.

Human rights ideas also address larger causal arguments about national interest. In foreign policy making, there is considerable uncertainty not only about what constitutes the national interest but also about how it can be promoted. For example, even if we agree that it is in U.S. interests to promote stable regimes in the Third World, it is far from clear what leads to stability. During the Cold War, U.S. policy makers believed they were promoting national interests by supporting anticommunist regimes, regardless of their internal human rights practices. By the mid-1970s, people began to question the causal assumption that support for repressive anticommunist regimes led to stability. An important group of "norm entrepreneurs" argued that the best way to promote stability was to defend human rights and democracy.[20] While some policy makers advocated human rights policy solely from a principled stance, most mingled principle and causal reasoning in their justification of the human rights policy. They argued that it was both immoral and counterproductive for long-term U.S. interests to support regimes that violated human rights. Social science research has produced good evidence to support the causal argument that promoting democracy furthers peace. Many quantitative historical studies have shown that although democracies are not peaceful per se, they do not initiate war with other democracies.[21] It is indeed likely, therefore, that it is in the long-term security interests of the United States to support democracy and human rights abroad.

Two Parts of a Human Rights Policy

A human rights foreign policy has two related but analytically separate parts: a bilateral policy and a multilateral policy. States have a bilateral human rights policy when their foreign policies systematically take human rights in other states into account. States have a multilateral human rights policy when they show they are willing to submit their *own* internal human rights practices to some international review.

States with both parts have a comprehensive human rights policy. The United States has a bilateral policy but not a multilateral policy. As a result, many other countries don't take our human rights commitments seriously because we aren't willing to submit our internal human rights practices to external scrutiny. The United States is a laggard in multilateral policy but a leader in bilateral human rights policy; it was the first country to explicitly incorporate human rights into bilateral foreign policy legislation.

States adopt a multilateral human rights policy when they ratify treaties or accept specific mechanisms for multilateral supervision of domestic human rights practices. To be categorized as having a multilateral human rights policy, countries must have ratified a human rights agreement with teeth: enforcement powers that permit a supranational institution like a regional human rights court to oversee internal human rights practices. Examples of such treaties with teeth include the European Convention of Human Rights, the American Convention on Human Rights, and the Rome Statute of the International Criminal Court. Signatory countries agree to submit their own human rights practices to the supervision of a court, whether the European Court of Human Rights, the Inter-American Court of Human Rights, or the International Criminal Court. Treaties with teeth allow individuals and other states some mechanisms for lodging complaints for alleged human rights violations by a state or by individuals acting on its behalf. The United States has been unwilling to ratify any international human rights treaty with teeth. We have not

---

IMPLEMENTATION OF BILATERAL HUMAN RIGHTS POLICIES

Implementation of bilateral human rights policies can take many forms, from private diplomatic discussions to the use of military intervention. We might think of bilateral human rights policies as arrayed along a continuum from mild to severe. The continuum includes:

- private diplomatic discussions;
- public diplomatic statements;
- information generation and dissemination, such as the State Department Reports on Human Rights Practices;
- reprioritizing aid decisions to reflect human rights goals;
- human rights training programs for military, police, or judicial personnel;
- sanctions, including trade sanctions and arms embargoes;
- implementing human rights policy through the judicial branch;
- participation in multilateral human rights verification and promotion missions; and
- military intervention to pursue a human rights goal.

These different policies are often used in coordination with one another.

---

ratified the American Convention on Human Rights or accepted the compulsory jurisdiction of our regional human rights court, the Inter-American Court of Human Rights. We have "unsigned" the Statute of the International Criminal Court and have even sought to undermine the court. As a result, many countries consider our support for human rights hypocritical.

The second part of a human rights foreign policy involves the projection of human rights values internationally through a bilateral human rights policy. A bilateral policy does not imply that human rights issues are taken into account in all bilateral foreign policy decisions. Rather, a country has a bilateral policy when it has adopted explicit mechanisms for integrating human rights concerns into foreign policy. Such mechanisms have significantly modified foreign policy decisions in some cases. For example, in the United States before 1973, human rights issues were rarely considered in the foreign policy calculus; after 1976, legislation and executive policy led to the explicit inclusion of human rights criteria in foreign policy (see box).

TABLE 1.
Four Possible Outcomes of Human Rights Policies

Does a country have a bilateral human rights policy?	Does a country have a multilateral human rights policy?	
	Yes	No
Yes	I. Comprehensive human rights policy (e.g., European Union, Canada)	II. External human rights policy only (U.S.)
No	III. Multilateral human rights policy only (e.g., most of Latin America)	IV. No human rights foreign policy

If we summarize the two aspects of human rights policy—bilateral and multilateral—in a 2 × 2 table, we see four possible outcomes of human rights policy (see table 1).

The United States is the only country in Europe and the Americas to have a bilateral policy but no multilateral policy. Most Latin American countries have accepted the compulsory jurisdiction of the Inter-American Court of Human Rights and/or have ratified the statute of the International Criminal Court, and thus have multilateral policies, but many do not yet have explicit bilateral human rights policies. The historical trend is a gradual but clear movement toward the adoption of human rights policies. Before World War II no country in the world had a human rights policy. By 2000 the United States, all countries of the European Union, and most countries in Latin America and Eastern Europe had some kind of human rights policy.[22]

Human rights ideas entered foreign policy debates in the immediate postwar period in the United States, Europe, and Latin America. These three regions differ, however, with respect to the timing of policy selection, the targets of human rights pressures, and the instruments or channels used to implement policy.

In Europe multilateral human rights policies have been present constantly since World War II, gradually increasing in their comprehensiveness throughout this period. In the United States, after a flurry of activity in the postwar period, human rights policies virtually disappeared for twenty years, only to resurface in the early 1970s. Latin American countries started earnestly enforcing a regional regime for the promotion of human rights and democracy only after the wave of the most repressive regimes in modern Latin American history ended in the mid-1980s and early 1990s. Yet by 2003, every major country in the region had a multilateral human rights policy except the United States and Cuba.[23]

Why Do States Adopt Human Rights Policies?

Human rights policies are puzzling. Why do states adopt multilateral policies that limit their discretion and infringe upon their sovereignty? Why do states adopt bilateral human rights policies that can prove costly and provoke hostility? Why should one government care how another government treats its own citizens? When we ask why states adopt human rights policies, we are actually asking two interrelated questions: Why do states adopt multilateral human rights policies? and Why do they adopt bilateral human rights policies? In particular, we are interested in why the United States is the only country to have a bilateral human rights policy but no multilateral one.

We will consider five different theories to explain the adoption of human rights: realism, critical theories, liberalism, institutionalism, and ideational theories. *Realists* argue that powerful states can do as they wish in international politics. Many countries are hostile to the idea of international supervision of their domestic human rights practices, but the most powerful state, or the hegemon, can afford to flaunt the rules. Realist theory leads us to expect that powerful states will adopt human rights policies only if they promote their interests, and other states will adopt such policies if they are embraced and espoused by the hegemon.[24] According to this view, human rights norms spread when they reflect the concerns of powerful states and when these states are willing to force weaker countries to adopt these principles and norms.[25] So, for example, some realists would argue that the United States supports civil and political rights because they help sustain a liberal capitalist order that benefits the United States economically.

But realist theorists don't provide a convincing explanation for why hegemonic states are willing to pursue human rights norms in the first place. Why did the British decide to use their naval power to end the slave trade, and eventually to end slavery, at great cost? Nor does realism help us understand why one powerful country that wasn't previously concerned with human rights adopted a human rights policy when it did. Why did the United States adopt a human rights policy in the 1970s but not before? What do we make of crucial episodes of human rights changes, such as women's suffrage, or the global campaign against apartheid, where hegemons were followers, not leaders?

Like realists, *critical theorists* see the adoption of human rights policies as instances of domination by the powerful, but they place more emphasis on how the powerful use language (or what they call discourses) to make the exercise of power possible.[26] For critical theorists, human rights discourses reflect and reinforce relations of power.[27] In one version of critical theory, wealthy countries of the North use human rights discourses to help them form their identities in contrast to developing countries of the South.[28] Countries in the North represent themselves as virtuous protectors of rights and portray peoples and countries in the South as "rights abusers," thereby justifying the North's political, economic, and cultural domination. Roxanne Doty, a critical theorist, sees human rights as a modern variant of historical discourses like colonialism, used to justify control by the powerful and the classification and surveillance of the Third World. For Doty, U.S. human rights legislation "has less to do with human rights and more to do with the promotion of U.S. security and the representation of the United States as a world power capable of exercising moral leadership."[29] Critical theorists believe their work unmasks domination, but they may fail to distinguish between the political implications of different types of language and policy. Are colonialism and human rights policies really so similar that it is useful to think of them as two types of domination and surveillance? Weren't human rights discourses used in the struggle against colonialism?

The critical theorists' position on human rights policy is questionable if we consider that human rights policies originated as part of a global movement in which actors from the developing world were key protagonists. Human rights discourses have been used effectively to criticize, condemn, and change U.S. practices of domination, such as offering military aid and training to repressive allies who commit human rights abuses. Critical theorists are correct that human rights policies lead to the surveillance of other countries but miss that these policies have also permitted critics to monitor U.S. practices as well. It doesn't make sense to treat all discourses of monitoring and surveillance as equally problematic. Is monitoring Uruguay for torture the same as monitoring it for labor union activism, as Philip Agee did as a CIA agent there in the 1960s? What is the alternative to monitoring—a return to the old understanding of sovereignty, where it is no one's business how a government treats its citizens?

Liberal theory places more emphasis on the domestic sources of state preferences. In this model, individuals and groups in domestic society determine the preferences of states, and the nature and intensity of state preferences determine the outcomes of international politics. Whether or not a state is democratic determines which groups and individuals it represents.[30] Liberal scholars identify a community of "liberal states" as a sphere of peace, democracy, and human rights, and distinguish between relations among liberal states and those among liberal and nonliberal states.[31]

The type of regime (democratic, newly democratic, or authoritarian) becomes a crucial factor for liberals in explaining the adoption of human rights norms. Andrew Moravcsik argues that states accept binding human rights treaties mainly as a means of political survival. A newly democratized state is likely to ratify legal human rights instruments to protect its still unstable democratic regime against opponents that might attempt to overthrow it.[32]

Liberals claim that it may be self-interested and rational for some states to accept long-term limits to sovereignty, since human rights treaties with teeth could create real costs for any group that tries to overthrow the existing government. Liberal theory would not lead us to expect mature democracies to be at the forefront of building binding human rights norms and institutions because they face the least threat from internal opponents. Yet in the Americas, as we shall see in chapter 1, mature democracies have been at the forefront of efforts to create binding human rights regimes.

Finally, *ideational theories* explore the role of ideas and norms in effecting political change. These are often called "constructivist" theories because they are concerned with how human consciousness constructs the social world. An ideational approach suggests that the origins of many international norms lie in strongly held principles, ideas about right and wrong. These ideas, in turn, shape state perceptions of both its interests and its identity, which in turn determine state policies. We can't know the interests of states independently of the ideas and norms through which states interpret their interests and forge their identities.

In one version of ideational theory, state elites and nongovernmental organizations adopt human rights policies because they believe in them. Human rights norms are seen as intrinsically appealing to many individuals. To the ordinary reader, it may seem deceptively simple and even obvious that people might press for human rights policies because they believe in them. Scholars of international relations, however, spend much energy and time explaining why such an obvious idea is wrong, naive, and perhaps even dangerous. It is perfectly acceptable for political scientists to suggest that all humans have a drive for power or wealth. But to suggest that many humans intrinsically find certain human rights ideas appealing is somehow more questionable. Yet it does not strike me as particularly odd to suggest that everyone would prefer to be alive, free, secure, and well fed rather than dead, imprisoned, tortured, and hungry. It is more complicated but still plausible to suggest that many humans realize that to enjoy such rights themselves, they need to make sure they are guaranteed for others. Some people have come to believe it is both good and necessary to enhance the rights of people around the world.

Another version of ideational theory argues that state beliefs and preferences are shaped by a world culture.[33] This world culture sets the model of appropriate forms of state behavior, and states emulate these models. In such a society, states may change their behavior because they care about what leaders of other countries think of them. International law and international organizations are the main vehicles for stating world culture norms. In this version of ideational theory, ideas have a profound effect on behavior, but change occurs not so much because people believe in the ideas, but because they want to imitate the dominant ideas. The popularity of the idea is more important than its content, and human rights ideas are treated as similar to ideas about science ministries, census bureaus, or primary education.[34] They are all things that modern states need to have, so state leaders that aspire to modernity imitate these behaviors. According to this perspective, there may be a large gap between the formal adherence to international human rights norms and the actual behavior of states. State actors are drawn toward the rhetorical acceptance of human rights norms, but once they adopt human rights norms, they receive the benefits from superficial conformity and do not feel compelled to implement these norms.

But these theories can't give satisfactory explanations about which norms are likely to be intrinsically appealing or when they are likely to have an influence. Many authors using an ideational approach have pointed out that new ideas often emerge in response to dramatic policy failures or crises. This relationship between crisis and failure and the adoption of new ideas has been found across issue areas, countries, and time periods. Human rights norms have made the greatest strides in times of war, revolution, and crisis.[35] For example, the common revulsion toward the Holocaust provided the consensus needed to adopt the Universal Declaration of Human Rights. Because such major wars and crises are also moments when power and hegemony shift, it may be difficult to sort out the influence of changing ideas from that of changing power configurations. But power shifts tell us only about the form of international order, not about its content. We need additional information about prevalent norms and ideas to know the content of a new order.[36] My own and my coauthors' contributions to ideational theories focus both on states and international organizations and on nonstate actors like nongovernmental organizations. We argue that it is not enough for ideas to be intrinsically appealing; in order to be converted into international norms, they need a strong advocacy movement on their behalf. Transnational advocacy networks constantly represent and express this universal appeal and push state actors not only to sign but actually to implement and comply with those universal values.[37]

Institutional theorists stress the importance of institutions and institutional rules. Institutionalists contend that ideas have strong and continuous influence on policy only if they become embodied in institutions. The ideas that have been successfully implemented and consolidated are those that have acquired an institutional home, where a team of like-minded people transform their individual ideas into an institutional purpose. In the United States, human rights ideas were given official homes in new state institutions, such as the Bureau of Human Rights in the State Department, now the Bureau of Democracy, Human Rights, and Labor (DRL). These institutional homes helped sustain human rights policies when less sympathetic governments came into office. Regional and international institutions have also played important roles in the transmission of ideas, especially the human rights institutions of the United Nations and the regional human rights organizations in Europe and the Americas.

Institutional theory also points to the role of bureaucratic politics in explaining policy outcomes. Foreign policy is often the product of struggles and compromises among different bureaucratic actors. The Bureau of Human Rights had a bureaucratic interest in getting human rights policies adopted. But other agencies, like the Department of Commerce, could be expected to oppose human rights policies if they called for actions that would interfere with trade and investment. The outcome of policy debates often depends on which bureaucratic actor is able to win out in a particular policy debate.[38]

What institutional theories may miss is how these different bureaucratic interests were created or empowered and why their ideas are persuasive in some settings. A small and relatively powerless institution like the Bureau of Human Rights would not be expected to win out in many bureaucratic struggles. The power of its ideas, and the resonance of those ideas with policy makers and publics, sometimes gave it an influence beyond what would be expected from bureaucratic politics alone.

Institutionalists also focus on how institutional rules can have a significant impact on policy outcome. They claim that the reason why some countries ratify human rights treaties and others don't has to do with ratification rules. Governments ratify treaties in different ways. In particular, difficult U.S. treaty ratification rules help explain our failure to ratify human rights treaties. From a legal point of view, any legal form of treaty ratification is equally binding. But from a political perspective, different types of ratification rules mean that ratifications are not all the same. We need to take ratification rules into account to understand why countries ratify human rights treaties and others don't. In an authoritarian regime a single leader or an appointed council might decide to ratify. Once an authoritarian leader decides to ratify a treaty, he can be sure of a rapid rubber stamp. Not all democratic regimes have the same ratification rules. Most countries with parliamentary political systems ratify treaties with a majority vote of parliament. The rules of parliamentary systems are designed to allow the government to secure majority votes in the parliament, so such ratification should be unproblematic. It is more difficult to ratify treaties in countries with presidential systems because an executive submitting a treaty to the legislature cannot be assured of ratification, since a party other than that of the president may be in control. But most countries with presidential systems ratify treaties with a majority vote, and such votes are not difficult in most circumstances.

The United States has one of the most difficult ratification rules in the world: a supermajority (two-thirds) vote of the Senate. Such a vote is extremely difficult, because organized groups with strongly held minority views can mobilize one third of the Senate to block ratification. Usually presidents must invest high levels of political capital to get a treaty ratified. Jimmy Carter spent much time and engaged in much pork-barreling to get the Senate to ratify the Panama Canal Treaty. Given these rules, it is surprising that the United States has managed to ratify any human rights treaties at all. Yet we did ratify the Genocide Convention in 1984, the Covenant on Civil and Political Rights in 1991, and the Torture Convention in 1994.

Overview of the Argument

In this book, I present an argument that emphasizes ideational factors. One cannot understand the emergence and adoption of human rights policies in the postwar period, I believe, without taking into account the central role of human rights ideas. Without these powerful principled ideas, which are of great intrinsic appeal to a circle of activists inside and outside of governments, human rights policy wouldn't exist. In Europe these ideas had a direct impact on policy, leading to the emergence of the European human rights regime in the postwar period. In the United States, in contrast, the impact of human rights ideas was delayed. A convergence of factors blocked the advance of human rights ideas in the United States during 1953–73, especially the attitudes of cold warriors, segregationists, and so-called states' rights advocates. It was not until détente, public disillusionment with Vietnam, and the initial successes of the civil rights movement that human rights ideas led to changing foreign policy in the mid-1970s.

Ideas do not explain everything. I argue that the best explanations of why countries adopt human rights policies require attention both to ideas and to institutions. The most interesting question is not whether ideas and institutions matter for the adoption of human rights policies but *which* particular ideational and institutional arguments are most persuasive for explaining outcomes. So, for example, a focus on the ideas of policy makers would lead us to expect that human rights policy would have disappeared during the Reagan administration, when policy makers came into office who did not believe that human rights should be a part of foreign policy. Indeed, during the first years of the Reagan administration, policy makers first attempted to remove human rights from the central importance it had attained during the Carter administration. This effort failed in part for institutional reasons: human rights ideas were already embedded in U.S. law and in foreign policy institutions. The most important part of the U.S. bilateral human rights policy was the legislation that created the Bureau of Human Rights in the State Department and mandated that the bureau produce reports on human rights practices around the world. This legislation created the institutional home and the standard operating procedures that helped human rights policy be sustained and grow over time. Institutionalist theories are also essential to understanding U.S. failures to adopt a multilateral human rights policy. If the United States had a majority ratification rule, I believe it would have ratified many of the human rights treaties endorsed by European and Latin American states, including at least one with enforcement power.

A better understanding of the emergence and diffusion of human rights norms on a global scale represents a crucial contribution to international relations scholarship. However, such norms matter in the world only if rhetorical commitments actually lead states to improve their human rights practices. The second part of the book therefore asks under what conditions a human rights policy can be effective. When do human rights policies and norms lead to improvements in human rights behaviors? There is not a clear linkage between the ratification of human rights treaties and actual human rights practices. Because ratification is easiest in an authoritarian state, countries that ratify human rights treaties don't necessarily treat their citizens well.[39] So, why should we care about ratifying human rights treaties if they don't lead directly to better human rights practices? Because ratification of human rights treaties is seen as an important symbol of a country's commitment to the human rights idea. We need to be aware that for many people around the world, U.S. failure to ratify these treaties undermines our capacity for leadership in the area of human rights. Recently, the United States has not only failed to ratify human rights treaties but the administration of George W. Bush "unsigned" the statute of the International Criminal Court and actively lobbied other governments not to abide by its provisions. Officials in the administration claim that they were responding to flaws in the statute. Because of the symbolic importance of these treaties, however, such action is often interpreted abroad as reckless disregard for international rule of law.

The emergence of human rights policy is not a simple victory of ideas over interests. It demonstrates the power of ideas to reshape understandings of national interest. The adoption of human rights policies does not represent a neglect of national interests but rather signifies a fundamental shift in the *perception* of long-term national interests. Indeed, human rights policies emerged because policy makers began to question the causal assumption that U.S. national interests are furthered by supporting repressive regimes that violate the human rights of their citizens and the related assumption that other countries' internal human rights practices are not a legitimate topic of foreign policy.

I also point to the importance of nongovernmental human rights organizations in introducing human rights ideas and reinforcing human rights policies. Transnational advocacy networks are important both for adopting human rights policies and for helping ensure that states actually abide by these norms. By the 1980s, these groups had become so well organized and internationally integrated with like-minded organizations that one can speak meaningfully of a transnational human rights movement. This is a variant of the ideational-institutional approach. Human rights networks were the primary carriers of human rights ideas into policy debates and acted as a lobby for human rights policies in the United States and Latin America.

Once human rights policies were introduced into the foreign policy arena, they had an unusual resonance among both publics and policy makers. This is because of the intrinsic appeal of the idea of human rights to U.S. and Latin American audiences. Why did this idea appeal to the U.S. audience? John Ruggie suggests that successful efforts to achieve American engagement in the world "entailed the role of imagery, ideas, and justification." At each moment leaders "linked the pursuit of American interests to a transformative vision of world order that appealed to the American public." But the American public was not willing to buy just any vision of world order. Those visions that were most congruent with America's understanding of its own founding principles were most likely to appeal to the public.[40]

The idea of basic rights of the individual is a key part of U.S. identity. A human rights policy thus resonated with long held understandings of state identity. But human rights policy also came into conflict with long-held foreign policy traditions and practices, in particular the practice of respecting state sovereignty. It also came up against another powerful vision of American identity that resonated with the very same founding myths: anticommunism as a global crusade for freedom.

In a society traumatized by the moral, political, and military failure in Vietnam in the late 1960s and early 1970s, the perceived moral and political failure of U.S. anticommunist policy in Brazil, the Dominican Republic, Greece, and Chile became the seed of U.S. human rights policy. People and policy makers increasingly asked, What do we stand for in the world? and How can our foreign policy better reflect our values? Nowhere did these two understandings of U.S. identity—human rights and anticommunism—come more in conflict with each other than they did in Latin America. Thus, a study of U.S. human rights policy toward Latin America is more than a narrow regional study of a single policy issue. To refocus U.S. policy on human rights and democracy required a rethinking of the entire foundational premise of U.S. policy. Human rights could not just be added to anticommunism in our policy toward Latin America. It required policy makers to choose between policies designed to defeat communism at any cost and those that remain within the bounds of the rule of law.

Human rights were a new lens through which policy toward Latin America was reinterpreted. The idea of human rights was transformational to the individuals and groups that began to espouse it. Latin America is the region in which that transformation was first carried out by both policy makers and nongovernmental organizations. The experience in Latin America was then diffused to other regions in what I believe to be the most important change in U.S. foreign policy in the final quarter of the twentieth century.

This policy change has once again been called into question since September 11, 2001. Some observers believe that the human rights era may be over; others fear that the war on terrorism is also going to be a war on democracy.[41] There is no doubt that human rights policy is receiving the most severe questioning since its inception in the 1970s. Antiterrorism appears likely to replace anticommunism as the new guiding force of U.S. foreign policy. And yet, exactly because the United States was never the main initiator or promoter of global human rights policy—and because human rights norms are embedded in regional and international institutions and in the foreign policies of diverse states around the world, and are promoted by a wide range of groups in global and domestic civil society—human rights policy is far more resilient than some pundits suggest. The new policy of antiterrorism is likely to provoke the same kind of identity conflict that anticommunism provoked when it clashed with human rights policy. For some time, antiterrorism may be justified in terms of the immediate security interests of the United States. U.S. citizens have indeed granted the government wide support and permission to pursue this policy. As the immediate security threat subsides and a long-term antiterrorism policy has to be justified and sustained, leaders will need to stress not only what we fear (terrorism, authoritarianism, fundamentalism) but also what we believe and take pride in (freedom, human rights, and democracy). As such, an antiterrorism policy that is seen to ignore and undermine human rights and democracy will come under attack from Congress and the public, and we may see debates similar to those over U.S. policy toward Brazil, Argentina, Chile, El Salvador, and Guatemala in the 1970s and 1980s.

This book is not just about the past. It offers a cautionary note for those who think or wish that the human rights era is over. The key lesson of human rights policy is that any "war against subversion" or "war on terrorism" must be conducted within the bounds of the rule of law, both domestic and international.

CHAPTER TWO

The Idea of Internationally Recognized Human Rights

Both Hernán Santa Cruz and Eleanor Roosevelt were unlikely champions of international human rights. When Roosevelt was asked by President Truman to be a member of the U.S. delegation to the United Nations in 1945, she doubted whether she could make a contribution because she had "no background or experience in international meetings."[1] Likewise, when the president of Chile asked Santa Cruz to serve as Chile's permanent representative to the United Nations in 1946, he protested that he did not have the necessary experience in international affairs and diplomacy to carry out the job. The president explained that neither the Chilean diplomatic service nor that of most countries was prepared to take on the new multilateral diplomacy. The UN was a newborn that the delegates had to nurture and strengthen.[2]

Both Roosevelt and Santa Cruz accepted the jobs and demonstrated extraordinary commitment and skill in helping to establish strong international human rights norms and laws. The awkward and intensely shy daughter of an elite American family, Eleanor Roosevelt had taken on an increasingly outspoken political role during her husband's career, especially on issues of social policy, women's rights, and racial discrimination. After FDR's untimely death Eleanor embodied the great international and domestic prestige of the Roosevelt legacy. When President Truman named her a member of the U.S. delegation to the United Nations, he hoped to keep the Roosevelt prestige associated with his administration.[3] But it was her commitment and hard work that earned

Eleanor the respect of U.S. diplomats and delegates from other states. Elected as chair of the newly established UN Human Rights Commission, Eleanor oversaw the early work of the commission to draft a statement of international human rights standards: the Universal Declaration of Human Rights (UDHR).

Recent books have told the story of Roosevelt's role in drafting the UDHR.[4] But Roosevelt was only one among an extraordinary group of diplomats from different countries who helped create human rights norms after World War II. Latin American countries were among the most important protagonists in this process. I can't do justice here to the careers of the dozens of Latin American diplomats and leaders who championed human rights at this time, but by focusing on one, Hernán Santa Cruz, we might gain some insight into the background and motivations of this generation of leaders.

Photographs from the period show a tall, dapper man with dark hair and a mustache, an aquiline nose, and the good looks of a movie star. Santa Cruz came from an elite Chilean family with a long record of intellectual contributions and public service. One of his grandfathers had been minister of justice and president of the Supreme Court, the other a senator who had also written dictionaries of the Quechua and Mapuche languages. Santa Cruz had worked for twenty-four years as a public servant dedicated almost solely to domestic political topics, especially penal, military, administrative, and social security law. In the late 1930s, Santa Cruz had become friends with a group of young leftist politicians including Salvador Allende, with whom he formed a lifelong friendship.[5] With these colleagues he had passionately debated the plans for the postwar period and the future of Latin America. "All of us shared the hope that the triumph of the Allies would bring democracy to all the countries of the continent." For Santa Cruz, the experience in the United Nations was like a university that increased his knowledge and strongly reaffirmed his basic convictions: "my faith in democracy, in the value and respect of the dignity of human beings and in the right of peoples to determine their own destiny, in a framework of free and pluralist societies." In the following years, the United Nations was full of debates about the primacy of political and civil rights versus economic, social, and cultural rights. Santa Cruz was a firm advocate of the *indivisibility* of rights: you couldn't have one type of rights without the others. Santa Cruz believed that liberal political regimes couldn't secure sustained progress without assuring economic, social, and cultural rights. He also thought it was illegitimate "to suppress liberty under the pretext of satisfying material needs."[6] These convictions would make him one of the most effective advocates for including economic, social, and cultural rights in the Universal Declaration of Human Rights.

Precursors to International Human Rights Policies before World War II

Before the Second World War, human rights were not considered an appropriate topic for international scrutiny and rule formation. Precursors to the international human rights issue included the movement for respect for human rights during armed conflict, the campaign for the abolition of the slave trade and slavery, the work within the League of Nations for the protection of minority rights, the early work on the rights of workers in the International Labor Organization, and the movement for women's suffrage.

In four of these cases—antislavery, women's suffrage, labor rights, and rights in war—nongovernmental organizations (NGOs) played a central role in bringing the issue to public attention and promoting international action.[7] NGOs have been the main actors responsible for inserting new ideas into the international political arena and mobilizing support for them. Despite their importance, none of the single-issue campaigns, such as the antislavery movement or the campaign for women's suffrage, demanded the international promotion of human rights for everyone. This broader demand began to emerge in the interwar period but was not institutionalized internationally until after the war.

Between 1917 and 1920 Woodrow Wilson articulated some human rights concerns in his campaign for global democracy and the rights of national self-determination. But the Convention of the League of Nations contained no mention of human rights, although it did mention "fair and humane conditions of labour" and "just treatment" of native inhabitants of dependent territories. Some delegates had raised human rights issues during the drafting of the convention, but they did not receive widespread support and were not incorporated into the document.[8] The U.S. decision not to ratify the Versailles Treaty and not to participate in the League of Nations weakened the new international organization and U.S. influence in world events.

Lawyer-diplomats first introduced and promoted the idea of internationally recognized human rights. For example, the Chilean jurist Alejandro Alvarez, the Russian jurist and diplomat Andre Mandelstam, and the Greek jurist and diplomat Antoine Frangulis first drafted and publicized declarations on the international rights of man as part of their work with nongovernmental legal organizations: the American Institute of International Law, the International Law Institute, and the International Diplomatic Academy.[9] At the same time, a Jewish Polish lawyer named Raphael Lemkin was struggling to develop an international law against racial massacres, for which he coined the word "genocide."[10]

Both critical theorists and leaders from some developing countries some-times present human rights discourse as a Western imposition upon weaker states with distinct traditions. In this context it is interesting that a Chilean, a Greek, a Pole, and a Russian, individuals from countries at the periphery of the European system rather than at its cultural core, were responsible for insert-ing the idea into global debates in the early twentieth century. Both Frangulis and Mandelstam were political refugees, the former from the Greek dictator-ship, the latter from the Bolshevist regime, and thus saw in human rights a means of protecting individuals from the repressive practices of their own gov-ernments.[11]

In general, human rights received little attention from policy makers and intellectuals before World War II. Although many were deeply concerned with democracy and freedom, they did not frame these issues in the language of hu-man rights, nor did they call for international protection of these rights.[12] Yet jurists and intellectuals in Latin America held human rights and democracy as ideals and turned to international law for help in realizing them.

The Inter-American Tradition of Support for International Human Rights

Sometimes Latin Americans also suggest that human rights are an "Anglo-Saxon" export inappropriate for their countries. For example, in 1996, when an Amnesty International report criticized the Panamanian government's de-cision to pardon nearly one thousand of the worst human rights offenders during the dictatorship of General Manuel Antonio Noriega, a prominent Panamanian government party legislator said that the organization was "brazenly and shamelessly at the service of Anglo-Saxon imperialism."[13] Such criticism ignores that Latin American intellectuals, policy makers, and activists have a long history of support for international human rights. It seems partic-ularly ironic that a Panamanian would make such a statement, because Panama's representative was one of the most eloquent spokesmen for interna-tional human rights standards in the UN charter.

In Latin America, there was also a tradition of support for international law as a means by which weaker countries might find protection against the inter-ventions of the more powerful, especially the United States. As Hernán Santa Cruz recognized, an intellectual elite had emerged in Latin America that "gave enormous importance to international law"; moreover, "many of these inter-nationalists had contributed significantly to the progress of international law at the world level and had distinguished themselves in the League of Nations."[14]

Many Latin American intellectuals were leaders in promoting international human rights law, through which they aimed to thwart rather than serve the domination of powerful states.

Yet there was a contradiction at the heart of this legalist tradition in Latin America. Legalism had primarily been used to support concepts of sovereignty and nonintervention. Because Latin American countries had been targets of U.S. intervention in the past, they were ardent supporters of the legal doctrine of nonintervention. Yet regional promotion of human rights and democracy could undermine the doctrine of absolute sovereignty and nonintervention. Before World War II this contradiction was resolved in favor of nonintervention, but support for sovereignty coexisted with a desire to promote human rights and democracy.

The idea that Latin American countries should work together to oppose authoritarian rule and support democracy is not a recent invention. As early as 1837 a Chilean, Pedro Felix Vicuña, published a plan calling for a Great American Congress to support democratic governments and oppose tyrants. Juan Bautista Alberdi, a framer of the Argentine constitution of 1853, supported Vicuña's idea and proposed an American Court with the right of collective intervention to oppose tyranny. An Ecuadorian diplomat, Carlos Tobar, proposed in 1907 a policy of collective nonrecognition of governments coming to power by other than democratic means.[15] After the First World War, most Latin American states joined the League of Nations and accepted the jurisdiction of the International Court of Justice. Some Latin American legal experts and diplomats saw international law and prodemocracy policies as a means of restraining tyrants in their own societies as well as those abroad.

The Chilean jurist Alejandro Alvarez was part of this tradition, as were other noted Latin American jurists like Carlos Calvo and Luis Drago, authors of the Calvo and Drago doctrines, which sought to use law to limit intervention in the region.[16] Alvarez in particular worked to codify international law, and one of his most important texts on the topic included a section on the "International Rights of the Individual," which mentioned the "right to life, liberty, and property, without distinction of nationality, sex, race, language, or religion," and the rights to freedom of religion and belief.[17]

At a conference of the Inter-American Bar Association in Mexico City in 1944, resolutions emphasized the "necessity" of a Declaration of Rights of Man, and the importance of international machinery and procedures to put the principles in the declaration into action. In late 1945 and early 1946, the American states considered a proposal by Eduardo Rodriguez Larreta, foreign minister of Uruguay, calling for collective intervention to oppose dictators and promote democracy and human rights. Rodriguez Larreta was most explicit about the potential conflict between nonintervention and the international protection of human rights.

> The principle of non-intervention by one State in the affairs of another, in the field of inter-American relations, constitutes in itself a great advance achieved during the last decades; this principle was inspired by noble and just claims. We must maintain and affirm that principle whenever the need arises. It must, however, be harmonized with other principles. . . . "Non-intervention" is not a shield behind which crime may be perpetrated, laws may be violated . . . and binding obligations may be circumvented. Otherwise, at the very time when, since Mexico and after San Francisco, we should be creating a new international and humanitarian conception, we would find ourselves tolerating a doctrine capable of frustrating and destroying that very conception.[18]

The Uruguayan plan was motivated in part by a fear of intervention from Argentina, then under Perón, but it generated a broad debate in the region. The measure received the support of the United States and six Latin American governments, but the remaining states, concerned about its implications for sovereignty, rejected it. In February 1945, at the Conference on War and Peace in Mexico City, Guatemala recommended that the countries of the region refuse to grant recognition or maintain relations with antidemocratic regimes, particularly those that came to power through coups. The Guatemalan government declared that "WWII had created a worldwide demand that the rights of man should be recognized and protected on the international level, and that the Inter-American movement therefore should support this universal yearning by recognizing that antidemocratic regimes were the primary cause of denial of human rights and freedoms."[19] The reformer Juan Jose Arévalo had been elected president of Guatemala just three months earlier but had not yet taken office. His election marked the beginning of the so-called Guatemalan democratic revolution of the presidencies of Arévalo and Jacobo Arbenz. The irony is that if the Guatemala proposal had been accepted, the countries of the Americas could have applied it against the Guatemalan government that came to power in the CIA-supported coup in 1954 that overthrew Arbenz.

This legal tradition led Latin American states to support human rights language in the UN charter and to draft and pass an American Declaration on the Rights and Duties of Man at the Bogotá Conference in 1948, months before the United Nations passed the Universal Declaration of Human Rights. The Santiago Declaration and other proposals calling for regional responses against coups, which the OAS finally adopted in the 1990s, reflected this continuing aspiration to develop effective policies in support of democracy and human rights. The policies of the Cold War further delayed the development of effective policies. Many Latin American governments who had been advocates of policies promoting human rights and democracy were overthrown by coups, sometimes with the support of the United States, and governed by increasingly authoritarian regimes. For example, the authoritarian regime that took over in Guatemala after the coup in 1954 became increasingly repressive over the next half century. Guatemala transformed from a country advocating regional promotion of democracy in 1945 to a fierce critic of human rights and prodemocracy policies in the 1970s.

Human Rights and the Preparations for a Postwar World

The British author H. G. Wells helped reinsert human rights issues into the wartime debate over the aim of war. "If many of us are to die for democracy," he stated, "we better know what we mean by the word."[20] But Franklin Roosevelt's "Four Freedoms" State of the Union speech in January 1941 was the most important statement on the place of human rights in the postwar order. The concept of a world founded upon four essential freedoms—freedom of speech and expression, freedom of worship, freedom from want, and freedom from fear—was Roosevelt's direct contribution, which he dictated personally to his speech writers after the speech had already gone through three drafts.[21] Roosevelt repeated these concepts frequently, and they were later reaffirmed in the Atlantic Charter endorsed by Churchill and Roosevelt.[22] In the Atlantic Charter, the Allies committed themselves to "respect the right of all peoples to choose the form of government under which they will live" and to "establish a peace . . . which will afford assurances to all peoples that they may live out their lives in freedom from fear and want." Roosevelt's concern with international human rights was in part an outgrowth of his New Deal beliefs but was also stimulated by the war and the need to articulate wartime and peacetime goals that would set the Allies apart from Nazi Germany and the Axis powers.[23] Roosevelt was a friend of H. G. Wells, and he was a member of the International Diplomatic Academy, which had actively studied and promoted the cause of international human rights under the leadership of Frangulis and Mandelstam.[24] It is likely that he turned to these sources when he formulated his Four Freedoms speech. Eventually, however, it was not Franklin Roosevelt but his wife, Eleanor, who became the leading U.S. government advocate and spokesperson for human rights, and who sustained the vision of human rights laid out in the Four Freedoms speech.

Roosevelt's speech heralded an explosion of intellectual, governmental, and nongovernmental activities to explore and promote the concept of human rights and to seek international protection of these rights. Intellectuals, activists, and policy makers collaborated in creating a new postwar order, one of the pillars of which was to be the international protection of human rights. There were four key moments in the development of global human rights in the postwar world:

- The Dumbarton Oaks meeting of the great powers (August–October 1944)
- The San Francisco meeting to prepare the Charter of the United Nations (April–June 1945)
- The drafting of the Universal Declaration of Human Rights (1947–48)
- The drafting of the legal treaties based on the rights in the UDHR, especially the Covenant on Civil and Political Rights, and the Covenant on Economic, Social, and Cultural Rights (1948–66)

Dumbarton Oaks

The first step in the creation of a new postwar order was a meeting in 1944 of the Big Four great powers (United States, Great Britain, the USSR, and China) to be held at the Dumbarton Oaks estate in Washington, D.C. The Big Four would decide on a draft proposal for a new international organization in preparation for a conference that would be held in San Francisco in 1945. To prepare for the meeting, the U.S. government set up the Advisory Committee on Postwar Foreign Policy, which brought together executive branch officials, members of the Senate and House, and individuals from the media, academia, and nongovernmental organizations.

In addition to participating in the advisory committee, nongovernmental organizations continued their parallel efforts to prepare for the postwar order. The American League of Nations Association was especially active through its Commission to Study the Organization of Peace. The roster of officers and members of this commission reads like "a who's who in international relations scholarship."[25] The commission collaborated closely with the Department of State to come up with proposals for the postwar order. Some NGO leaders served on both the commission and the Advisory Committee on Postwar Foreign Policy, thus providing an interconnection between nongovernmental and governmental efforts at planning the postwar order.

The domestic campaign for postwar international organization and the intense cooperation between the State Department and citizens' groups in this period can be understood as a response to the administration's fear of a repeat of the U.S. failure to ratify the Versailles Treaty. Many analysts attributed the failure of the League of Nations to the lack of U.S. participation and support. The Roosevelt administration was determined to avoid a similar situation and thus throughout the war, and especially in the preparations for the postwar international organization, put a premium on involving the public and Congress in planning the postwar order.

United States policy makers were divided on the human rights issue. Cordell Hull, secretary of state, had been willing to invoke human rights during the war to help clarify war aims, but he opposed any efforts to promote human rights that would undermine national sovereignty. Other members of the U.S. government—especially Sumner Wells, undersecretary of state—were more deeply committed to incorporating human rights into U.S. foreign policy and into a new international organization. Wells had played an important role in articulating human rights as part of the Allies' war aims. As one of the architects of Roosevelt's Good Neighbor policy, he had long experience in Latin American politics. Hernán Santa Cruz described him as "a decided pan-americanist."[26] Wells chaired one of the most important subcommittees of the Advisory Committee on Postwar Foreign Policy. Under his leadership, the group produced an international bill of human rights in 1942. At a postwar planning meeting Secretary Hull attacked the proposed international bill of human rights, contending that no country would permit others to regulate how it treated its citizens. The United States, he declared, would oppose "any proposal requiring a derogation of national sovereignty."[27]

Hull eventually carried the day, and Wells was forced to resign in 1943. Hull instructed the U.S. delegation to the Dumbarton Oaks meeting to avoid any detailed discussion of human rights.[28] As a result, the initial U.S. drafts of the UN charter made no reference to human rights, while the proposals that emerged from the Big Four meeting at Dumbarton Oaks contained only one reference.[29] The failure of the Big Four to include more references to human rights calls into question both the realist and the critical theory explanations for the origins of human rights norms. If human rights emerged primarily from the goals and needs of powerful states, as realists claim, then why didn't these powerful states include human rights language in the Dumbarton Oaks draft? Only China, the weakest of the four, pressed for inclusion of some human rights language. But China's effort to include an explicit statement against racial discrimination was rejected by the other great powers.

Nongovernmental organizations and a group of small countries (particularly the Latin American states but also New Zealand and Australia) tried to rectify the limitations of Dumbarton Oaks. Latin American countries felt betrayed, both because they had not been consulted before Dumbarton Oaks about a postwar organization and because the Dumbarton Oaks draft did not incorporate various ideals they supported, including human rights.[30] To promote their concerns and formulate a collective policy, Latin American countries called an extraordinary meeting in Mexico City in February 1945, the Inter-American Conference on Problems of War and Peace, which ended a few weeks before the opening of the San Francisco Conference. Delegates at the meeting raised a series of important issues about great power dominance, the importance of international law, regional agreements for security, and economic and social problems. Human rights issues figured prominently in the speeches and resolutions, and the conference called upon the Inter-American Juridical Committee to prepare a draft declaration of human rights.[31]

Meanwhile, NGOs in the United States organized a campaign to promote support for U.S. membership in the postwar international organization and to ensure that the new organization would have mechanisms to protect human rights.[32] They called it a "second chance campaign," because, as a letter announcing an NGO meeting to consider the Dumbarton Oaks proposals said, "All of us who support a 'general international organization' with power to prevent another war, face the greatest challenge of our lives. We have the 'second chance' to establish such an organization with the United States as part of it."[33] Each NGO worked to educate and mobilize its members and the general public, and to pressure the U.S. government. For example, Judge Joseph Proskauer, president of the American Jewish Committee, wrote to the secretary of state calling for the adoption of "an International Bill of Rights" and "setting up machinery to implement and protect those rights" in the form of a specific commission on human rights.[34] The American Jewish Committee circulated a declaration calling for an international bill of rights, which was signed by over thirteen hundred prominent Americans, and brought these proposals to the San Francisco Conference.

The San Francisco Conference

Delegates from forty-six countries gathered in San Francisco in April 1945 amid an atmosphere of optimism and urgency. The great human cost of the war motivated leaders to find a way to prevent future wars. The sudden death of FDR only a few weeks before the conference left the United States without his vision and experience. The new Truman administration worked to carry out the plans of its predecessor and preserve the unprecedented level of cooperation between the executive branch, both parties in Congress, and nongovernmental organizations that existed during the Roosevelt administration.

Congressional leaders from both the Democratic and Republican parties and nongovernmental leaders were represented in the official U.S. delegation to the San Francisco Conference. In addition, over forty NGOs and interest groups were invited to serve as "consultants" to the U.S. delegation. This involvement of NGO consultants was totally unprecedented and was considered an "experiment"—what one participant called "an experiment in democracy in action on the diplomatic level."[35] This experiment is one of the forerunners of the UN practice of granting NGOs consultative status and involving NGOs in meetings parallel to its own. At the same time, conference officials accredited 2,500 press representatives from the United States and around the world. The glare of publicity highlighted the work of the delegates and NGOs.

The NGO consultants to the U.S. delegation represented a broad range of religious, business, farm, labor, veteran, and professional associations, as well as activist groups. They included leaders from the American Federation of Labor (AFL) and the Congress of Industrial Organizations (CIO), representatives of the International Chamber of Commerce, and key international relations scholars. "They were, for the most part, highly capable thinkers about problems of international organization and public affairs, and veteran practitioners of negotiation, propaganda, and community education."[36]

These nongovernmental organizations, along with the delegations of some Latin American and other countries, played a pivotal role in securing the inclusion of human rights language in the UN charter, language that served as the basis for all further UN efforts in the human rights area. As we saw earlier, the U.S. delegation was divided about the wisdom of incorporating human rights and democracy into international organizations and foreign policy. Even though human rights concerns had lost out in the internal debate within the U.S. government before Dumbarton Oaks, groups in civil society helped resurrect human rights issues at the San Francisco Conference. According to one close observer of the UN human rights regime, these groups "conducted a lobby in favor of human rights for which there is no parallel in the history of international relations, and which was largely responsible for the human rights provisions of the Charter."[37]

In a meeting with the secretary of state, Edward Stettinius, the consultants urged the U.S. delegation to support four amendments to the Dumbarton Oaks proposals that would further institutionalize and incorporate human rights concerns and language into the UN charter. The most important of these amendments held proposals to add the phrase "to promote respect for human rights and fundamental freedoms" to chapter 1 of the charter, which outlined the basic purposes of the new organization, and to include a specific provision calling on the Economic and Social Council to set up a human rights commission.[38] These activists were aware of the importance of finding an institutional home for the human rights idea.

The consultants said that these amendments had to be included if the charter was to be ratified, and because they represented such a wide range of public opinion, their words carried weight. For example, the president of the CIO, Phillip Murray, stood up and proclaimed his conviction that he was speaking not only for the CIO but for all labor in stating that "we are 100 percent behind the argument for the human rights language."[39] At the end of the meeting, Stettinius rose to his feet and declared that he would try to convince the rest of the delegation.

At the same time as the NGO consultants were pressuring the U.S. government, many delegations, including Uruguay, Panama, Mexico, New Zealand, and Australia, were also urging the United States to add human rights language to the charter. Eventually Stettinius was able to rally his colleagues around the human rights issue, and together they convinced the other Big Four powers as well.[40] The British government gave the Latin American bloc credit for changing the U.S. government position on human rights at San Francisco.[41] Latin American countries made up twenty of the fifty states present at the San Francisco Conference.[42] At this historical moment Latin America held an unusually large number of democratic countries, and their shared worldview favoring democracy and human rights made them the most important voting bloc at San Francisco.[43] For Hernán Santa Cruz, the initiatives of the Latin American countries helped extend the economic, social, and human rights objectives in the charter, in particular articles 55 and 56, upon which so much later human rights work of the organization rested.[44]

But even this "pincer" motion of pressure on the U.S. government from below (the NGO consultants) and from outside (the Latin American governments and New Zealand and Australia) couldn't have changed U.S. policy had there been no allies within the U.S. government. The group within the U.S. government that had been committed to incorporating human rights concerns into the postwar international order had lost influence in the drafting of the Dumbarton Oaks proposal, as we learned earlier. So the combination of external and internal pressures was particularly effective because it supported and reinforced a position already held by a minority faction within the U.S. government.

The final UN charter has seven references to human rights, including the key amendments the NGO consultants proposed. A member of the U.S. delegation later told the consultants, "If you had been at Dumbarton Oaks where we struggled for weeks literally to get just the two words 'human rights and fundamental freedoms' somewhere into the proposals, you would realize what enormous progress has been made during the last six months. . . . It has largely resulted from the action of this group . . . which really changed history."[45]

If the charter, adopted at a high point of postwar collaboration, hadn't contained references to human rights and specifically to a human rights commission, it is quite likely that the Universal Declaration of Human Rights would not have been drafted in 1948. The inclusion of the human rights language in the Charter of the United Nations was a *critical juncture* that channeled the history of international human rights in the direction of setting international norms. The inclusion of human rights language was not the preferred option of the great powers, and was finally adopted by them only in response to pressures from NGOs and small states.

The record of the United States at San Francisco was mixed. Although it eventually supported the effort to include human rights language in the charter, the United States delegation resisted attempts to include references to economic human rights and expressed concern over possible UN intrusion into domestic jurisdiction. The two other key governmental actors, the USSR and the United Kingdom, shared the U.S. concern to limit possible infringement on domestic jurisdiction.[46]

Neither realism nor critical theory can help explain this critical juncture in human rights history, initiated by the less powerful and by a convergence of interests between mainly U.S.-based NGOs and small states. If human rights was a discourse that powerful states used to reaffirm their identity as superior to the weaker nations and to promote monitoring and surveillance, why did more powerful states initially resist the adoption of human rights discourses and less powerful states promote it? Realism and critical theory have misunderstood and misrepresented the history of human rights ideas and policies. Often it has been the less powerful who have sought to restrain the more powerful by embracing human rights ideas. These less powerful groups sometimes succeed, when they have allies *within* powerful states.

The small states that advocated the inclusion of human rights in the charter—Uruguay, Chile, Canada, Mexico, Panama, New Zealand, and Australia—were for the most part democracies committed to the idea of human rights. Some of them tried but failed to secure stronger human rights provisions with enforcement powers in the charter. The Uruguayan delegation, for example, proposed that countries that persistently violated human rights be suspended from the organization.[47]

The final language of the charter called only for promoting and encouraging respect for human rights, rather than assuring or protecting rights. This compromise characterized UN human rights work from 1945 until 1973. The United Nations was expected to promote human rights but not protect them, unless such violations could be seen to threaten peace.[48] The alternative vision of a United Nations with stronger human rights enforcement presented at the

San Francisco Conference would have to wait another forty years to begin to be realized. Nevertheless, the charter, by assigning institutional responsibility for human rights to the General Assembly and the Economic and Social Council and by specifically recommending the creation of a human rights commission, paved the way for later human rights actions within the UN.

The careful bipartisan strategy of the Roosevelt administration in all its preparations for the new international organization helped secure an 89 to 2 vote in favor of the UN charter in the U.S. Senate.

Drafting the Universal Declaration of Human Rights

The human rights language in the charter was only a starting point. The new Commission on Human Rights, mandated in the charter, had to begin the task of defining what the United Nations meant when it talked about human rights. To do this, the commission drafted first a Universal Declaration of Human Rights and later two binding human rights treaties: the Covenant on Civil and Political Rights, and the Covenant on Economic, Social, and Cultural Rights. Eleanor Roosevelt was named chair of the new Commission on Human Rights to oversee these tasks.

The dramatic story of the drafting of the Universal Declaration of Human Rights and Eleanor Roosevelt's role has been told elsewhere.[49] The drafting was guided by an exceptional circle of leaders, especially Roosevelt, Charles Malik of Lebanon, Peng-Chun Chang of China, René Cassin of France, and Hernán Santa Cruz of Chile, each representing a different corner of the world. Although conflicts were not infrequent within this core group, Charles Malik would later recall that "Mrs. Roosevelt, Mr. Cassin, Mr. Chang, Mr. Santa Cruz and I, together with our respective advisors and assistants, soon achieved a fairly close identity of aims and objectives. We worked more or less as a team."[50] They received essential assistance from John Humphrey of Canada, director of the UN Division on Human Rights. The effective cooperation of the core group rested on shared values and some personal friendships. Santa Cruz and Humphrey shared democratic socialist ideas and "enjoyed an excellent working and social relationship."[51] Santa Cruz also developed a personal though less close friendship with Roosevelt that lasted "until the end of her days." Eleanor invited him to Hyde Park, visits that Santa Cruz said produced "great emotion" due to his admiration for President Roosevelt.[52]

Roosevelt shared Santa Cruz's idea that political and civil rights should be balanced with economic, social, and cultural rights. "Nowhere was Eleanor Roosevelt's ability to influence U.S. policy more evident than in her success in persuading a reluctant State Department to accept the inclusion of social and economic rights in the Declaration."[53] Even so, Roosevelt and Santa Cruz frequently disagreed on the specifics of the language on economic, social, and cultural rights. Santa Cruz presented the position of economically developing countries "with great energy, a practice that often brought him into conflict with Western industrial powers."[54] For example, during the debate over the right to work, the United States argued that everyone should have the "opportunity to work," while Santa Cruz preferred the language of the right to work, which ultimately prevailed in the declaration.[55]

Once again, Latin American countries and NGOs played a behind-the-scenes but important role in drafting the Universal Declaration of Human Rights. When Humphrey wrote the Secretariat Outline (a draft bill of rights) for the Human Rights Commission to use during its deliberations, he modeled it on a score of drafts the Secretariat had collected from law professors and legal and social NGOs as well as from other intergovernmental organizations and from governments.[56] Cuba, Panama, and Chile were the first three countries to submit full drafts of bills of rights to the commission. The Panamanian draft was prepared by the American Law Institute (ALI) and the Chilean draft was prepared by the Inter-American Juridical Committee of the Organization of American States. Each of these contained references to the right to education, food, health care, and other social security provisions.[57] "Humphrey took much of the wording and almost all of the ideas for the social, economic, and cultural rights in his first draft from the tradition of Latin American socialism by way of the bills submitted by Panama and Chile." Once these rights were in the draft declaration, Latin American delegates made sure they stayed in. Among these guardians, Santa Cruz "was the greatest."[58] The very influential Latin American lobby dominated the drafting history of the UDHR on work-related rights. They were influential both because John Humphrey was sympathetic to their point of view and because they were able to "speak with one voice (usually that of Hernán Santa Cruz)."[59]

In the end, the General Assembly endorsed the Universal Declaration of Human Rights with an overwhelmingly robust vote on December 10, 1948. The UDHR bore the strong imprint of many countries and traditions, including the New Deal liberalism of Eleanor Roosevelt and the democratic left position of many Latin American intellectuals, embodied in the ideas of Hernán Santa Cruz.

Drafting the Human Rights Treaties

The UDHR was a declaration: a statement of aspirations and norms without binding legal force. Eleanor Roosevelt and others thought the UDHR would be shorter and more eloquent if it were a declaration instead of a legal document. They also believed it would be easier to ensure the rapid approval of a declaration. But the next task was to translate the norms of the UDHR into binding legal treaties that countries could ratify. The very first human rights treaty adopted by the United Nations was the Convention on the Prevention and Punishment of the Crime of Genocide, passed on December 9, 1948, one day before the United Nations approved the UDHR. Panama, Cuba, and India sponsored the original resolution. To the great disappointment of human rights advocates, the United States, the first government to sign the treaty, then failed to ratify it.[60] The Senate's failure to ratify the Genocide Convention was a signal of troubled times ahead for human rights in U.S. foreign policy. As the Cold War intensified, human rights concerns were increasingly subsumed to anticommunism.

The period 1945 to 1953 nevertheless represented a historical high point in U.S. participation in the work of the United Nations on the issues of human rights, not to be equaled again until the Carter administration. During this period, the United States continued to negotiate the content of UN human rights treaties under the leadership of Eleanor Roosevelt. Roosevelt's prominence in the drafting of international human rights documents and her frequent and outspoken criticism of racial discrimination in the United States symbolized, for some conservative political leaders, the link between UN human rights work and the issues of segregation and states' rights in the United States. This link would later lead the United States to withdraw from the drafting of the covenants.[61]

Over the next few years it became clear that human rights language in the UN charter and the UDHR created norms and expectations that could bring pressure to bear even on a powerful country like the United States.[62] In the context of decolonization in Africa and Asia, U.S. civil rights practices were coming under increased international scrutiny and criticism. The United States was trying to exercise leadership among the recently independent countries of Africa and Asia, but its claims to moral leadership were undercut by its domestic practices of institutionalized racism. Domestic social movements and civil rights organizations in the United States decided to use the human rights language in the UN Charter to bring a petition before the United Nations against the U.S. government for racism and discrimination.

W. E. B. Du Bois and Walter White of the National Association for the Advancement of Colored People (NAACP) had served among the consultants to the U.S. delegation to San Francisco. They were disappointed that they weren't able to secure stronger language against discrimination and colonization in the UN charter. But the knowledge of the United Nations they gained and the international contacts they made served them well in their campaign after the war to bring international pressure to bear on U.S. practices of racial discrimination. Under their leadership, U.S. civil rights organizations filed three petitions with the United Nations between 1946 and 1951. Although the United Nations refused to act on them, the petitions helped mobilize foreign public opinion against U.S. segregation. Many delegates of African and Asian states at the UN were sympathetic to the petitions because they had personally suffered overt discrimination while at UN meetings in New York and in their travels around the United States. The new states, together with many European countries, urged the United States to change its domestic practices. State Department officials complained that "no American problem receives more wide-spread attention than our treatment of racial minorities, especially the Negro."[63]

These international pressures influenced key executive and judicial decisions about civil rights during the Truman and Eisenhower administrations. The executives appointed civil rights committees to study the problem and recommend solutions, and filed briefs with U.S. courts. The Supreme Court made a series of landmark decisions to end institutionalized discrimination, many based on cases initiated and litigated by the NAACP. In all these cases after 1946 "either the Justice or the State Department, or both submitted amicus briefs that identified racial segregation and discrimination as obstacles to U.S. foreign policy interests."[64]

The combination of internal pressures from domestic civil rights organizations and external pressures from states in Europe, Asia, and Africa led factions within the U.S. government—especially the State Department and the Justice Department—to support reform policies that they would have been unlikely to support without such external pressures. Such successes, however, may have contributed to a backlash in conservative U.S. political circles against the United Nations. As it became clear that international human rights norms and institutions could have an impact on U.S. domestic politics, conservative political groups in the United States organized a campaign that would lead to U.S. withdrawal from UN efforts to promote human rights for twenty years.

Anticommunism Replaces Human Rights in U.S. Policy

During the Cold War, Europe and the United States took different approaches to human rights. Whereas the United States largely abandoned human rights promotion, the Europeans moved quickly and consciously to build a regional human rights regime. Human rights issues were present in the earliest discussions of the postwar European order. NGOs promoting European unity focused on human rights issues,[65] and their call for a European human rights charter and court was taken up by the newly created Council of Europe. In contrast to other international references to human rights, the statute of the Council of Europe does not merely affirm its commitment to human rights, but makes respect for human rights and the rule of law conditions of membership in the council, the violation of which may result in suspension from the organization.

In the fifteen months between August 1949 and November 1950, the Europeans drafted the European Convention for the Protection of Human Rights and Fundamental Freedoms and opened it for ratification. The European Convention and its protocols are limited basically to civil and political rights.[66] This regional human rights regime, which only applies to the European signatories, granted very strong monitoring powers to the European Commission of Human Rights, and authoritative decision-making powers to the European Court of Human Rights. By September 1953 the Convention entered into force. Most of the countries in Western Europe initiated a multilateral human rights policy during this period when they accepted the compulsory jurisdiction of the European Court of Human Rights.

In contrast, human rights issues essentially dropped out of the U.S. foreign policy agenda from 1953 to 1973. During the Cold War, human rights was subsumed to anticommunism as part of a broader policy calling for the "containment" of the Soviet Union and its allies. This framework was summed up in the National Security council document NSC-68, "the single most important statement of the creed of containment."[67] NSC-68 affirmed that any means were justified to increase American power relative to that of the USSR:

> Our free society, confronted by a threat to its basic values, naturally will take such action, including the use of military force, as may be required to protect those values. The integrity of our system will not be jeopardized by any measures, covert or overt, violent or non-violent, which serve the purposes of frustrating the Kremlin design, nor does the necessity for conducting ourselves so as to affirm our values in actions as well as words forbid such measures, provided only they are appropriately calculated to that end and are not so excessive or misdirected as to make us enemies of the people instead of the evil men who have enslaved them.[68]

The philosophy of NSC-68 was distrustful of democracy. It considered free society "vulnerable," even in the United States, but especially in those countries without a strong tradition of democracy. The diplomat George Kennan, an architect of the policies of the Cold War, after a tour of Latin America in the 1950s, concluded,

> We cannot be too dogmatic about the methods by which local communists can be dealt with. These vary greatly, depending upon the vigor and efficacy of local concepts and traditions of self-government. . . . Where the concepts and traditions of popular government are too weak to absorb successfully the intensity of the communist attack, then we must concede that harsh government measures of repression may be the only answer; that these measures may have to proceed from regimes whose origins and methods would not stand the test of American concepts of democratic procedure; and that such regimes and such methods may be preferable alternatives, and indeed the only alternatives, to further communist successes.[69]

Containment fully dominated U.S. foreign policy from 1950 to 1973 and then became the major framework against which a human rights approach would have to struggle. Kennan justified the policy in Latin America by claiming that "it is not entirely possible for us to know which institutions of government are morally commendable, and which are not, in a Latin American country." In particular, he argued that it was difficult to distinguish between democratic and authoritarian regimes in the region. "A policy based on the attempted maintenance of such distinctions is apt to be a source of endless confusion and controversy, here and abroad," he reasoned.[70]

In the case of U.S.–Latin American relations, the switch from the noninterventionist Good Neighbor policy of the Roosevelt administration to the more interventionist anticommunist policies of the Cold War was most clearly marked by the U.S. covert intervention that overthrew the democratically elected government of Jacobo Arbenz of Guatemala in 1954. The Guatemalan intervention was a clear symbol of precedence that the anticommunist agenda of the Cold War took over concerns about human rights and democracy. The United States initiated and supported the overthrow of a democratically elected president undertaking a program of reform because it could not accept Arbenz's sympathy for the Communist Party, contacts with Eastern Bloc countries, and curtailing of the privileges of the United Fruit Company.[71]

But issues other than anticommunism blocked the adoption of a human rights policy in the United States. In 1951 Senator John Bricker of Ohio sponsored a constitutional amendment to protect states' rights against treaties authorizing "any international organization to supervise, control, or adjudicate rights of citizens of the United States."[72] The coalition supporting the Bricker amendment, almost the necessary two thirds of the Senate, included not only cold warriors but also a group of conservative senators concerned with states' rights, some traditional isolationists, and segregationists who feared that the ratification of UN human rights treaties would give the federal government the authority to impose civil rights standards on the states.

One of Bricker's main allies in the struggle against the human rights covenants was the American Bar Association (ABA). Frank E. Holman, president of the ABA, had attacked the UDHR as a "manifesto on pink paper" that would "promote state socialism, if not communism, throughout the world."[73] The ABA opposed Senate ratification of the Genocide Convention and the other human rights conventions.

The Eisenhower administration, worried that the Bricker amendment would tie the hands of the executive in foreign policy, successfully blocked its passage. But in turn, the administration also asked for Mrs. Roosevelt's resignation from the UN Human Rights Commission, and Secretary of State Dulles formally declared to the Senate in 1953 that the United States would not become a party to UN human rights covenants. Senator Bricker had emphasized that the purpose of his amendment was "to bury the so-called covenant on human rights so deep that no one holding high public office will ever dare to attempt its resurrection."[74] Although his coalition was unable to pass his amendment, it did succeed in blocking attempts to ratify the human rights covenants for almost forty years.

For the next twenty years, U.S. policy makers paid little or no attention to human rights.[75] Occasional references to human rights appear in the *Congressional Record* during this period, but the overall trend is one of indifference and opposition to UN human rights efforts and of refusal to incorporate human rights concerns into bilateral policy. In 1957 Henry S. Reuss, congressman from Wisconsin, complained that the United States "stands almost alone in opposing in principle treaties relating to human rights."[76] In 1967 Senator William Proxmire, discouraged by Senate refusal to ratify the Genocide Convention, vowed to speak daily about human rights until the convention was ratified. He was an exception, however, and his comments rarely initiated debate or support.

Some authors suggest that the Kennedy administration's program for Latin America, the Alliance for Progress, was an early human rights policy.[77] But the thrust of this program was quite different from that of a human rights policy. The goals of the Alliance for Progress were economic and social development, which were seen as the necessary preconditions for democracy and stability in Latin America. The program was motivated by a fear of the spread of communism and a belief that only material progress could stem the tide of rebellion. Kennedy stressed initially that the Alliance for Progress "must work to eliminate tyranny" and took action in 1961 to prevent a coup in the Dominican Republic. But the period of the Alliance for Progress witnessed a succession of military coups in the region, and neither the Kennedy nor the Johnson administration developed any direct or specific policy to defend democracy or promote human rights. Indeed, under Johnson an explicit policy was adopted "to show no preference, through aid or otherwise, for representative democratic institutions."[78]

It was not until the domestic and international situation changed in the late 1960s and early 1970s that the United States could overcome the legacy of the Bricker coalition of cold warriors and states' rights advocates to design and implement a human rights policy.

The Inter-American Human Rights Regime

At the same time as human rights dropped out of U.S. foreign policy, the Americas were slowly creating a regional human rights regime. After proclaiming the far-reaching but nonbinding American Declaration of Human Rights in 1948, American states took no action until 1959 to create an institutional mechanism to protect the rights set forth in the declaration. Partly in response to the Cuban revolution of that year, the member states of the OAS created the Inter-American Commission on Human Rights (IACHR) to promote awareness and respect for human rights. But the commission, created by a resolution rather than a binding treaty, reflected the unwillingness of OAS member states to accept legally binding human rights obligations.

In the 1960s, states began negotiations on a legally binding treaty—the American Convention on Human Rights, which was eventually adopted and opened for ratification in 1969. The American Convention is a comprehensive treaty for civil and political rights. Economic, social, and cultural rights were set out in an additional protocol to the American Convention, the Protocol of San Salvador, which was drafted later and opened for ratifications in 1988. The American Convention incorporated the IACHR and created the Inter-American Court of Human Rights. Eleven states had ratified the American Convention by 1978, and it entered into force in July of that year. At this point, individual states could choose to accept the jurisdiction of the newly created Inter-American Court of Human Rights. Table 2 gives the date when countries of the Americas ratified the American Convention and the date when they accepted the jurisdiction of the court.

TABLE 2.

Countries That Have Ratified the American Convention on Human Rights (ACHR) and Accepted the Compulsory Jurisdiction of the Inter-American Court of Human Rights

Country	Acceptance of court	Regime type at time of acceptance	Legal system
Argentina	1984	Newly democratic	Civil
Barbados	2000	Democratic	Common
Bolivia	1993	Newly democratic	Civil
Brazil	1998	Newly democratic	Civil
Chile	1991	Newly democratic	Civil
Colombia	1985	Democratic	Civil
Costa Rica	1980	Democratic	Civil
Dominican Republic	1990	Democratic	Civil
Ecuador	1984	Newly democratic	Civil
El Salvador	1995	Newly democratic	Civil
Guatemala	1987	Newly democratic	Civil
Haiti	1998	*Not* Democratic	Civil
Honduras	1981	*Not* Democratic	Civil
Mexico	1998	Democratic	Civil
Nicaragua	1991	Newly democratic	Civil
Panama	1990	*Not* Democratic	Civil
Paraguay	1993	Newly democratic	Civil
Peru	1981	Newly democratic	Civil
Surinam	1987	*Not* Democratic	Civil
Trinidad and Tobago	1991	Democratic	Common
Uruguay	1985	Newly democratic	Civil
Venezuela	1981	Democratic	Civil

Note: The regime type is taken from the Freedom House political rights ranking. A ranking of 1, 2, or 3 leads to a democracy listing. A ranking of 4 to 7 or above is coded as *not* democratice. If the country has been a democracy for 10 years or less, it is listed as newly democratic. If it has been a democracy for more than 10 years, it is listed simply as democratic. Because Freedom House rankings are given in mixed years (e.g., 1984–85), I have averaged two years to arrive at a score.

How well do the main contending approaches—realist, critical, institutional, liberal, or ideational—help explain the patterns of adoption of the human rights regime in the Americas? A realist approach is not useful here because the United States did not initially take leadership in creating the inter-American human rights regime and its institutions. U.S. treaty ratification rules made it unlikely that the United States would ratify the American Convention.

To evaluate a liberal approach, we need to determine the nature of the regimes in countries that ratified the American Convention on Human Rights and accepted the competence of the Inter-American Court of Human Rights. Acceptance of the court's jurisdiction gives teeth to the convention, since the court can consider cases presented by individuals and other states. Table 2 sug-

TABLE 3.
Countries That Have Neither Ratified the American Convention nor Accepted
the Jurisdiction of the Inter-American Court of Human Rights

Country	Regime types	Legal system
Antingua and Barbuda	Democratic	Common
Bahamas	Democratic	Common
Belize	Democratic	Common
Canada	Democratic	Common
Guyana	Democratic	Common
Saint Lucia	Democratic	Common
S. Vincent and the Grenadines	Democratic	Common
St. Kitts and Nevis	Democratic	Common
United States	Democratic	Common

gests that democracies are more inclined than authoritarian regimes to accept effective human rights treaties. Liberal theory predicts that new democracies will embrace human rights treaties but old democracies will not. In Latin America, not only were two old democracies (Costa Rica and Venezuela) deeply involved in the drafting of human rights treaties, they were among the first to accept the compulsory jurisdiction of the Inter-American Court of Human Rights. It is interesting to note, however, that countries with common-law legal systems—found in the United States, Canada, and the former British colonies of the Caribbean—have been more reluctant to accept the compulsory jurisdiction (see table 3). Only two countries with common-law systems, Barbados and Trinidad and Tobago, have joined the court.

The most important trend revealed in the ratification data, however, is the great regional trend toward embracing human rights norms. By the year 2000, all the countries of the Americas with civil-law systems had ratified the American Convention on Human Rights and had accepted the compulsory jurisdiction of the Inter-American Court. This is what I call the "human rights norms cascade" in Latin America.

The countries that have not accepted the jurisdiction of the Inter-American Court are all former British colonies with common-law legal systems. This supports the finding that common-law systems are generally more hesitant to ratify treaties than are civil-law systems.[79] So, what at first glance may appear to be a tendency for old democracies not to ratify human rights treaties is better explained by the nature of the legal system.

Two patterns thus emerge. In general, democracies are more likely to ratify binding human rights treaties in the Americas than are nondemocracies. However, democracies with common law may be more hesitant to do so than other democracies. Democracies and legal systems are particular types of institutions that also involve ideas. Democracies have both particular institutions for government and powerful ideas about the relationship between citizens and governments. Common-law legal systems involve not only particular types of laws, courts, and judges but also ideas about the nature and proper place of laws and judges. In civil-law systems, the autonomy of judges is more limited. Judges are supposed to apply the law but not create it, and there are no legal precedents that bind future judges. As a result, it is perhaps not surprising that countries in the civil-law tradition are less worried about the role of international or regional courts: what they see in an international treaty is essentially what these countries expect to get. In common-law systems, however, judges have more power; they not only apply law but also interpret it. Through their decisions, they create legal precedents that bind future legal decisions.[80] Because legal precedents are sources of law and because courts have a more activist function, leaders in common-law systems may be more concerned about the potential role of international judges in creating more far-reaching international law. International courts are themselves hybrid legal systems, with elements of both civil and common traditions. It seems likely, however, that political leaders from different types of legal systems interpret the role of international courts in light of their own legal tradition.

These *institutional* and *ideational* factors help us understand why countries in Latin America support human rights treaties. Leaders and citizens in democratic countries are more likely to believe in human rights, which form the basis of democratic culture and institutions. But institutional rules and roles also shape the willingness and ability of leaders to secure ratification of human rights treaties.

Many people in the United States, in government or not, are increasingly hostile to international treaties and to the United Nations. But in the 1940s the United States was at the forefront in setting up the United Nations and providing a vision of a new postwar order in which nations would cooperate to prevent future wars and promote human rights. Despite their many differences, policy makers from around the world came together and constructed an extraordinary set of institutions and norms. Franklin and Eleanor Roosevelt exercised a form of international leadership that didn't erase these differences but drew upon them to build international institutions that would advance both U.S. and international interests. The support for the United Nations and its human rights mission was not limited to the Democratic Party. Republican internationalists in San Francisco and in the Senate played crucial roles as well.

But the U.S. government did not act spontaneously or unilaterally to include human rights in international institutions. Human rights were included in the UN charter due to the work of myriad civil society organizations and a handful of governments who believed in the concept and lobbied for its inclusion. Latin American countries were among the most forceful advocates of rights and formed a crucial part of the coalition that put human rights on the international agenda.

Today the United States is no longer exercising this form of international leadership. Instead of building and cooperating with international human rights institutions, we are trying to undermine them from within and from without. This current trend resembles the attitude in the United States during the height of the Cold War from the mid-1950s to the mid-1970s, when human rights issues vanished and were replaced by anticommunism and containment as central organizing principles of policy. As we will see in the next chapter, the U.S. foreign policy of disregard for human rights during the Cold War provoked a backlash internationally and domestically. This backlash eventually led policy makers to realign foreign policy once again with ideals more consistent with U.S. identity.

By the 1970s, most of the original drafters of the UN charter, the Universal Declaration of Human Rights, and the covenants on human rights were dead or retired. But Hernán Santa Cruz continued to work in the United Nations until 1973, when he resigned after the coup that overthrew his longtime friend Salvador Allende, president of Chile. Chile, which through Santa Cruz had played an important role in the drafting of human rights norms, was now to become one of the flashpoints that would push activists to translate those norms into specific foreign policies. Santa Cruz lived to see the whole process. He returned to Santiago in 1980 when Pinochet, still ensconced in power, was the object of a global human rights campaign. He witnessed the transition to democracy in 1990 and the arrest of Pinochet in London in 1998. When Santa Cruz died in 1999 at ninety-two, his career had spanned the entire period of the emergence and evolution of the global human rights regime that he had helped build.

CHAPTER THREE

The Reemergence of Human Rights in U.S. Foreign Policy in the 1970s

In the seven years from 1973 to 1980 the United States fundamentally altered its external policy by explicitly incorporating human rights criteria into the foreign policy calculus. Although a robust human rights policy is usually associated with the Carter administration, it actually began in Congress well before Carter was even a presidential candidate. When Carter took office, the essential human rights legislation was in effect already in place. Thus any inquiry into the origins of U.S. human rights policy must examine the 1968–77 period, when Congress was holding the hearings that gave rise to the bulk of human rights legislation. The United States adopted a bilateral human rights policy in the 1970s but made no progress in adopting a *multilateral* human rights policy.

Before 1971 no legislation instructed U.S. policy makers to take human rights into account in bilateral relations. There was only one officer in the entire Department of State whose full-time responsibility was human rights. By 1977, when the Carter administration took office, an assistant secretary of state for human rights and humanitarian affairs presided over a new State Department bureau with over thirty staff.[1] One of the responsibilities of the new bureau was to prepare annual human rights reports for each country receiving U.S. assistance. Congress had enacted general human rights legislation governing U.S. military and economic aid and multilateral loans, and it approved country-specific human rights provisions banning military aid to Argentina,

Chile, and Uruguay. An important transformation had occurred in U.S. policy: human rights concerns had become embodied in the laws and the institutions implementing U.S. foreign policy.

One of the key Congressional leaders responsible for the new legislation was Donald Fraser, a representative from my home district in Minneapolis, whose hearings on human rights in Uruguay had been published in all the censored Uruguayan newspapers. Like Eleanor Roosevelt, whose work he took up almost exactly twenty years after Eisenhower asked her to resign from the UN Human Rights Commission in 1953, Fraser was a soft-spoken internationalist with strong, principled commitments.

In 1971 Fraser became chair of the Subcommittee on International Organizations of the House Foreign Relations Committee. Fraser's Minneapolis home district was liberal, but not particularly concerned about human rights when Fraser first turned to the issue in the early 1970s. "I don't think for the most part that people in the district were aware of the extent I immersed myself in human rights issues. . . . The level of interest and involvement in the district was modest."[2]

When asked how he became absorbed in human rights, Fraser replied that at the time a number of events around the world—military coups in Greece and in Chile, the Vietnam War, the situation in South Africa, and the U.S. intervention in the Dominican Republic—had heightened sensitivity to human rights issues. Fraser concluded that Congress needed a more systematic forum and criteria for responding to these issues than the case-by-case cutoffs of military aid that were being discussed. "The conservatives were offering amendments to curtail aid to left-leaning regimes, and the liberals were offering amendments to cut off aid to right-wing regimes, and it seemed to me that there must be a more objective way to incorporate human rights into U.S. foreign policy."[3] The hearings that Fraser held in his subcommittee on U.S. policy and human rights violations around the world led to a report that became the blueprint for human rights policy. Many of the policy innovations that we now take for granted—a human rights bureau in the State Department, annual country reports on human rights practices, cutoffs of military aid to rights-violating regimes, and a UN high commissioner for human rights—were recommended in this committee report in 1974.[4] Although Fraser received little pressure from his home district, he was influenced by NGOs working on human rights and, in particular, by advocates of human rights who testified before his subcommittee.

One of these human rights advocates was Senator Wilson Ferreira of Uruguay. Senator Ferreira never intended to be part of a transnational human rights advocacy network. He had prepared his whole life to be the President of Uruguay. He was often described as a "caudillo" after the old-style Latin American leaders on horseback, both because he had a larger-than-life political style and because he represented the Blancos, or National Party, with its roots in the Uruguayan countryside. Although Ferreira received the most votes in the 1971 presidential elections, his main opponent, Juan María Bordaberry, won the presidency as a result of intricate Uruguayan election laws. In 1973, President Bordaberry was faced with an economic crisis, an increasingly violent urban guerrilla movement, and a political stalemate. He subsequently carried out a "self-coup" with the support of the Uruguayan military, closing the legislature and the Supreme Court. Three days after the coup, Senator Ferreira and some of his colleagues from the Uruguayan Congress went into exile in Buenos Aires.

Not long after the Argentine military coup of March 1976, the Uruguayan and Argentine military began collaborating in repression. In May of that year, Argentine security forces kidnapped and later killed two of Ferreira's friends and colleagues, Héctor Gutiérrez Ruiz, the speaker of the Uruguayan Chamber of Deputies and a member of Ferreira's Blanco Party, and Senator Zelmar Michelini, one of the most eloquent spokesmen of the leftist opposition coalition, the Broad Front. When the kidnappers bungled an attempt to capture Ferreira, he went into exile in London. He sent his son Juan Raúl Ferreira to Washington, where he worked on Uruguay with the Washington Office on Latin America, a human rights organization. Wilson Ferreira and Juan Raúl brought the situation in Uruguay to the attention of U.S. congressional leaders like Donald Fraser and Edward Koch, representative from New York. The Ferreiras, whose lifeblood of Uruguayan politics had been cut off by exile, now replaced that passion with the transnational politics of human rights. But in contrast with some human rights activists who came to the work without strong political party commitments, the Ferreiras believed that working for human rights in Uruguay and working for the future of the Blanco Party were fully consistent. Ferreira's message to Fraser's subcommittee was simple and forceful.

> We do not come—and I am sure I speak on behalf of all my countrymen—to ask for either the help or the intervention of the U.S. government in overthrowing the dictatorship which oppresses us. That is our task as Uruguayans and ours alone. . . . We ask that you stop supporting the dictatorship openly and publicly. . . . The U.S. Embassy in Montevideo acts as a public relations agent for the Uruguayan government by publicizing throughout the world false information about conditions in Uruguay; by denying true allegations and evident facts; by claiming that subversion cannot be curbed without the suppression of liberties. . . .

[W]e object to the material and technical aid which contributes daily to the growth and increased sophistication of the repressive apparatus; and to the direct and indirect forms of financial aid which keep power artificially in the hands of tyrants. . . . We are struggling in every way possible to defend principles, ideals and a way of life that our country learned from the Constitution of the United States. No Uruguayan would ever understand if the very nation that defined those ideas 200 years ago, and today celebrates them with joy, were to continue to exercise its enormous influence in support of the enemies of our people."[5]

Following the tradition of Hernán Santa Cruz and many other Latin American politicians and diplomats, Ferreira saw human rights policy not as intervention in the internal affairs of his home country, but as a way to get the United States to *stop* intervening through its support for the dictatorship. He used the language of human rights to critique U.S. policy in the region and to plead for an alternative.

The Origins of U.S. Human Rights Policy in Congress

The crucial question in this chapter is why the United States adopted a human rights policy in the mid-1970s. As Senator Ferreira pointed out to Congressman Fraser's subcommittee, U.S. policy in the region in the 1960s had been to support dictatorships publicly and openly. Ferreira noted the contradiction between U.S. history and identity and its support for dictatorships. In 1976, the year of the Uruguayan coup and the year Ferreira testified, the United States was celebrating the bicentennial of the Declaration of Independence, which can be seen as a salute to human rights.

Rights ideals had long been perceived as part of U.S. tradition and identity, so it is not surprising that these ideals would shape foreign policy. But what caused these ideals to be activated at this particular historical moment? Why did the United States support dictatorships in the 1960s and yet come to criticize them in the 1970s? And if human rights policy was uniquely related to U.S. tradition, why did other countries adopt human rights policies around the same time? As we saw in the last chapter, U.S. human rights policy was not unique: it was part of a broader global movement.

In the United States the initial postwar belief in the promotion of human rights as a means of preventing future conflict gave way in the 1950s and 1960s to the dual pressures of anticommunism in foreign policy and states' rights and segregationist sentiment in domestic matters. Not until both of these powerful imperatives had waned could human rights ideas reemerge in U.S. policy. Even then, human rights ideas did not totally displace earlier interpretations of national security, but rather coexisted with them in Congress, in the executive, and in the public mind. The outcomes of many policy debates depended on which advocates happened to win out in that particular debate.

The United States didn't relinquish its identity as a rights-promoting state, but rather subordinated it to its Cold War anticommunism. Anticommunism, it was supposed, was the most effective way to promote rights; human rights and anticommunism were complementary, not at odds. But in the late 1960s and 1970s, alternative sources of information became available that called U.S. identity as a human rights–promoting state into question. This information was provided by an increasingly independent international and domestic press corps, and by civil society groups (NGOs) in Latin America and the United States that provided conduits for information critical of traditional U.S. policy in the region.

At the same time, generational change and shifting rules in the U.S. Congress empowered a new group of representatives and senators whose political ideals had been shaped by the protests against the Vietnam War, Watergate, and the civil rights movement. This new generation in Congress, armed with alternative sources of information, invoked traditional perceptions of U.S. identity to forge a new foreign policy, one where human rights and democracy would have a more prominent place.

In the backlash to the foreign and domestic policies of the Nixon / Kissinger years, including the fallout of Vietnam and Watergate, congressional activism in foreign affairs increased substantially, particularly in the area of human rights. The human rights issue provided a vehicle for Congress to attack the executive and assert greater control over foreign policy. The enabling conditions for this activism were in part institutional changes within Congress that allowed junior representatives and senators to play an unusually important role in the formation of foreign policy. The ability of new members to influence foreign policy was especially pronounced with respect to Latin America, where few congressmen professed much knowledge or interest.[6] In the aftermath of the Vietnam War and the civil rights movement, international human rights became a cause with significant public and congressional support. Domestic groups with an interest in human rights issues found receptive ground in Congress and testified at dozens of hearings.

From the mid-1960s to the early 1970s, two groups in Congress began to be concerned with human rights.[7] One focused on human rights violations in the Soviet Union, Eastern Europe, and other communist countries. This group is sometimes referred to as the Jackson Democrats because of the leadership role of Senator Henry "Scoop" Jackson, though it also included Republicans. Their strand of human rights thinking became particularly influential during the second Reagan administration. Human rights and anticommunism did not pose a problem of U.S. identity conflict for the Jackson Democrats, as their focus on rights violations in communist countries meant they rarely had to choose between their anticommunist and human rights ideas.

The other group, mainly liberal Democrats, was more concerned about right-wing authoritarian regimes that were U.S. allies and received substantial military and economic aid from the United States. Senators Edward Kennedy and Frank Church as well as Representatives Donald Fraser and Tom Harkin were leaders in this group. The invasion of the Dominican Republic, the Vietnam War, the situations in Rhodesia, South Africa, and in East Pakistan, and the coups in Brazil, Greece, and later in Chile all focused their attention on human rights. It was this group that highlighted a profound identity conflict. They argued that prioritizing anticommunism had led the United States to support regimes engaged in extensive violations of human rights. But when they criticized the human rights practices and called for a cutoff of military aid, they were accused of ignoring the dangers of communist subversion. These two tracks of an emergent human rights policy, which mutually influenced each other, would eventually converge uneasily to produce a genuine human rights policy rather than ad hoc responses to country-specific concerns.

The U.S. invasion of the Dominican Republic in 1965 provoked early concern over the impact of U.S. policy on human rights in Latin America. When the democratic government of nationalist Juan Bosch was overthrown by a military coup in 1963, the United States did nothing to prevent the coup. But when a "constitutionalist" civil and military uprising in 1965 attempted to bring Bosch back to power, U.S. marines landed in the Dominican Republic on April 28 to prevent what the U.S. administration referred to as a potential "second Cuba."

This intervention generated a small but influential backlash in U.S. intellectual and policy circles. Eleven years earlier, when a CIA-sponsored invasion overthrew the elected government of Jacobo Arbenz in Guatemala, virtually no one in the United States protested.[8] The Senate passed a resolution in support of the Guatemala invasion with only one negative vote. Meanwhile "the credulity and the complicity of the American press" allowed the Eisenhower administration to present the fall of Arbenz as a victory for the "idea of freedom," rather than the grave undermining of that idea it was later understood to be.[9]

By 1965, however, sectors in the United States were less prepared to respond with "credulity and complicity" to the invasion of the Dominican Republic. While the U.S. action in Guatemala in 1954 was clandestine, the United States overtly sent 22,000 troops to the Dominican Republic, the first American troops on Latin American soil since the early 1930s. When the invasion occurred, few voices protested, but as the intervention dragged on, a handful of policy makers, intellectuals, and journalists began to question the government's motives, justifications, and information. The Johnson administration had justified the intervention on the grounds that the Dominican revolt was in the hands of "communist conspirators," but according to Tad Szulc, the *New York Times* reporter covering the story in the Dominican Republic, "no U.S. official could name visible communists in positions of command, although a list of 58 communists allegedly connected with the movement was widely circulated by U.S. sources."[10] The American embassy in Santo Domingo fed the American press with such "obvious falsifications" that journalists were able to expose them "with devastating effect." Szulc continues:

> Having arrived in Santo Domingo ready to believe in the integrity of their embassy and the correctness of their government's policy, [the journalists] became bitter critics. . . . Most of these critics would have approved the landing of marines had there been a Communist danger, but once they understood that no danger existed, they condemned the intervention. They were shattered by the realization that their president was lying to them. The credibility gap had been opened. It would never close.[11]

At the beginning of the twenty-first century, with Vietnam, Watergate, Iran-contragate, and the Monica Lewinsky scandals all behind us, it may be difficult to imagine that in the mid-1960s sophisticated individuals might indeed be "shattered by the realization that their government was lying to them." But this realization is crucial for the history of human rights policy. The press and nongovernmental organizations (NGOs) would come to play an increasingly influential role as providers of information to Congress and the public, information that would come to be seen as more reliable than that which Congress was getting from the executive branch.

The Dominican invasion influenced a number of key people later involved in human rights work. The Latin America Committee of the National Council of Churches issued a strong statement protesting the invasion, which represented the beginning of a different approach within church groups to international policy.[12] Liberal scholars were also influenced by the Dominican invasion. Abraham Lowenthal was a Ford Foundation officer in the Dominican Republic when the U.S. marines invaded. He later wrote the most influential book on the intervention, in which he concluded that the U.S. military intervention was a "tragic event, costly to the Dominican Republic, to the United States, and to inter-American relations." Lowenthal located the sources of the tragedy in the U.S. policy apparatus, and especially "the adoption of dubious analogies, the bureaucratic reinforcement of such analogies, the domestication of dissent, and the uncritical acceptance of established conceptual frameworks even when they are severely flawed."[13] The main dubious analogy in the case of the Dominican Republic was "another Cuba." Lowenthal argued that "conscious, forceful, and repeatedly critical questioning of the dubious analogy from within or from outside the bureaucracy might undermine its power, but such questioning rarely occurs. . . . On the contrary, the dubious analogy is preserved, given sanctity and power by public rhetoric. . . . Policy makers are prisoners of their own and others' language and concepts."[14]

Within the U.S. government, questioning had also started. As a new congressman from Minnesota and junior member of the House Foreign Affairs Committee, Donald Fraser visited the Dominican Republic shortly after the invasion in 1965. Fraser recalls that the Dominican episode

> clearly influenced my thinking about the Vietnam war. I came to understand that we weren't fighting for people's right to self-government. We didn't have an interest in what the Dominican people wanted. Our policy was based on what we didn't want, and I thought that was an inappropriate objective of U.S. policy. That perception allowed me to discard the overwhelming rationale for Vietnam, which was the "Munich" analogy, the need to hold the line and avoid appeasement. But in trying to learn from history so as not to repeat it, there is also a need to test that against one's vision of the future. I had come to believe firmly that people had the right to choose their own governments.[15]

Some questioning even started within the CIA. The reaction to the Dominican crisis of CIA agent Philip Agee, watching from his post in Uruguay, reveals his increasing disenchantment with U.S. policy toward the region. "Nobody's going to believe Johnson's story of another Cuba-style revolution in the making. . . . Uruguayans don't understand either. People here think Bosch stands for the kind of liberal reform that brought social integration to Uruguay. Already the street demonstrations against the U.S. have started."[16]

While none of these responses to the invasion of the Dominican Republic added up to a significant domestic opposition to U.S. policy, they suggested that the U.S. policy makers and public would not grant the government the complete "credulity and complicity" that had characterized the debate over Guatemala in 1954.

Although international human rights norms already existed before the 1970s, they were not implemented, nor did activist groups in Latin America and the United States frequently use human rights terms to frame their concerns or demands. But in the late 1960s and early 1970s such groups rediscovered the language of human rights as a way to express their concerns. This language came to resonate in policy circles because it invoked traditional understandings of U.S. identity.

The issue of human rights provided a common ground for diverse groups to frame their concerns and work together.[17] To understand the shift in U.S. human rights policy toward Latin America, we need to look at the common role of NGOs as behind-the-scenes providers of information and testimony that instigated questioning of past policies and policy change. Human rights groups in repressive countries began to link up with a variety of international actors—international NGOs, international and regional organizations, and private foundations—to protest violations and pressure for change. We cannot understand U.S. human rights policy in Latin America without exploring the connections between U.S. policy and these international groups and domestic human rights organizations.[18] International and regional actors were in turn connected to domestic human rights organizations in Latin American countries, which served as sources of information and inspiration for organizations and individuals in a transnational advocacy network.[19]

NGOs played a particularly significant role in the origins of U.S. human rights policy. NGOs helped initiate concern about human rights, provided information to U.S. policy makers about human rights abuses, helped initiate specific human rights policies (in some cases actually drafting legislation), and lobbied for more consistent implementation. Because NGOs often worked behind the scenes and didn't claim credit for their successes, their importance may be overlooked or underestimated.

Amnesty International, founded in 1961, had a mandate limited to prisoners of conscience, torture, the death penalty, and unjust trials. The focus on rights of the person found an echo in the liberal ideological tradition of Western countries, where the human rights movement had the bulk of its members. But the focus on basic rights of the person was also consonant with the human rights problems in the main target countries of the early movement. With the focus on cases of Chile, Uruguay, Argentina, and Brazil, it seemed imperative to address the problems of execution, torture, disappearance, and political imprisonment committed by military regimes in these countries.

Human rights policy originated from the "conscious, forceful, and repeatedly critical questioning" of the existing foreign policy framework that Lowenthal found absent in debates about the invasion of the Dominican Republic. In the Senate in the early 1970s, key senators like Edward Kennedy, Frank Church, and Jacob Javits began to focus on human rights issues, although they didn't always use the language of human rights. In the Senate, rights debates started over the issue of embargoes on Rhodesia and sanctions against South Africa, they continued in regard to the Greek military junta and the military regime in Brazil, and they culminated in the hearings on Chile. Vietnam formed the backdrop of the foreign policy debate of the time. The early debates to curtail military aid to specific repressive regimes are indicative of the ideological universe of the time. The Greek case was one of the first instances where parallels were made between the executive's failure to respond to our nation's values in Vietnam and elsewhere.[20] As one congressman maintained,

> The very ideals that we seem to be professing and the ones that we say we are concerned about achieving in South Vietnam are the ones that get set aside in countries like Greece. . . . I am distressed about what it means not just to those of us who might sit on committees like this and have a chance to see this close up, but to our young people today. . . . You people come in and justify money for Greece and we find a way to live with these things that we don't like. But, every time we do that, it undercuts the credibility of these institutions, of your job, of yourself, the State Department, and the Federal Government.[21]

In 1971, critics in Congress presented legislation to suspend all military assistance to Greece, in response to human rights violations and the suspension of democracy after the coup in 1967. Those who favored sending military aid argued that "at least the present [Greek] government is pro-United States and pro-Western in an area where this is rare. We should let well enough alone and not invite chaos and communism."[22]

Supporters of the legislation to suspend aid to Greece stressed questions of U.S. identity: "There are those who will view this amendment as an undue interference in the domestic affairs of the Greek government. But let me remind them that this is American taxpayers' money we are talking about—not the Greek regime's—and it is the responsibility of Congress to insure that these funds are not squandered on governments which mock our democratic ideals."[23] The 1971 attempt to cut off aid to Greece was defeated, but these arguments would reappear more frequently.

In the Senate, Edward Kennedy played a central role in the attempt to put Latin American human rights issues on the foreign policy agenda, with the help of his main staff person on this issue, Mark Schneider. Schneider's interest in human rights had developed through a series of formative experiences. As a student, he got involved with the civil rights movement and worked with the American Civil Liberties Union while studying at Berkeley. He went to El Salvador with the Peace Corps in the mid-1960s and later was awarded an American Political Science Association Fellowship to work in Edward Kennedy's office on issues relating to foreign relations and Latin America. One of his first assignments was to write a speech for Kennedy to deliver as the first Mansfield lecture at the University of Montana. Entitled "Beginning Anew in Latin America," it sketched out a new kind of relation with Latin America. The *Saturday Review* published an article based on the speech in October 1970, and Kennedy's colleagues put it in the *Congressional Record*. This early attempt by an important congressional leader to assemble individual cases, such as Greece and Brazil, into a general policy statement signaled a new way of thinking about human rights and U.S. foreign policy.

> Despite our strong tradition of democracy, the United States continues to support regimes in Latin America that deny basic human rights. We stand silent while political prisoners are tortured in Brazil. . . . I point this out . . . because Brazil is ruled by a government that we fully support with money, arms, technical assistance, and the comfort of close diplomatic relations.
>
> The Council of Europe has condemned the Greek military dictatorship for political oppression and the torture of political prisoners. The Organization of American States can do no less. It is the responsibility of the nations of the hemisphere to focus the spotlight of international opinion on the outrages being committed in Brazil. . . .
>
> Much of the $673 million in military aid granted in the past nine years has gone to those governments that displayed their contempt for democratic principles. The premise has been that anti-Americanism, subversion, and communist insurgency will end if police and military forces are better trained and equipped. . . .
>
> We cannot prevent change. The only rational policy for American assistance to Latin America is to direct our effort to responsive, representative governments, reflective of the needs of their people. The destiny of Latin America is for Latin Americans to decide, not the United States. But we can make it clear that, although we will not intervene, neither will we be party to any form of repression of the people and their aspirations.[24]

This speech is interesting in many ways. Kennedy is using the human rights idea to make a pointed critique of U.S. Cold War policy in the region and to suggest an alternative based on democracy and human rights ideals. He is aware of European human rights policies as a model that could be emulated. Kennedy's statement differs from later human rights policies in that he advocates sweeping alternatives: "immediate withdrawal of all of our military missions," "phasing out our military assistance programs and halting sales of arms on credit to Latin America," and reserving "economic assistance for development programs designed to produce social justice and not solely those projects aimed at economic growth."[25] These policies are far more ambitious than the targeted cutoffs of military and economic assistance to repressive countries that were later incorporated in human rights legislation.

The speech is also interesting for the prominence the Brazilian case receives. On May 5, 1964, only one month after the military coup in Brazil, Lincoln Gordon, the U.S. ambassador, made a speech before the Brazilian National War College heralding the Brazilian "revolution" (coup) as an event that encouraged the cause of freedom in the world and that "may well take its place alongside the initiation of the Marshall Plan, the ending of the Berlin blockade, the defeat of communist aggression in Korea, and the solution of the Cuba-missile base crisis as one of the critical points of inflection in mid-twentieth century world history."[26] Gordon served as ambassador to Brazil until early 1966, after which he was assistant secretary of state for inter-American affairs and then president of Johns Hopkins University. In this speech he offered policy makers in Brazil and elsewhere a high-profile cue that was consonant with U.S. anticommunist policy and national security doctrine. The United States would not only support military coups but would embrace and justify them.

The Brazilian coup of 1964 was indeed a critical "inflection point" in U.S. relations with Latin America, but not in the way Gordon suggested. Rather, the repressive practices of the Brazilian military (and the unambiguous support offered to the military government) led key policy makers, intellectuals, church leaders, and foundations in the United States to question the fundamental premise of foreign policy toward Latin America and to put forward an alternative vision that incorporated human rights and democracy.

The most repressive period of the Brazilian military regime that came into power in 1964 was under General Emílio Médici in 1968–74. Almost two thousand individuals later testified in military courts that during this period they had been tortured while being interrogated.[27] By 1970 Americans were becoming aware of the extent of repression in Brazil. An early network of individuals and organizations in Europe, Latin America, and the United States organized a campaign to publicize the torture of political prisoners in Brazil. In the United States, a handful of academics and members of religious organizations who had lived and worked in Brazil and elsewhere in Latin America initiated the campaign.

Brady Tyson, a political scientist and Methodist minister, initially learned about human rights issues in his work in the 1950s in the civil rights movement with Martin Luther King. The work of southern Methodist women in their campaign against apartheid in South Africa in the 1950s introduced him to the international dimension of human rights. While serving as a missionary in Brazil after the 1964 coup, Tyson began sending circular letters to his friends in the States, describing the increasingly repressive situation in Brazil. Forced to leave Brazil in 1966, he began teaching at American University in Washington, D.C., where his home became a way station for Brazilians and for Americans returning from Latin America. In late 1969 and early 1970, after reports about torture in Brazil became more alarming, Tyson met with William Wipfler, the assistant director of the Latin American Department at the National Council of Churches, and with Ralph Della Cava, a historian at Queen's College and an expert on the Catholic Church in Brazil, along with other academics, to try to organize a strategy to bring the situation in Brazil to public attention. When the Church became a target of repression in Brazil, Della Cava received reports of human rights abuses from his contacts there. In 1966 Tyson and his academic colleagues decided to launch a publicity campaign about torture in Brazil and publish as many articles as possible in a short time.[28] Within weeks of each other, Tyson and his colleagues published a series of articles including an article in the *Washington Post*.[29] This flurry of publications attracted surprising attention from U.S. policy makers. Lincoln Gordon, the former ambassador, wrote a long letter to the editor in response to Della Cava's article in *Commonweal*. In the letter Gordon clarified his position on Brazil: "During the period before mid-1967, no cases of torture were brought to my attention. I would have condemned them if they had been."[30]

Della Cava's letter in response to Gordon pointed out that many cases of torture and other human rights abuses were in fact documented in the Brazilian press during the time Gordon was ambassador in Brazil. Della Cava continued:

> But, even if we accept unquestionably Dr. Gordon's view of it, we can have no doubt about his own choice in the matter: in order to avoid a left-wing dictatorship he urged (and continued to urge) moral and material support of a right-wing dictatorship. When that regime followed the course of repression and terror right-wing regimes are wont to follow, Dr. Gordon expresses shock; regrets his helplessness before the trend of events; assigns culpability to the failures of a deceased leader of the Brazilian military; and disclaims all personal responsibility for the regrettable outcome. . . . Dr. Gordon's letter should be read as a model of what ails U.S. foreign policy.

This exchange, and all the documents created and published by the group of activists and academics working with Tyson, Della Cava, and Wipfler, were published as an appendix to the hearings before the Appropriations Subcommittee on the Foreign Assistance Programs for 1972. As one activist later pointed out, "suddenly, the issue [of torture in Brazil] was on the table."[31]

Wipfler got Tom Quigley of the U.S. Catholic Conference (USCC) involved in human rights work, and the National Council of Churches and the USCC together brought a case before the Inter-American Commission for Human Rights (IACHR) against the Brazilian government for torture. Wipfler and Quigley had been receiving testimonies of torture in Brazil. Sometimes, the victims told them the stories directly; other testimonies arrived through surprising channels. Most surprising, Wipfler recalled, was testimony from women about torture at a women's prison, written in tiny writing on toilet paper and rolled up inside a ball-point pen. The writing had to be translated with a magnifying glass. Eventually the National Council of Churches and the USCC presented 150 such testimonies of torture in Brazil as part of their case against the Brazilian government in 1970–71. The IACHR's charter allows it to receive cases from NGOs, but the staff was startled to receive such detailed data from Brazil by way of two U.S.-based church groups.[32]

The network contacts in Brazil were made primarily through the Catholic Church, the Brazilian Bar Association, and the Brazilian Press Association, as compared to the later networks in Argentina and Chile, where explicit human rights organizations were the central nodes. The most important of these network contacts were Brazilian churches. In 1968 Brazilian bishops created the Brazilian Commission of Justice and Peace. After 1972, under the leadership of Cardinal Paulo Arns, the São Paulo branch of this commission became one of the most important centers of human rights activity in Brazil.[33]

The campaign succeeded in attracting the attention of some key members of Congress, especially when reports charged that U.S.-trained Brazilian police were the main perpetrators of torture and repression. The United States had been training Brazilian police since 1959 through the Public Safety Program of the U.S. Agency for International Development (AID). In 1970 Senator Church began an investigation into U.S. financial support for the Brazilian regime and the use of torture in Brazil. Although the senators were not yet using the language of human rights, many of the concerns that characterized the later debate were raised in these early hearings. Questions about sovereignty and intervention pervade the discussion. The U.S. ambassador to Brazil, testifying before a Senate subcommittee, quoted approvingly President Nixon's statement that "we deal with governments as they are."[34] Senator Church's response captures the concerns that some members of Congress were grappling with at this time.

> We not only deal with them, we extend lavish amounts of money, in the case of Brazil, $2 billion to support Brazilian programs under the auspices of this country. . . . Now when I go to American colleges and talk to young people they ask why have we spent $2 billion in Brazil when the government there is dictatorial in character, run by military men, and numbers of Brazilians are said to be mistreated in the jails, where there are recurrent reports of human torture. Why should the United States give such lavish support to a government of this kind? . . . They say, "What does this have to do with the kind of society we are supposed to stand for?" Those questions are not easily answered, and since ultimately public support will be necessary to sustain any foreign policy, what happens when that foreign policy falls out of contact with the traditional values of our country in such a way that people can no longer understand its purpose nor justify their support for it? Young people say, if we are not against this kind of thing then what is it we are for in the world that is worth supporting? This is the ultimate test of a foreign policy and frankly, public support for the American foreign policy is rapidly eroding away.[35]

Church makes a forceful statement about the importance of U.S. identity. He expresses both his own opinion of what the United States should stand for and the demand coming from the public, especially the young, that U.S. foreign policy reflect "traditional values of our country." In two key early debates over human rights in Greece and in Brazil, members of Congress evoked this image of trying to explain U.S. policy to young people. This image highlights some dilemmas of the government when its policies diverge from the country's values. These debates of course took place against the backdrop of a very vocal and increasingly radical student movement in opposition to the Vietnam War. The Vietnam War, and the protests against it, are indeed a crucial context for understanding the emergence of human rights policies. Even when the war and the protests were not directly invoked, concern about disaffected young people, the loss of values, and the deteriorating legitimacy of government institutions were the grand themes pervading human rights debates.

These debates over U.S. identity were provoked by new policy frameworks and alternative sources of information that questioned what was happening in Brazil and asked who was responsible. If U.S. policy makers had to depend solely on information from the U.S. State Department via the U.S. embassy in Brazil, as they had in the past, they would not have raised the issue of torture in Brazil. Ambassador Gordon and his staff were not seeking such information and would not have conveyed it. Instead, the information was arriving from groups of victims in Brazil by way of Brazilian churches to U.S. church groups and academics, who brought it to the attention of the U.S. press and policy makers.

In the debates over Brazil members of Congress criticized the AID Public Safety Program, which sent U.S. police officers abroad to help train the police in other countries.[36] Critics of the Public Safety Program argued that U.S.-trained police officers were directly involved in torturing prisoners. This same AID Public Safety Program gained notoriety in Uruguay as well. In 1970, the Tupamaro guerrillas in Uruguay kidnapped an AID Public Safety Program officer, Daniel Mitrione, accused him of training Uruguayan police in torture techniques, and eventually murdered him.

Mitrione's stated task was to "professionalize" the Uruguayan police. Professionalization often meant training the police to be more violent rather than less so. In the 1960s, when confronting a criminal, Uruguayan policemen were allowed to return gunfire but prohibited from initiating it. Mitrione aimed to change that restriction. He also sent seven Uruguayan policemen to take a CIA course in the United States that included instruction in techniques for building bombs.[37] The CIA was encouraging Chilean, Brazilian, Argentine, and Uruguayan military and police officers to share intelligence and training. Subsequently, the Chilean intelligence service came to play an important role in organizing these contacts among the Argentine, Bolivian, Chilean, Paraguayan, and Uruguayan intelligence organs and, to a lesser extent, those of Brazil. This coordination developed into a network of physical repression called Operation Condor, which was implemented most enthusiastically by Argentina, Chile, and Uruguay. Sometimes referred to as the Condor Plan, this network led to "the surveillance, the harassment, and finally the assassination of political exiles."[38] The Uruguayan military used their contacts with the Argentine military to ask them to murder Wilson Ferreira's colleagues, the Uruguayan congressmen Gutiérrez Ruiz and Michelini, in 1976.

The Brazilian and Uruguayan police already knew how to torture before the advent of the Public Safety Program. One of the most knowledgeable and fiercest critics of the CIA in Latin America, the former CIA agent Philip Agee, wrote that in 1964, before the start of the Public Safety Program in Uruguay, "torture of communists and other extreme leftists was used in interrogations by our liaison agents in the police."[39] In 1965 Agee reported that he and the CIA station chief had heard moans and screams at the police station, and they had realized it was torture. Agee's most damning accusation was against himself for inaction. "Why didn't Horton or I say anything to Rodriguez? We just sat there embarrassed and shocked. I'm going to be hearing that voice for a long time."[40] He resolved that he would pass no more names to the police as long as the current Uruguayan deputy chief of investigations remained. While Agee accuses himself and the U.S. government of passivity in the face of torture, four years later the accusation against Mitrione was that he contributed to teaching torture. After Mitrione's murder, a member of the Uruguayan police who had worked with him gave an interview to a Brazilian journalist in which he said that Mitrione advocated psychological torture and that he had introduced scientific methods of torture to the Uruguayan police. A carefully researched book-length treatment of Mitrione's life presents these facts but stops short of actually confirming that Mitrione taught torture to the Uruguayan police.[41]

Whether Mitrione taught torture or not, he was undeniably part of an overall U.S. government policy that supported authoritarian regimes and justified whatever methods were necessary to combat communism. The NSC-68 directive says it clearly: "The integrity of our system will not be jeopardized by any measures, covert or overt, violent or non-violent, which serve the purpose of frustrating the Kremlin designs." U.S. policy during this period expressed a deep distrust for democratic politics in the developing world and a disregard for civil liberties.

One of the clearest expressions of this overall policy was the U.S. Army School of the Americas, located in the Panama Canal Zone. Established in 1946 as the Caribbean Training Center and renamed the School of the Americas in 1963, it focused on training Latin American military officers to defend against "communist subversion." Later, the School of the Americas would become a symbol of U.S. support for dictatorships in Latin America. The campaign to shut it down will be discussed in chapter 5. In the late 1960s, however, it was the Public Safety Program for training police that attracted the attention of activists, not the School of the Americas.

Not all members of the U.S. Congress shared the belief that anticommunism could be used to justify any foreign policy. When James Abourezk, senator from South Dakota, criticized the Public Safety Program, the executive agreed to close it down without even a campaign (which would have led to congressional hearings). Congress ended the AID Public Safety Program in Brazil, but other United States military or economic aid to Brazil was not suspended until much later during the Carter administration.

In these early debates, all congressional activity was on a country-by-country basis. No general vision of alternative policies or doctrines guided foreign policy. Applying a human rights lens, however, some members of Congress saw that peoples they had thought to be *disparate* (e.g., Greeks and Brazilians) were all suffering from *similar* conditions. What connected these cases was the substantial support and training these rights-violating governments had received from the United States, which implied that the United States was implicated in the violations.

The early efforts to cut off aid to right-wing dictators in Greece and Brazil need to be seen in the context of human rights sanctions that were later applied to the Soviet Union. In 1974 Congress passed the Jackson-Vanik amendment to the trade act, which was designed to deny most-favored-nation status, credit, and credit guarantees to any country with a "nonmarket economy" (i.e., a communist economy) that denied its citizens the right to emigrate. First introduced in early 1973, the Jackson-Vanik amendment drew upon an article in the Universal Declaration of Human Rights affirming that anyone has the right to leave any country, including his own. Although it focused on one specific right, it was "the first piece of US legislation consciously and deliberately inspired by the Universal Declaration."[42] Designed primarily to respond to Soviet restrictions on Jewish emigration, the amendment nevertheless set a congressional precedent in linking human rights practices to trade. Initially resisted by the executive branch, the amendment eventually received broad support from both parties and from both the executive and legislative branches.[43]

The Jackson-Vanik amendment was narrow in both the right it focused on and the range of countries to which it applied. It did not constitute anything like a general statement on human rights policy. In late 1973 such a general vision began to emerge out of a set of hearings under Fraser's leadership.

The Work of the Fraser Subcommittee

After Fraser was appointed to chair the House Subcommittee on International Organizations in 1971, he decided to hold a series of hearings on human rights.[44] Institutional changes in the House in 1971 had recently allowed subcommittees to have their own staff. In June 1973 Fraser hired the human rights scholar and activist John Salzberg to prepare a series of hearings from August to December of 1973.[45] Salzberg had written his doctoral dissertation on the UN human rights machinery and had worked for years with the New York office of the International Commission of Jurists. Fraser claims that his own knowledge of human rights at the time was "very modest." "I had strong feelings, but as we got to work on the subcommittee, I got introduced to the U.N. system and human rights standards. . . . the hearings helped clarify my views."[46] According to Salzberg, Fraser's interest in human rights arose from "strong moral or ethical principles in terms of our country's beliefs." Fraser was concerned by the dichotomy in the United States between professed beliefs and foreign policy, especially policy toward countries closely linked by military alliances or military aid. In addition, his long-standing interest in the United Nations and ample contacts with European parliamentarians had given him ideas about new ways to respond to human rights abuses.[47]

Between August 1 and December 7, 1973, the subcommittee held fifteen hearings with forty-five witnesses, including government officials, lawyers, scholars, and representatives of NGOs. The early hearings invited legal scholars and knowledgeable activists to provide an overview of international human rights. Although most of the hearings focused on the general issue of the international protection of human rights, the witnesses also discussed a number of country cases, including Burundi, South Africa, Brazil, Northern Ireland, the Soviet Union, Bangladesh, and Chile.[48] Fraser questioned at length the very first witness, Niall MacDermot, secretary-general of the International Commission of Jurists, about the European human rights system and the role of the Council of Europe and the European Court of Human Rights. Fraser was particularly interested in the report of the European Commission for Human Rights on torture by the military government in Greece.[49] The commission's report eventually led Greece to withdraw from the Council of Europe, to avoid being expelled for its human rights practices.

The hearings clarified the institutional position of human rights in the early 1970s. Aside from the European reporting on Greece, very little government attention was devoted to human rights. No countries had external human rights policies or even human rights offices within their foreign ministries. NGOs were still relatively weak, underfunded, and uncoordinated, although efforts at coordination were under way. Although the United Nations had made excellent progress in defining human rights and codifying human rights norms and standards, it was virtually paralyzed when it came to preventing human rights violations. Fraser understood these weaknesses. "We are engaged in . . . what is known as a consciousness raising process . . . trying to elevate this subject matter and explore ways in which we can strengthen our own participation. I don't know what the ultimate conclusion will be, but we are probing for specific ideas to advance with respect to the executive branch as well as the Congress itself."[50]

On September 11, 1973, after the first Fraser hearing and just days before the second series of hearings was to open, the Chilean military brutally overthrew the elected government of the socialist president Salvador Allende. The coincidence threw human rights into high political relief. There was a sense that if such violations could take place in Chile, one of Latin America's oldest democracies, they could take place anywhere. But the Chilean coup made a great impact because the debates had already supplied a way to understand it. The coup was important not as an isolated event but as an experience juxtaposed to others, such as U.S. support for the repression in Greece and Brazil, the war in Vietnam, and the legacy of the civil rights movement.

As Salzberg prepared for his hearings, he met with Wipfler, Quigley, and other church activists who had formed a group to work on U.S. human rights policy toward Latin America. After the Uruguayan and Chilean coups in 1973, the group decided to set up an office in Washington, since they realized they needed a base from which they could talk to people in Congress. When they set up the Washington Office on Latin America in 1973, it was one of very few organizations working in Washington on human rights.

The Fraser hearings were not always well attended. Some members of the Foreign Affairs Committee were indifferent or hostile. At times, Fraser was the only representative present. Wayne Hays, a representative from Ohio who was a member of the Foreign Affairs Committee and the chair of the House Administration Committee, tried to hold up the paycheck of Fraser's staff director after hearings on human rights violations in Indonesia, which included testimony from a human rights activist who had been a member of the Indonesian Communist Party.[51] Other committee members were more sympathetic, especially the Democrats Benjamin Rosenthal, Jonathan Bingham, and Lee Hamilton and the Republicans Charles Whalen, John Buchanan, and Paul Findley. According to Fraser, "by churning the subject over and over, you create an environment more aware and more supportive when you propose legislation."

Another benefit of the hearings was to sensitize the State Department to congressional concern with human rights issues. Many hearings consisted of testimony from NGOs, from State Department officials, and from individuals who had suffered human rights abuses. Often State Department officials were ill at ease when testifying, showing a lack of interest, concern, and awareness of human rights issues. For example, in hearings on human rights in Chile, Harry Shlaudeman, deputy secretary of state for inter-American affairs, said at one point in an uncharacteristically sharp exchange with Fraser that "I find myself in the position of doing what I really do not want to do, which is defending the Chilean government."

> **Fraser:** You have done it very effectively this afternoon, Mr. Secretary, and your last statements are the most astonishing of all. . . . If there were a coup d'etat by the U.S. military forces, and they exercised governmental power, suspended the Constitution, recessed the Congress, issued preemptory decrees and tried people without appeals, or habeas corpus, you would not call that a totalitarian government either I gather?

Shlaudeman: I think we have a difference in semantics.

Fraser: Probably it is a fairly important difference for one who is being tried.[52]

The hearings were educational, not only for Fraser but also for some of the human rights activists who attended. Joe Eldridge, a Methodist missionary who had left Chile after the coup, remembers that he "vented his fury" about the situation in Chile but knew little about human rights issues generally. "The Fraser hearings were like my Bible, my introduction to human rights. I didn't know what it was about. I just knew it really got debate started. Don Fraser and John Salzberg helped me understand how U.S. policy could give articulation to international standards. . . . I really learned the limits of indignation and how to put it in a language that Washington can digest."[53] When the Methodist church agreed to pay Joe's salary to work with the new Washington Office on Latin America, he put the new language of human rights to good use as he lobbied Congress.

Some of the testimony had a didactic quality reminiscent of a classroom. The Berkeley law professor Frank Newman, who had recently led the Amnesty International mission to Chile, clarified that the Covenant on Civil and Political Rights had an "escape clause" that allowed governments to take some exceptional measures in time of public emergencies. Newman also stressed that the covenant was very clear on the inviolability of certain rights, no matter what the situation, including the right to life, freedom from torture, freedom from slavery, and freedom of thought and religion. When asked if human rights policy could violate the prohibition in the UN charter on intervention in the domestic affairs of a government, Newman responded that "violations of human rights of the kind we are talking about, gross violations of human rights, are no longer matters essentially within the domestic jurisdiction of states."[54] Fraser and his staff noted the importance that witnesses placed on the international consensus around certain "gross violations of human rights" and would later write this distinction into U.S. human rights legislation.

What is unique about the Fraser committee hearings of 1973 is the quality of the conversation between Fraser and many of his witnesses. Through his carefully crafted questions, the chair invited the witnesses to think aloud with him about the shape of a new policy. A new policy agenda was in the making, with international lawyers like Thomas Burgenthal and Frank Newman, church activists like Thomas Quigley, and lawyer/NGO types like Niall McDermott, all part of a process of articulating and thinking through alternatives. Through these conversations, Fraser came to believe that the United States needed to assert a general or blanket position on human rights based on principle, rather than dealing with them on a case-by-case basis. The principled position needed to reflect the values of the American public and be consistent with the basic international consensus on human rights. Whenever possible, this policy could be articulated through U.S. participation in multilateral and international organizations. Fraser also concluded that a "respectful and proper bilateral relationship should include a strong affirmative position in defense of human rights. Our concern should be limited to those rights which are internationally recognized. Consequently, we would not be imposing our value system on them."[55]

Despite some indifference and hostility demonstrated by certain members of Congress, these hearings produced a set of legislative initiatives that were to transform U.S. foreign policy over the next decade. Upon the conclusion of the first round of hearings, the subcommittee issued a slim report titled *Human Rights in the World Community: A Call for U.S. Leadership,* which served as a blueprint for human rights policy over the next two decades.[56] Significantly, the report immediately situated itself above the left/right ideological divide that permeated the early debates over cutoffs of aid to specific countries. "Government oppression is not limited to any particular ideological persuasion. Governments of the right, center, and left have been responsible for violating the fundamental rights of men and women."[57]

U.S. Human Rights Legislation

The three most important pieces of U.S. legislation that arose out of the 1973 hearings and were recommended in the *Call for U.S. Leadership* report were (1) the creation an Office for Human Rights within the State Department (later called the Bureau for Human Rights and Humanitarian Affairs, and today called the Bureau for Democracy, Human Rights, and Labor); (2) the requirement that the State Department prepare annual country reports on the "observance and respect for internationally recognized human rights in each country proposed as a recipient of security assistance" (later extended to all member countries of the UN); (3) insertion of language in section 502B of the Foreign Assistance Act governing military aid, demanding for the first time that no security assistance be provided to countries that engaged in "a consistent pattern of gross violations of internationally recognized human rights." The language of the section was carefully drafted by Fraser and his staff, who wanted to refer to international human rights standards, not just U.S. standards, and who were especially concerned about consistent patterns of gross violations, not just incidents.[58] The influence of UN language is evident. The section begins, "The United States shall, in accordance with its international obligations as set forth in the Charter of the United Nations and in keeping with the constitutional heritage and traditions of the United States, promote and encourage increased respect for human rights and fundamental freedoms throughout the world without distinction as to race, sex, language, or religion."[59] Fraser and his staff stressed the constitutional heritage and traditions of the United States in an effort to evoke identity and garner support for their legislation.

Section 502B goes on to define a gross violation of internationally recognized human rights as "torture or cruel, inhumane, or degrading punishment, prolonged detention without charges and trial, and other flagrant denials of the right to life, liberty, or the security of the person." (Later the legislation was amended to add disappearances as another specific example.)

Critics have sometimes complained that U.S. legislation has an exceedingly narrow conception of human rights as a result of its political bias toward civil and political rights. In the drafting of the legislation, however, Fraser and his staff were much influenced by Frank Newman's interpretation of international law: gross violations of human rights are no longer essentially within the domestic jurisdiction of states, and thus actions to protest them cannot be construed as intervention under the UN charter. In other words, the narrow wording was an attempt to follow an international consensus so that U.S. policy would not violate the charter's prohibition on intervention in domestic affairs.

All future U.S. human rights policies flow from and are based on these three early pieces of legislation. The Bureau of Humanitarian Affairs and Human Rights in the State Department institutionalized the human rights idea. It bore the responsibility for assuring that human rights concerns were brought into all aspects of U.S. foreign policy. The country reports created a process of information gathering that had far-reaching implications for U.S. policy; and section 502B remains the legislation at the core of the human rights policy.

The report *A Call for U.S. Leadership* also made many prescient recommendations that the U.S. government considered and adopted over the next two decades, including the ratification of some of the international human rights treaties, efforts to promote the status of women, and efforts to strengthen international organizations that deal with human rights, such as the UN Commission on Human Rights and the Inter-American Commission on Human Rights. Other recommendations anticipated global debates by over twenty years: for example, the report calls for a UN high commissioner for human rights and calls on the United States to convene a diplomatic conference to consider the restriction or prohibition of the use of specific weapons that cause unnecessary suffering, such as delayed-action weapons like land mines.[60]

An unusual coalition of liberals and conservatives supported human rights legislation. In Congress, votes in favor of cutting assistance to violators came from liberals dedicated to reducing American ties to repressive regimes, from anticommunists who supported human rights policy against communist regimes, and from conservatives with a more general interest in reducing U.S. expenditures on foreign aid. Opposition to such sanctions came from administration officials in favor of "flexibility," from career Latin American specialists, especially in the State Department, from members of Congress who believed such actions were contrary to traditional interpretations of U.S. national security, and from some business interests. The proponents of human rights policy, as we see in the debates discussed above, over and over again invoked "identity" language in defense of human rights policy. They spoke of the heritage and traditions of the United States, the values of the American public, the "kind of society we are supposed to stand for," and our democratic ideals. Although different words were used, each speaker ventured that foreign policy should in some way be more consistent with visions of who we Americans are as a people and what we stand for and take pride in—in other words, visions of national identity.

In 1975 the Helsinki Final Act was signed, and what has come to be known as the "Helsinki process" was initiated, a process that, contrary to what the drafters anticipated, came to have human rights at its core, and that contributed to the undermining of political and ideological structures in Eastern Europe and the Soviet Union.[61] The main supporters of the Helsinki process were different from, and sometimes antagonistic to, supporters of human rights policy toward Latin America. David Forsythe's study of human rights voting in Congress from 1977 to 1984 concludes that few members of Congress voted for human rights across the board. Instead, conservatives tended to vote for human rights policies punishing leftist regimes, and liberals, right-wing regimes.[62] The most consistent support for initiatives aimed at Latin American countries came from liberal Democrats. Opposition came from members who voted frequently in favor of "pro-security" legislation, such as increases in the defense budget and support for major weapons systems.[63] Simply put, party affiliation and ideology were the best predictors of human rights voting, and region and other constituency factors were weak predictors.[64]

Nevertheless, the convergence of human rights debates about the Soviet Union and Eastern Europe, on one hand, and about Latin America, on the other, began to create some impetus for synergy and consistency that led to the emergence of a more comprehensive human rights policy. After the initial round of hearings that led to the *Call for U.S. Leadership* report, the Fraser subcommittee continued its hearings on human rights practices in diverse countries.

Fraser was particularly concerned with human rights practices of governments to which the United States was providing military aid. For Fraser the imperative was not only to improve human rights practices but also to lessen U.S. responsibility for such practices and distance it from repressive regimes. This meant that initially his subcommittee focused almost entirely on right-wing authoritarian governments, since these were the countries with human rights violations that received U.S. assistance. Salzberg argued that they were not "soft on the left, but the U.S. government did not give assistance to leftist repression."[65] The conservatives protested, and Fraser and Salzberg soon realized that, to be credible, the subcommittee needed to be concerned with violations on the left as well as the right, so they would not be accused of political bias.

The additional piece of legislation that created the core human rights policy was the Harkin amendment. Previous legislation had mandated cutoffs of military aid to repressive regimes but had ignored economic aid. In 1975 Joe Eldridge of the Washington Office for Latin America and Edward Snyder of the Friends Committee on National Legislation drafted an amendment to the Foreign Assistance Act that would halt economic aid to countries engaged in gross violations of human rights unless the aid would directly benefit needy people. Representative Tom Harkin and Senator George McGovern respectively agreed to sponsor the amendments, which passed with backing of an odd coalition of human rights advocates with conservative opponents of any foreign aid.[66]

It was in this context that Fraser's subcommittee decided to hold hearings on the human rights situation in Uruguay. Near the end of Senator Ferreira's testimony, Fraser asked him if the U.S. government had ever spoken out against the 1973 coup and the human rights violations that had occurred. Ferreira replied that he had "no direct or indirect knowledge of any representation regarding the preservation of human rights or the maintenance of our democratic institutions." Ferreira said that even for him, getting a U.S. visa to come to the hearings "was like something out of a novel." Fraser asked him if he believed the United States should end its military aid program to Uruguay. Ferreira responded, "The military aid program is a form of aggression, . . . [an] artificial stabilization of tyranny. . . . This is not a question of suspending assistance, it is a question of ceasing to be the aggressor. And of remembering that while diplomatic relations exist between governments, friendships exist between peoples."

Later in the same hearings, a spokesperson from Amnesty International provided detailed testimony about political prisoners and the use of torture in Uruguay. Amnesty estimated that there were about five thousand political prisoners in Uruguay, and massive evidence of torture. He included a list of 105 Uruguayans who had suffered from torture, along with two photographs of individuals being tortured that had been sent to Amnesty by an anonymous Uruguayan police officer.[67] The next week, a representative of the U.S. State Department, Mr. Ryan, presented testimony.

Mr. Fraser: Mr. Ryan, there is torture in Uruguay, is there not?

Mr. Ryan: There has been apparently. The Government of Uruguay has admitted that there have been occasional cases of this, but they tell us they have taken steps to prevent its recurrence.

Mr. Fraser: Do you believe it?

Mr. Ryan: It is what the Government tells us. We have no reason to doubt them at this moment.[68]

Lawrence Pezzullo, who would later serve as ambassador to Uruguay but at this moment was in the Congressional Office at the State Department, recalls that there was "almost hooting and hollering" at the hearings because the State Department personnel appeared to be so uninformed about the human rights situation in Uruguay.[69] After his arrival as ambassador in Uruguay, Pezzullo mobilized the embassy to gather human rights data. They determined that there were approximately 4,300 people in jail in 1977, very close to the Amnesty International estimate of 5,000 in 1976.[70]

Congressman Koch sponsored an amendment cutting off military assistance to Uruguay on human rights grounds, which passed in September 1976. The Uruguayan leaders strongly condemned the amendment as a slanderous attack.[71] Ernest Siracusa, the U.S. ambassador, told the Uruguayan newspaper *El País* that both he and the State Department strongly opposed cutting off aid to Uruguay. He stated that the congressional decision to cut off aid for human rights reasons was "due to some kind of lack of communication" and vowed he would do everything possible to get aid resumed.[72]

But if Ambassador Siracusa thought that he would easily get aid restored to Uruguay, he underestimated the sea change that would happen after Jimmy Carter won the 1976 elections. Although U.S. human rights policy had its origins in the four-year period before Carter's presidency, its institutionalization and durability remained uncertain until Carter took office. After the Carter administration gave the policy a high profile and institutional status, it proved difficult for later administrations to dismantle it. Carter's advisers and speech writers stressed that his human rights policy reflected his religious and moral beliefs.[73] But the origins of Carter's human rights policy are not that simple. Carter had a political and moral predisposition to embrace the cause of human rights, but he did not have the content of human rights as part of his foreign policy agenda until well into his presidential campaign. What had happened to introduce Carter to the issue of international human rights?

Human rights emerged in Carter discourse after the 1976 Democratic platform was written, only ten days before Carter's speech to the Foreign Policy Association on June twenty-third in which he first articulated a human rights policy. During the drafting of the Democratic platform, Carter's staff observed that a general emphasis on human rights was one of the few issues that could (temporarily) unite a deeply divided Democratic Party.[74] The right wing of the party, including Senator Henry Jackson and Patrick Moynihan, favored an active human rights policy directed against "totalitarian" regimes such as the Soviet Union, Vietnam, and Cambodia. The left wing of the party supported a human rights campaign directed against "authoritarian" regimes such as those in Latin America. This pattern reflected the nature of voting for human rights sanctions in Congress. Moynihan later wrote about the Democratic platform meeting: "'We'll be against the dictators you don't like the most,' I said across the table to [Sam] Brown, 'if you'll be against the dictators we don't like the most.' The result was the strongest platform commitment to human rights in our history."[75] Both the right and left wings of the party had a longer experience working on human rights issues than did Carter and his team. Jackson was the author of the Jackson-Vanik amendment. The left wing had been at the forefront of congressional efforts to ban U.S. aid to regimes that engaged in gross violation of human rights.

As soon as he incorporated human rights into his foreign policy agenda, the issue of human rights gave Carter tangible political benefits, as well as fitting in with his own view of the proper purposes of U.S. foreign policy. As National Security Adviser Zbigniew Brzezinski explained, "The commitment to human rights reflected Carter's own religious beliefs, as well as his political acumen. He deeply believed in human rights. . . . At the same time, he sensed . . . that the issue was an appealing one, for it drew a sharp contrast between himself and the policies of Nixon and Kissinger."[76]

Surveys by Carter's campaign pollster had also shown that human rights was a strong issue with voters "across the board" and united liberal and conservative Democratic voters.[77] So, as one researcher summed it up, "the impetus for Carter's human rights campaign was that the issue had resonance, both in Carter's soul and in his polls."[78]

During the campaign, Don Fraser's staff had sent a package of material on the human rights hearings from the subcommittee to the Carter campaign. Carter had identified Fraser with the human rights issues, and at one point in the campaign Carter called him to ask for examples of successes of the human rights policy.[79] Some of Carter's human rights language in the campaign speeches is reminiscent of the Fraser committee's *Call for U.S. Leadership* report.

Once Carter took up the theme of human rights, he made it his own. Carter mentioned human rights frequently after the June 23 speech and gave two further speeches mainly on this theme.[80] Although most references were quite general, he outlined a series of specific commitments, including a commitment to seek ratification of the Genocide Treaty and the human rights covenants, to refrain from giving military or economic aid to repressive governments, and to "lend more vigorous support" to the human rights efforts of public and private bodies.[81] Latin America occupied a special place in Jimmy Carter's discussions of human rights. Carter invoked the case of Chile seven times—more than any other issue—in his campaign debate on foreign policy with President Ford.[82] In his speeches Carter usually mentioned Chile as one in a list of countries, including Vietnam, Cambodia, and Angola, where U.S. policy failures had led to citizen disillusionment with their government's secretiveness and its failure to reflect American ideals in foreign policy.[83] But sometimes Carter elaborated specifically on the Chilean case, both to point to U.S. complicity in overthrowing an elected government and to underscore the problems of torture and political prisoners.[84]

Much of the world identifies the emergence of human rights in U.S. foreign policy with Jimmy Carter because he was a high-profile spokesman. Teddy Roosevelt called the presidency a "bully pulpit," and there are few recent examples of a more effective use of the bully pulpit to spread a concept than Carter's embrace of human rights. In Latin America Carter quickly became identified with the human rights position. On election evening, when it became clear that Carter was elected, members of the Uruguayan military government left the election party at the U.S. embassy in disgust.

In his memoirs Carter wrote that he had studied the records of abuses in many countries as reported by Amnesty International, and that he had reviewed congressional legislation on human rights, but even as he launched his administration's human rights policy, "In spite of my own study of the past and planning for the future, I did not fully grasp the ramifications of our new policy."[85] One ramification that neither Carter nor his staff yet grasped was how fully the theme of human rights would capture popular imagination in this country and abroad. Later Secretary of State Cyrus Vance reported to Carter after the first press conference that he was "struck by the degree of interest, even sharpness, on human rights issues." Judging from mail, news coverage, and poll results, Carter concluded that "human rights had become a central theme of our foreign policy in the minds of the press and the public. It seemed that a spark had been ignited and I had no inclination to douse the growing flames."[86] What is striking about the language used here is the sensation that the policy led the policy makers rather than the other way around.

Their participation in path-breaking human rights legislation won neither Rep. Fraser nor Senator Ferreira enduring political benefits. Fraser was defeated in the Democratic primary in 1979 in his bid for a Senate seat. The citizens who voted against him were mainly unaware of his work on behalf of human rights. Some were outraged, however, about his support for gun control and a ban on snowmobiles on public lands. Yet when Fraser left Washington he left a legacy of a new U.S. human rights policy, now embraced by President Carter.

Wilson Ferreira didn't live to carry out his dream of being president of Uruguay. Although the military prohibited Ferreira from participating in the 1982 primaries, a slate associated with him was the overwhelming winner, making Ferreira the front-runner for the 1984 presidential elections.[87] But the military hated Ferreira for his effective campaign against them abroad during the dictatorship, and above all wanted to avoid his victory. When Ferreira returned from Buenos Aires to Montevideo in June 1984, the military immediately arrested him and imprisoned him in a barracks in the countryside. While Ferreira was in jail, representatives of the Colorado Party and the left-wing coalition, the Frente Amplio, negotiated an agreement with the military for a transition to democracy. Presidential elections were held while Ferreira was still in jail and barred from participating. The rival Colorado Party candidate won. "A few days later, Wilson Ferreira, who now had fair claim to consider himself robbed of the Presidency for a second time, was released."[88] But Ferreira was still the head of the Blanco Party. In 1986, to the consternation of the human rights advocates with whom he had worked for over a decade in exile, he swung the Blanco Party behind a sweeping amnesty law that protected all of the military from prosecution for human rights violations committed during the dictatorship. At the time, some said that Ferreira was smoothing the way for yet another presidential bid in 1989. A few weeks later, Ferreira discovered he had terminal cancer, and he was dead within a year.[89]

Human rights activists find it hard to forgive Ferreira for this final betrayal. Yet Ferreira was first and foremost a Blanco Party leader. Different types of people make up a human rights movement. Wilson Ferreira spoke out against human rights violations in Uruguay when few prominent Uruguayans were able or willing to do so. He broke a nationalist taboo and asked the U.S. Congress to stop military aid to a government he considered a tyranny. Together with U.S. politicians like Donald Fraser, he contributed to a new human rights policy against the vehement opposition of Secretary of State Kissinger, Ambassador Siracusa, and the Uruguayan generals.

PART TWO

Effectiveness of Human Rights Policies

CHAPTER FOUR

Introduction to the Effectiveness of Human Rights Policies

In Chapter 1 we explored the origins of human rights policies, and in Chapters 2 and 3 I discussed the adoption of human rights policies in greater detail. But ultimately, we care about the origins of a policy only if we have some reason to believe that the policy made an important difference in the world. The second part of this book is about the effectiveness of human rights policy. I introduce the topic in this chapter and explore it in Chapters 5 to 8 by examining the implementation of human rights policies in Latin America. I do not attempt to be comprehensive, since it would be impossible to explore twenty-five years of policy toward a large, complex region.[1] Instead, I focus on critical junctures and examine key factors that strengthen or undermine human rights and democracy. By "critical juncture" I mean a period of significant change that starts a country on one path instead of another.[2] Among the most lasting legacies of authoritarian rule are those caused by human rights violations. To evaluate the effectiveness of human rights policies, therefore, I will focus on U.S. policy during periods in Latin America when the scale of repression rose or fell dramatically. Because increases in repression often followed military coups, I will examine U.S. policy in response to such interruptions of democracy.

I begin by discussing criteria for evaluating human rights policies. What does it mean to say that human rights policies worked? Next, I discuss theories of repression, because understanding the causes of human rights violations may be useful in explaining why and under what conditions human rights policies may be effective. Finally, I give an overview of the patterns of repression we are trying to explain, particularly the unprecedented waves of repression in Latin America in the 1970s and 1980s.

Criteria for Evaluating U.S. Human Rights Policy

U.S. human rights policy can be evaluated in terms of its impact on human rights in Latin America and its effect on U.S. national interests. We are concerned with policies that are effective in limiting human rights violations in the short and long term. Pragmatically, we would also expect that effective human rights policies do not harm traditional understandings of U.S. national interests by alienating important allies or undermining the economic or security interests of the United States. Of course, interests are not always obvious, nor are they fixed. Changing ideas about what constitutes U.S. interests shaped the history of U.S. human rights and democracy policies. Nevertheless, any pragmatic evaluation will want to ascertain at the very least that a human rights policy does not undermine existing understandings of U.S. interests.

When we say that effectiveness means limiting human rights abuses, we need to clarify what kinds of human rights violations we are talking about. The human rights documents we have considered so far, such as the Universal Declaration of Human Rights, enshrine a broad definition of civil, political, economic, social, and cultural human rights. For the purposes of evaluating effectiveness, I will use a much narrower definition of human rights, focused on the basic rights of the security of the person, including freedom from genocide, summary execution, torture and cruel and inhumane treatment, disappearances, and prolonged detention without charges. I call this narrower range of rights violations "repression."

Why do I choose to focus on a narrow range of human rights? First, these were the kinds of rights violations that the Latin American human rights movements first denounced and organized around, in the 1970s and 1980s. So a focus on repression responds to the urgent concerns of those human rights activists. Second, framers of U.S. human rights policy, such as Donald Fraser, designed legislation to take into account "gross violations of internationally recognized human rights," which they saw as comprising cruel, inhuman, or degrading treatment or punishment, torture, prolonged detention without charge or trial, disappearances, and "other flagrant denial of the right to life, liberty, or security of person." It makes sense to evaluate U.S. policy in relation to its own goals. A policy is effective, at least in the short term, if fewer people are killed, tortured, disappeared, or imprisoned without charges. Truth commissions in the region have also focused on this range of basic rights of the security of the person, so we have data to evaluate effectiveness. Latin American governments gave their truth commissions a relatively narrow mandate to focus primarily on deaths, disappearances, and torture, underscoring the primacy granted these rights in the region.

When people evaluate a human rights policy, they are not concerned only with consequences and effectiveness. They also ask normative questions about complicity, consistency, and responsibility. So we need to consider the ethical and legal principles that we can use to evaluate human rights policies. Some realist foreign policy analysts claim that ethical criteria have no place in a foreign policy. But foreign policy elites and the general public constantly invoke ethical criteria to justify or critique foreign policy decisions. If we assume such discussions are more than window dressing, it may be useful to spell out ethical obligations. In addition, many moral criteria have become embodied in international human rights treaties that the United States has ratified, thus obligating itself legally as well as ethically.

With regard to human rights policy, the highest ethical (and legal) obligation is for the United States to ensure that its own agents do not engage in, facilitate, or encourage human rights violations at home or abroad. The great bulk of human rights treaties impose obligations on governments not to commit human rights violations themselves. In the domestic realm, these obligations are buttressed by the Constitution and myriad domestic laws. In the international realm, obligations not to violate rights are clearly spelled out in international treaties. Our greatest obligation is to ensure that U.S. personnel, and foreign persons whom we train or fund, do not commit human rights violations. Our obligation is greatest in those countries and areas where we have the most involvement and influence. This is why Latin America is such a crucial case for U.S. human rights policy, since it is a region where we have deep historical and current involvement. Clearly the United States has less responsibility for human rights violations in Cuba than for the gross violations carried out by the Latin American military establishments that we supplied with aid and training. Likewise, we have more responsibility in Latin America than we did in Rwanda, where we failed to stop genocide but also had little involvement in the training and support of the individuals who carried it out. This is not to say that U.S. policy toward Cuba or Rwanda is insignificant, just that the highest obligation in the human rights realm is similar to that of a medical doctor: Do no harm.

U.S. policy makers and Latin American governments sometimes justified human rights violations in Latin America using consequentialist arguments:

some persons' rights had to be violated in order to secure or protect national security. The essence of both the containment and national security doctrines is that violations of individuals' rights might be necessary to fight communism and internal subversion. I argue that U.S. personnel cannot be permitted to carry out gross human rights violations, nor can they be allowed to condone such violations or recommend them to a foreign government, even if they believe that they are doing so in the service of a greater end.

The first and foremost obligation is to stop policies that contribute to human rights abuses. Once the "do no harm" obligation is met, we can turn to the next level of obligation: positive actions that promote human rights. At this level, an effective or successful human rights policy is one that has an immediate impact on the victims of human rights abuses. It saves lives, stops torture, and helps political prisoners get released. This is what I call the short-term impact of human rights policy.

We cannot limit our definition of success only to the direct impact on victims of repression. As important as it is to help victims, human rights policy has broader objectives. It must address the root causes of human rights violations as well as the proximate suffering of victims. This is what I call the long-term impact of human rights policy. In order to evaluate both the short- and long-term impact of policy, we need to know more about the causes of human rights violations.

Why Do Human Rights Violations Occur?

Much of the debate over human rights policy today is not a debate about *whether* we should stop human rights abuses but over *how* to stop them. This involves evaluating different causal ideas about what really contributes to human rights abuses.

A human rights approach always begins with, and has as its essence, a concern with individual victims of rights abuses. Social scientists sometimes skip over this first step of starting with the victims and their families. We are trained to explain phenomena using abstract theories. It is second nature to us to immediately ask "why?" and begin the search for deep and proximate causes of puzzling events. But before we begin our search for explanations, a prefatory comment: A search for explanation does not imply justification. There can be no justification for human rights abuses. Nor can any explanation remove the perpetrators' moral and legal responsibility for these criminal acts.

Hannah Arendt was concerned about exactly such a point in the last pages of *Eichmann in Jerusalem*.

> Another such escape from the area of ascertainable facts and personal re-
> sponsibility are the countless theories, based on non-specific, abstract,
> hypothetical assumptions . . . which are so general that they explain and
> justify every event and every deed: no alternative to what actually hap-
> pened is even considered and no person could have acted differently from
> the way he did act. . . . All these clichés have in common that they make
> judgment superfluous and that to utter them is devoid of all risk.

She importantly underscores that such theorizing is a symptom of "the reluctance evident everywhere to make judgments in terms of individual moral responsibility."[3]

In this vein, we need to begin by stating that human rights violations are consciously committed by individuals who could have chosen to act differently, and
who bear moral and legal responsibility for their actions. Individuals and governments make a choice to repress. Whatever theory we use to examine the
deep causes of human rights violations, the actual individuals who made the
decision to repress still bear individual responsibility for their actions. The victims of repression and their family members are entitled to seek justice in
courts by determining which individuals and governments are responsible for
repression, and by obtaining convictions, punishment, and reparations.

Having said this, I believe that any effort to limit human rights violations is
most effective when it is informed by a credible theory of the causes of repression. The substantial literature on the causes of human rights violations
tries to identify the conditions under which governments and people will commit large-scale murder, torture, and arbitrary imprisonment. This literature
can serve as a starting point for thinking about what policies are most likely to
promote human rights. The literature researches economic, political, ideological, and psychological explanations; some of it is quantitative and some qualitative. Economic explanations focus on such factors as poverty, inequality, and
globalization. The political explanations mainly explore whether particular
regime types—democratic, authoritarian, totalitarian, or military—are more
likely to have human rights abuses. An additional set of political explanations
looks at the impact of war or threats to the regime from challengers. Finally,
ideological and psychological factors focus on the individual or collective ideas
and mental states that make repression and genocide possible.

So, what do these theories tell us about the causes of repression? First, almost
all the studies have shown that democracies are less likely to violate rights than
undemocratic states.[4] Thus a policy of promoting democracy is a key policy for
improving human rights. But, although democracies have overall a better human rights record, the process of transition to democracy can be a perilous one

for human rights. The occurrence of human rights violations increases when undemocratic states make the transition to democracy, perhaps because ethnic conflict and its consequent human rights violations are most likely to occur during the early stages of transition to democracy.[5] Policy makers need to be aware that when they try to improve human rights by promoting democracy, in the short term the situation is likely to get worse before it gets better.

Many democracies, however, fail to protect human rights, and it is essential to understand that establishing democracy in and of itself is necessary but not sufficient to secure respect for human rights. There are many examples of democratic countries (or at least countries with free and fair elections) that do not have good human rights performance, such as Colombia, where an electoral system coincides currently with the highest levels of repression in the western hemisphere. Many of these countries, including Colombia, are beset by civil war, which may counteract the impact of democracy.

There is a strong connection between involvement in both civil and international war and human rights violations.[6] Countries at war are much more likely to repress their citizens. In Latin America many of the cases of severe human rights violations coincided with either civil wars or significant guerrilla movements: for example, El Salvador, Guatemala, Argentina, Uruguay, and Colombia. This strong connection between war and repression should make us think twice before advocating military solutions to human rights violations. Since war almost always leads to an increase in human rights violations in the short term, military solutions are likely to make the situation worse rather than better. Left-wing guerrilla groups in Latin America have also failed to appreciate the connection between civil war and human rights abuses. Many believed that guerrilla warfare was necessary to build a new society where social and economic rights would be fully guaranteed. In the process, they helped provoke civil wars that unleashed massive human rights violations, not only against their followers but against broad sectors of the population as well.

Military interventions may in rare circumstances be necessary to prevent human rights disasters, through what is called "humanitarian intervention." But policy makers should seek to use all options short of military force to prevent human rights violations and only turn to humanitarian intervention in the face of large-scale violations such as genocide when all other options have failed.

Economic factors also are important in understanding the causes of repression. Poor countries are more likely to have inferior human rights records than richer countries.[7] Some research suggests that both absolute poverty and high levels of inequality are associated with human rights violations.[8] Despite the connections between the economy and human rights, it takes a very substantial increase in the GNP to make an important difference in human rights performance, so economic growth and increased economic equality can only be a long-term remedy for repression.[9] The worst repression in Latin America occurred both in richer countries like Chile, Argentina, and Uruguay and in poorer countries like Guatemala and El Salvador. In Central America, Nicaragua and Honduras were as poor as or even poorer than Guatemala and El Salvador and yet suffered less repression.

Scholars used to stress that economic development was a necessary precondition for democracy. Recent work has reconfirmed the strong correlation of democracy and wealth but has suggested that political freedoms are as likely to contribute to the generation of wealth as the other way around.[10] Hence, democracy and the protection of basic human rights should be of particular concern in and of themselves rather than assumed to be a natural outcome of economic development.

There are two opposing arguments about the link between human rights and globalization. The first claims that expanding free trade and capitalist investment will lead to improvements in human rights conditions.[11] This is the argument used to justify U.S. policy toward China, where the U.S. government claimed that expanding trade relations would also contribute to improved human rights. This argument is not invoked, however, to justify human rights policy toward Cuba. A complete U.S. trade embargo has been in effect against Cuba for decades, justified on human rights grounds. An opposing argument has been made by authors such as Noam Chomsky and Edward Herman, who contend that those countries with more extensive involvement with the capitalist center are more likely to engage in human rights violations.[12] The most convincing study to date concludes that there is little connection between levels of trade and direct foreign investment and repression.[13] Such conclusions suggest it will not work to try to use free trade policies as a proxy or substitute for a human rights policy. Promoting free trade will not in and of itself lead to better human rights practices. But the results also contradict the claims that globalization or free trade exacerbates repression.[14]

Politics and economics aren't the only factors known to contribute to repression. Once again, ideas matter as well. Groups may promote ideologies that dehumanize their opponents or exclude them "from the realm of obligation" as a way of preparing the ground for repression against them.[15] Ideologies that depict other groups as animals or diseases have the effect of dehumanizing victims and making repression possible. For example, military leaders throughout Latin America referred to subversion as a cancer that had to be cut out of the body politic in order for the society to heal. As part of this process, groups may engage in scapegoating, that is, blaming a specific group of people for the ills of society and thus targeting them for repression.

Ideologies in which the ends are seen to justify the means may contribute to repression. In these ideologies, some desired endpoint is so compelling that repressive means are seen as justified or indeed necessary for achieving those ends. Studies of ideologies as diverse as Nazism, the Khmer Rouge dogma in Cambodia, and the national security doctrine in Latin America have shown that whenever ends are believed to justify the means, repression is likely.[16] Researchers have found that humans have a predisposition to obey authority, even if this involves administering pain to another individual. When soldiers are trained in ways that reinforce this tendency to obey authority, they may be more likely to engage in human rights violations. These soldiers are often themselves brutalized in their training and, as victims of abuse, may themselves become abusers.[17]

While this literature on causes of repression has arrived at a series of accumulated findings, it does not add up to an integrated theory of repression. These theories tell us much about what may be the root causes of repression, but they don't give us an actual understanding of the proximate decision-making and foreign-policy interactions that could promote or undermine human rights. Ultimately, individual leaders choose to carry out human rights violations, but we assume that they could have decided otherwise. So we are concerned with what kinds of policy messages might alter the decisions to carry out human rights violations.

Efforts at such theory building are under way. One proposed theory of Steven Poe's uses a rational actor decision-making model. Poe starts with the assumption of a rational decision-maker engaged in choices of how much repression to use. This decision maker is influenced both by his perceptions of threat to the regime and by his perception of the strength of the regime.[18] The decision maker's perception of threat and strength may be diminished or heightened by other factors such as economic development or civil war. So, for example, economic crisis or civil war leads elites to feel the regime is threatened, while economic growth may enhance perceptions of regime strength. Decision makers are seen as choosing from a menu of possible policy alternatives. They are influenced both by variables that affect which alternatives appear on the menu and by variables that affect how they choose.

At first, this sounds like an unrealistic and mechanical view of repression. Yet many academics and NGOs writing about human rights implicitly adopt such a view, albeit in different language. So, for example, in one of the most exhaustive studies of the Rwandan genocide, Alison Des Forges concludes that the genocide was not the result of "ancient hatreds," but rather of deliberate choices made by modern elites whose power was threatened by the success of their opponents on the battlefield and at the negotiating table. The study concludes that the failure of international actors to raise the perceived costs of genocide permitted domestic actors to carry out their program of mass murder.[19]

Poe's theory is a good start, but it is not interactive and it doesn't take communication fully into account. We know that even dictators operate in settings where they are constantly in communication with other actors about their practices. Poe recognizes implicitly the importance of such ideational factors when he argues that "the communication process between the donor and recipient, the messages sent, and their strategic interactions are apt to be important to our understanding of the linkages between aid and repression overlooked by the analyses conducted to date."[20]

The "spiral model" of human rights change that I have developed with my colleagues Thomas Risse and Steven Ropp is an interactive model of repression that takes communication seriously. It starts with states that choose to use repression and conceives of them as actors with both interests and identities trying to decide how to act in a specific political context.[21] The spiral model is a phased model of human rights change that incorporates the interactions between the repressive state apparatus, groups in the domestic society of the repressive state, and the international realm. In the international arena, we look at the impact of pressures from other states, international organizations, and international nongovernmental organizations. When repression occurs, international actors often receive information about human rights violations from human rights groups within the repressive state. They use the information to invoke international human rights norms and to pressure the repressive state to change its practices. Repressive states, however, initially react to such pressure by denying the validity of the human rights norms and foreign pressures. If international and domestic actors are able to sustain pressure, they can increase the costs on the repressive state and bring about far-reaching human rights change.

International and domestic actors, in interaction with one another, impose costs for repression. The costs of repression include not only lost foreign aid but also lost reputation from shaming and stigmatization by international human rights campaigns. The states that are most likely to respond to such pressures are those that are most sensitive to such stigmatization. States that aspire to be members of a community of liberal states and whose identity as a liberal state is affected by stigmatization are the most likely to respond to pressure. For example, when the Argentine military carried out its coup in 1976, they announced that they were doing it in defense of "Western and Christian civilization." This identity made it more difficult for them to disregard reputational costs when Western states denounced their human rights violations.

What the spiral model does not yet adequately portray is how this process of human rights change is affected by ambiguous or contradictory signals from powerful international actors like the United States. In this book I offer an addition to the spiral model: a better understanding of how interactive communication contributes to or thwarts human rights change. In doing so, I draw on the "sensemaking" approach in organizational studies, which has explored how decision makers in organizations respond to new stimuli.[22] This literature points out that since communicative cues are not easy to make sense of, actors call upon existing ideological frameworks and understandings of identity.

In order to understand fully the costs and benefits of repression, leaders interpret the communications they receive from other countries in relation to their own identities and ideology, and to their expectations about the identities and policies of those countries. Latin American policy makers choosing to use repression in the 1970s and 1980s were militaries that were deeply socialized into national security ideology and saw themselves as struggling against a dangerous internal enemy. Containment or anticommunism as practiced in Latin America had various names. It was called a "national security ideology," the "doctrine of anti-subversive war," or "counterinsurgency doctrine." These all refer to a common doctrine that emphasizes two points: (1) the country is engaged in permanent warfare, "in which there is no distinction between periods of peace and periods of war, no formal declaration of the start or end of hostilities," and "no distinction between the civil front and the military front"; and (2) this war is total in scope, morally justified, and conventional, "involving two antithetical visions of the world," the objective of which is the annihilation of the adversary.[23] I will refer to this doctrine as *national security ideology*. The doctrine legitimated far-reaching political and military action by the military, which was viewed as the "last hope of the West—the bulwark, support, and repository of the good order as attacked by internal Communist subversion."[24] Latin American militaries believed that U.S. policy makers shared and supported this worldview, and they interpreted the communication they received from the United States in light of these expectations.[25]

Human rights policy, however, aims to affect these decisions by providing information, alternative types of socialization, and economic and political pressures. In other words, international human rights activism increases the "cost" of repression so that it is a less attractive choice of action. In the past, policy makers may have chosen repression because it was effective and a relatively cheap policy alternative. There were few domestic costs. Repression silenced or eliminated domestic opponents and allowed the coup makers to consolidate power. Once repression ended and a new regime came to power, there were few legal or political consequences for the repressors. They were not tried for past human rights abuses, nor were their careers negatively affected.

But policy makers are never fully rational calculators; they are groups with interests and identities trying to interpret often contradictory messages. They interpret the information available to them through the conceptual filters of their ideology. U.S. policy makers also operate within their existing policy frameworks. When human rights policy was introduced, it was a new foreign policy framework that came into conflict with national security doctrine. Because there was a conflict between these two frameworks, U.S. policy makers gave deeply contradictory cues about human rights issues. Latin American policy makers saw themselves as engaged in a heroic battle against terrorism, and they found it difficult to accept those parts of U.S. policy that would require them to think of themselves as violators of human rights.

Repression became an increasingly costly policy by the late 1970s. New human rights advocacy networks generated negative international publicity about countries that violated human rights. As states adopted bilateral human rights policies, this negative publicity translated into real or potential costs in terms of diminished military or economic aid or trade credits. Human rights practices affected levels of U.S. military aid in particular.[26]

Human rights policy also affected how "threats" were interpreted. Norms and ideas help actors interpret threat and provide a menu of options for a response to threat. Thus norms and ideas can both contribute to increasing repression or to limiting it, depending on the content of the ideas. Certain ideologies associated with repression, such as national security ideologies, encourage a military solution to domestic unrest and often justify repression. They heighten perceptions of threat and validate a decision to treat internal protesters as legitimate military targets. These ideologies have had international as well as domestic origins and have been transmitted through foreign aid, training programs, and diplomatic communications.

By the 1990s, international and regional norms in favor of democracy played an important role in virtually removing certain options—such as military coups—from the policy menu in Latin America. The military coup, long an accepted and even respected political option in the region, became more costly and less common.

To further develop this addition to the spiral model, I explore the connection between changes in U.S. policy and changing levels of human rights violations in the region. The remaining chapters in Part II are case studies of critical junctures in key Latin American countries in which I identify policies and factors that appear to have contributed to improved human rights. Before we turn to these cases, however, we need an overview of repression trends in the region over the last thirty years.

Trends in Repression in Latin America, 1970–2000

In the 1970s and 1980s, many countries in Latin America suffered a wave of intense repression, including widespread executions, disappearances, political imprisonment, and frequent use of torture. In almost all cases, military governments committed these human rights violations either directly through security forces and police or through paramilitary groups closely linked to the government. Executions, disappearances, torture, and imprisonment were the most severe and visible human rights abuses, but these governments also closed parliaments, curtailed political and civil rights of citizens, and severely limited the freedoms of speech and assembly. This was a time of intense fear and insecurity for many citizens in Latin America.

Contrary to popular perceptions in the United States, this wave of repression was unprecedented. Most Latin American countries had not witnessed such levels of state repression in the twentieth century. We have to go back to the colonial and independence periods to find comparable violence.[27]

This wave of repression and human rights abuses occurred in Argentina, Brazil, Chile, El Salvador, Guatemala, Honduras, Nicaragua, Bolivia, Paraguay, Uruguay, Peru, and Mexico. When we look closer at the pattern of repression in four cases for which precise data are available—Argentina, Chile, El Salvador, and Guatemala—a striking pattern stands out. In all four, deaths and disappearances peaked during a relatively short two- to three-year period preceded and followed by serious and systematic but lower-level violations. These peaks of repression occurred during a single decade between 1973 and 1982 (see figure 1).

Argentina and Chile, relatively wealthy countries of the Southern Cone of Latin America, have little in common with El Salvador and Guatemala. The same repressive trend in the four very different countries indicates that there might be a common explanation, not rooted in distinct national histories but in some set of factors that all share. Such an explanation would need to account for the peculiar intensity of repression within a single decade and the eventual decline of repression throughout the region (with the important exception of Colombia). Explanations of repression generally stress domestic causes such as poverty, authoritarianism, inequality, and war. But these factors, while present in some of the countries some of the time, are not unique to the 1970s and 1980s.

In virtually all cases, the repression was carried out under military regimes that had come to power through the wave of coups that swept the region in the 1960s and 1970s. But Latin America had experienced authoritarian regimes before, and though repressive, the human rights abuses then did not reach the

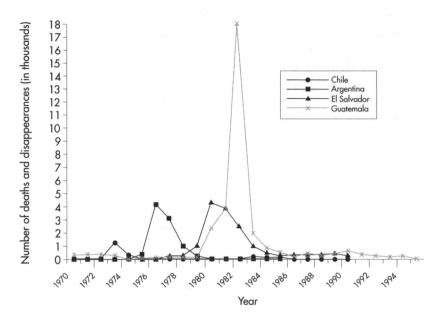

Figure 1. State-sponsored Deaths and Disappearances, 1970–1995

levels of the 1970s and 1980s. What was it about the regimes of the 1970s and 1980s that made them more repressive? In both Argentina and Chile, human rights violations peaked in the period immediately following the military coups. In Guatemala and El Salvador, after decades of different forms of authoritarianism, repression peaked in the 1979–83 period.

The concentration of repression within a single decade leads us to think about whether there is a generational effect. Because military promotions in Latin America follow a relatively formal pattern of seniority, a similar generation of leaders was in power throughout the region during this decade of repression. The military leaders in power during this decade all received their formative military training and early experience at approximately the same time in the late 1950s and early 1960s.

If indeed there is a powerful generational effect in the repression in Latin America in the 1970s and 1980s, then much of the search for causes of repression in the region has been short-sighted. Most often the literature on causes has looked to events that directly preceded the repressive period—economic downturns, military aid, or human rights pressures. I do not dispute that such factors are significant. But in most of Latin America, repression was carried out by centralized states led by military leaders within a hierarchical chain of command. So rather than only asking whether, for example, a cutoff in military aid in 1978 led to a reduction of repression in 1979, we also need to think about the formative influences on the individuals that were leaders of repressive states in the 1970s and ask what permitted or inspired them to carry out an unprecedented wave of repression against their own population.

In three of the four cases—Argentina, El Salvador, and Guatemala—the repression responded to a significant emergence of or increase in leftist insurgency. In Argentina, the Montoneros and the Ejército Revolucionario del Pueblo (ERP) emerged in the late 1960s and early 1970s and increased their activities during the mid-1970s prior to the coup in 1976. In El Salvador, the failure of the reformist coup of 1979, and the murder in 1980 of the leading leftist opposition political party leaders, convinced the left that peaceful political activity was futile. This led to the growing strength of guerrilla organizations, eventually united in 1980 in the Farabundo Martí Front for National Liberation (FMLN). In Guatemala, the guerrilla movement reached a new peak in 1981.[28] The connection between repression and the increase in insurgency in all three countries supports the idea that repression is often a response to a perceived threat to the regime in power, as Poe argued in his rational actor model of repression. Chile, however, does not fit this pattern, because repression there occurred when there was no civil war or significant guerrilla insurgency. But organized nonviolent protests or rebellion may also constitute a threat to a regime.[29] In Chile, the victory of the left in the 1970 elections threatened traditional political and economic interests. What made the Chilean case unusual is that the "threat" had been elected to office and was using conventional means to bring about a significant change in political institutions.

To say that repression responded to threat does not mean necessarily that the state is a unified rational actor, that repression is inevitable, or that that repression is proportionate to the level of threat.[30] There were profound divisions within Latin American authoritarian states about the nature of the threat and the level of repression. Repression was often used by one faction within the state against others as a way to impose its view of the situation. Second, repression was not the only, or even the most logical, response. Alternative responses were possible and had been used previously. Governments could have attempted more reform or tried to co-opt their opponents. And finally, repression was not proportional in any sense of the word. The guerrilla movement in Guatemala was relatively small, with perhaps as few as six thousand combatants, and yet over a hundred thousand people were murdered. Nor was repression always an effective response to threat. Even in the short term, repression, far from silencing threats, may exacerbate them. In the case of El Salvador, for example, the guerrilla movement was the direct result of past electoral fraud and repression that led the political opposition to conclude that it could not seek to influence politics nonviolently. As repression increased, so did the power of the guerrilla movement.[31]

One dilemma with adopting a reaction-to-threat model of repression is that in many ways it echoes and legitimates the very discourse of the military. The Argentine military claimed that they were engaged in a "dirty war" against an unorthodox enemy and that in a dirty war any tactics are permissible. Human rights activists spent considerable time demonstrating that the great bulk of repression was not at all in the context of military confrontations but involved the abduction and murder of unarmed civilians. Either we assume that the military was hypocritically using the language of threat to hide their deeper political or economic interests and aspirations to power, or we try to get inside the minds of the military and see how their perceptions of threat *and* of the costs and benefits of repression made their decisions about repression possible.

The apparent convergence between the upsurge in guerrilla activity and the increase in repression is too compelling to ignore the reaction-to-threat model. But that does not mean that repression was natural or inevitable. Repression was chosen as a tactic within an international and domestic normative context that legitimated and naturalized it as a means of conducting state business: the Cold War in Latin America. In a different domestic and international normative context, an increase in threat could lead to very different responses. But within this Cold War normative context, elites interpreted external and internal cues to make calculations about the costs and benefits of repression. The perception of threat on the part of military leaders and economic and political elites was, like all perceptions, an interpretation. Granted, it had a factual basis—there were indeed guerrilla organizations operating with increased strength—but it was also a projection of fears and anxieties. Particularly where economic and political elites had been targets of guerrilla activities such as kidnapping and bomb attempts, they feared for their physical safety and their financial security. In many cases, these elites welcomed military coups and abdicated responsibility for helping maintain basic rights.

That this context allowed for the perception of threat becomes clearer when we examine the case of Chile. In Chile, the threat was electoral and not military. While the left-wing president, Salvador Allende, was making substantial changes to the social and economic system of the country, his opponents always had the possibility of using conventional political means to defeat him, such as elections and political alliances. But in the polarized Cold War world of the 1970s, Allende's election became yet another indication of a threat to "national security," which the military and the economic elite increasingly saw as dangerous.

Two powerful contrasting sets of ideas spread and clashed in the continent at this period. On the left, the belief in the necessity of armed struggle was increasingly common, regardless of the objective situation of the country. Young leftists in Uruguay, with its large middle class, strong electoral system, and basic respect for civil liberties, had come to believe that their political system was an illegitimate bourgeois democracy and incapable of delivering social justice and equality for all citizens. They advocated these beliefs with as much enthusiasm as the left in El Salvador, where political assassinations and violence made participation in the political arena increasingly untenable. On the right, meanwhile, many conservatives and the military, drawing on their national security ideology, saw the left as a threat to the nation and a legitimate target for military and repressive activity.

As these ideas clashed with each other, military repression reinforced the left's belief that bourgeois reform was impossible and that revolution was the only answer, which in turn provoked the military's sense of threat. As the conflict progressed, the middle ground was often emptied, either by a conscious policy of repression where centrist political leaders were murdered, or by a process of polarization, where people were forced to choose sides. The voices of advocates for democracy and human rights were muted or silenced.

The United States was directly involved in supporting and communicating this ideology through its diplomacy, military training, and military and economic aid programs. Since before the Cuban revolution, Latin American militaries had received extensive training on the internal threat of communism. National security doctrine, first introduced by French military advisors in the late 1950s, was later augmented by U.S. training in the wake of the Cuban revolution. It focused the military's attention on the "internal enemy" of communist subversion and justified repressive tactics against domestic political opposition.

I don't suggest that Latin American militaries were innocent and passive recipients of foreign ideologies. Latin American militaries embraced and furthered national security ideology because it fit with their own historic understanding of their central role in the nation.[32] The United States didn't simply dictate the outcome of crises in the region. Nevertheless, when domestic actors were divided and in conflict with one another, the positions that powerful external actors took often had the effect of empowering one internal faction vis-à-vis its opponents. Even as we accept that Latin American political actors had significant autonomy to determine their own fate, we also need to recognize that powerful foreign actors can often throw their weight behind particular internal factions, and thus help sway the outcome.

Chapters 5 – 8 of this book explore the U.S. role in critical junctures of human rights practices in Latin America. They also explore the broader normative and ideological context to which U.S. policy and training contributed. We ask not only what impact specific U.S. policy decisions had on repression but also how broader U.S. diplomacy and military training framed a worldview in which certain kinds of responses to political crisis seemed possible or desirable. Almost all research on the effectiveness of human rights policies involves some kind of counterfactual reasoning. We are usually trying to compare what happened in a country to what *would have happened* in the absence of human rights policies (the counterfactual). This kind of reasoning is difficult because we're not comparing one factual situation to another factual situation, but one person's estimation of what would have happened to what did happen. Counterfactual reasoning is common in the social sciences and the policy realm, but it can be controversial because reasonable people differ over what would have happened and thus make different evaluations. We cannot avoid counterfactual reasoning if we want to try to make causal arguments, but we need to be explicit about our counterfactuals and about our standards of evidence and proof.[33]

The basic counterfactual argument presented in the second part of the book is that without the rise of the human rights movement and the incorporation of human rights issues into foreign policy, Latin America would have more human rights violations and less democracy than it has today. I use various kinds of research design and evidence to explore this argument. First, I compare human rights practices over a relatively long time span in a series of countries, comparing each country historically to itself in earlier periods and to other countries. Second, I compare conditions in case countries before the introduction of human rights policy with what happened after the implementation of human rights policy. In other cases, I match the case of a country where the United States explicitly applied human rights policy with an otherwise similar case where the United States did not apply human rights policy. Finally, I examine critical junctures where the human rights situation worsened or improved dramatically and attempt to identify factors that appear to have contributed to the change.

Case Selection

The four main cases I study are Argentina, Chile, Guatemala, and El Salvador. I chose these cases because they show variation in the factors considered as possible causes or remedies for human rights violations: level of development, presence of civil war, regime type, and degree and type of U.S. involvement and assistance. They are also the four countries for which the most complete data are now available: data on human rights violations from extensive truth commission reports, and newly declassified documents from the United States government now in the National Security Archives. Because this is such a controversial topic and period, it is important to rely on cases where new and highly reliable data are available, and only these four cases provide that option. I have been asked why I did not include Cuba as one of the main cases for this book. As I said earlier in this chapter, the United States has little responsibility for repression in Cuba because it never provided military or economic aid or training for the Cuban regime. The embargo against Cuba was adopted well before the advent of human rights policy. Neither a truth commission report nor a release of State Department documents on Cuba policy has provided reliable data like that I use in my other cases.

I supplement these four main cases occasionally with material from other cases. The available data on these other cases are less systematic, but these other cases are important because as time progressed and the four main case countries underwent transitions to democracy, other countries such as Haiti, Peru, and Colombia became more important for U.S. policy makers.

Truth Commissions and New Information on Human Rights

In the four main cases much more comprehensive and complete qualitative and quantitative information on human rights violations is available today than in the past. All four countries had truth commissions that published definitive reports on repression, which focused on the most severe forms of human rights violations.[34] Both Chile and Argentina had nationally appointed truth commissions, whereas El Salvador and Guatemala had UN sponsored truth commissions. In addition to the officially sponsored commissions, nongovernmental data reports supplemented the official reports. These truth commissions probably underestimated the total amount of repression in each country, because they relied on exact lists of names and thus leave out the many victims of repression who never appeared on the lists. The overall trend of repression they signal is nonetheless the most reliable available. This information makes it more possible to try to understand the causes of repression and assess the impact of U.S. policy in these four countries.

In addition, the release of large sets of declassified U.S. State Department documents covering the critical period in all four cases allows me to complement the truth commission data with some insider information on the U.S. policy making process.[35] A full-fledged comparative assessment has not yet been done using this newly available information. The truth commission data on repression establish broad trends. It is necessary to combine an analysis of these broad trends with the qualitative and historical research presented in the next three chapters to make more convincing arguments about U.S. human rights policy and the trends of repression in these case countries. Before looking at the four case countries, I want to situate them in a brief survey or map of repression throughout the region.

A Map of Repression

If we could trace repression on a map of Latin America, it might appear that there were subregional waves of repression. The first wave, in the Southern Cone of South America, started in Brazil in the late 1960s, moved to Chile and Uruguay by 1973 and to Argentina and Paraguay after 1976, and reached Bolivia in 1980−81. The second wave, in Central America, began in Nicaragua in 1977 and engulfed El Salvador and Guatemala in the late 1970s and early 1980s. The third wave, in the Andean region, started latest, beginning in Peru in the late 1980s and continuing in Colombia and Venezuela throughout the 1990s. The Andean wave is distinguished from the earlier ones in that repression took place under governments that were formally electoral regimes, if not fully democratic.

The first wave of repression started in Brazil after the military coup in 1964. Although the Brazilian military government lasted twenty years, the level of repression, which peaked in the late 1960s and early 1970s during the Medici administration, was never as high as in the other three cases. Torture of political prisoners was the most widespread form of repression in Brazil. Using the actual records of the military government, a church-sponsored report documented over two thousand cases of torture of political prisoners, of which 81 percent occurred during the Medici administration.[36] The report also presents evidence of 10 cases of death under torture and 125 disappearances, which were denounced in military courts and officially registered in legal proceedings.[37] The military government in Argentina during the 1966−73 period was also more repressive than previous military governments there, but its repression was far milder than the military government that came into power in 1976.

The wave continued with the military coups in Chile and Uruguay in 1973, two countries with long democratic traditions and little past experience with repression. Repression in Uruguay was not characterized by large-scale mas-sacres and death squads, as in Guatemala, or by legions of disappeared people, as in Argentina. Instead the military implemented a program of far-reaching arrests, routine torture of prisoners, and complete surveillance of the popula-tion. In 1976, Amnesty International estimated that sixty thousand people had been arrested and detained in Uruguay, and one out of fifty Uruguayans had been through some period of imprisonment since the coup. Seventy-eight pris-oners died in prison, many of them as a result of torture.[38] Thirty-two Uru-guayans were disappeared domestically. But the Uruguayan case also illustrates the interconnected nature of repression, especially in the Southern Cone, where the military collaborated in repression through the secret "Condor Plan." Many Uruguayans had sought refuge in neighboring countries after the coup in Uruguay in 1973. After the coup in Argentina, 135 Uruguayans were killed or were disappeared in Argentina apparently as a result of their political activities in Uruguay. In addition, nine Uruguayan children were disappeared in Argentina, usually captured when their parents were disappeared. Of these, four later "reappeared," released by security forces or put up for adoption. An-other four Uruguayans were disappeared in Chile, and two in Paraguay.[39]

Repression in Chile was more overt than in Uruguay. According to the Chilean truth commission's report, *The Rettig Report: Report of the National Com-mission on Truth and Reconciliation,* government murders peaked in 1973, with 1,261 cases of death and disappearance during the final four months of 1973. The Rettig report discusses human rights violations during the seventeen years of military rule but devotes 350 of its nearly 900 pages to these four months alone.[40] The report documents that after the peak in 1973, there were on av-erage 189 deaths and disappearances per year between 1974 and 1976, 16 on average per year in the five-year period from 1977 through 1982, and an aver-age of 43 from 1983 until re-democratization in 1990. Government repression declined significantly after 1976 but did not end until the country returned to democratic government.

In Paraguay the Stroessner regime exercised repression mainly through widespread and arbitrary imprisonment and torture. A wave of human rights violations that began in 1976, during the thirty-year dictatorship of Stroessner, constituted one of the worst episodes of repression in Paraguayan history.[41] Likewise, in Bolivia the coup of General García Meza in July 1980 "stands out as the most bloodthirsty and cruel in Bolivia's history."[42] There were direct links between the García Meza regime and that of General Viola in Argentina, which provided logistical and political support for repression in Bolivia. Gar-cía Meza's regime lasted only thirteen months, but during this period it is estimated that the government assassinated 196 people, wounded another 554, disappeared 87, arbitrarily imprisoned 3,500, and forced between 440 and 1,500 into exile.[43]

The most serious case of human rights violations in the entire region was Guatemala. The UN Truth Commission Report on Guatemala estimated that security forces killed and disappeared perhaps as many as two hundred thousand people. For the purposes of this analysis, however, I will be working with a data set of human rights violations comparable to that available for Chile and Argentina, which is a list of cases of disappeared or dead collected by the International Center for Human Rights Investigations. The ICHR pooled data from the press and from testimony provided to human rights organizations. The total number of state-sponsored deaths and disappearances documented by the ICHR for the period 1959–95 is 36,906. The ICHR data, because it is broken down by year like the Argentine, Chilean, and Salvadoran data, can be used to assess the impact of human rights policies over time. As with the data from other truth commission reports, it underestimates the total number of deaths and disappearances in Guatemala. I nonetheless believe it is accurate about the overall trend of repression.

A handful of countries avoided the regional trend toward escalating human rights violations in the 1970s and 1980s. Many of the small island states of the Caribbean, under the parliamentary system, avoided the military coups and resulting violence of the continent. In Central America, only democratic Costa Rica remained an island of relative stability and freedom, though human rights violations in Honduras and Nicaragua were significantly lower than those in El Salvador and Guatemala. In South America, Ecuador and Venezuela bucked the regional trend, although the human rights situation in Venezuela began to worsen in the 1990s. The country that most completely avoided the waves of repression, Costa Rica, was not only democratic but the only country in the region without a military, having abolished it in 1948. Yet authoritarianism in and of itself is not a sufficient condition for explaining the massive human rights violations of the 1970s and 1980s. The military regimes of the 1980s were much more repressive than previous military regimes. In Colombia large-scale human rights violations have been carried out during a nominally democratic regime.

The final point to make about the map of repression is how much the situation improved in Latin America in the 1990s and the beginning of the twenty-first century. The decline in summary executions and disappearances has been particularly notable. In its first report in 1981, the UN Working Group reported that it had received information about 11,000 to 13,000 cases of disappearances from fifteen countries, ten of which were Latin American.[44] By 1996, however, the UN Working Group concluded that political disappearances had almost ended in the western hemisphere.[45] By the mid-1990s, most analysts agreed, torture was less widespread throughout the region than it was in the 1970s. Nevertheless, in 1997 Amnesty International reported torture was frequent or common in five countries in Latin America (Brazil, Colombia, Mexico, Peru, and Venezuela) and that some or several cases of torture had been reported in ten additional countries.[46]

The region has furthermore witnessed a dramatic change with respect to democracy. After a century of swinging between democratic and authoritarian regimes, every Latin American country except Cuba either retained or returned to electoral democracy between 1978 and 1991,[47] although these electoral regimes are far from perfect democracies. As a result of these changes, Latin America today faces a new set of issues—not the problem of military coups, but rather the dilemmas of deepening existing electoral regimes into fuller democracies.

U.S. Policy in Relation to Regional Trends in Repression

In this book my concern is with the relation between U.S. policy and this map of repression in Latin America. In particular, I'm interested in the role of U.S. policy at the critical junctures before and during the repression peaks shown in figure 1. What was U.S. policy toward Argentina in 1976–77, Chile in 1973–74, Guatemala in 1980–82, and El Salvador in 1979–80 and what difference did that policy make? The issue most often raised is the impact of U.S. military and economic aid on the human rights practices of recipient states. In three of the four main case countries studied here—Argentina, Guatemala, and Chile—military aid was eventually terminated and economic aid curtailed as a result of poor human rights practices. In some cases the U.S. government actually cut aid; in others, Latin American governments rejected U.S. aid after it was linked to human rights performance. In El Salvador, aid was cut off briefly under the Carter administration but later sustained and increased throughout the rest of the period under study, despite repeated attempts by congressional critics to reduce or cut off aid.

What was the human rights impact from these aid cutoffs? To answer this question, I chart the levels of U.S. military and economic assistance to the four case countries in relation to trends in deaths and disappearances (figures 2–5). Overall, the four charts are puzzling and do not yield a clear statement about the relation between human rights and levels of military and economic aid.

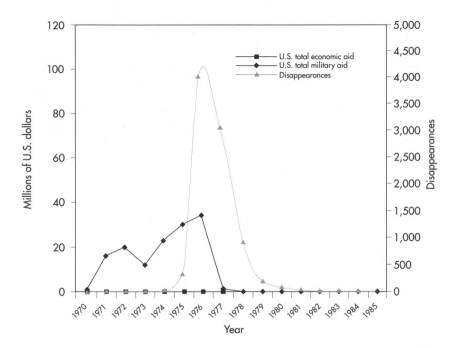

Figure 2. Argentina: Disappearances and U.S. Aid

In the case of Argentina, a dramatic increase in disappearances provoked a cutoff of both military and economic aid, and aid levels stayed low during the entire period of the military regime (see figure 2). In Chile, Congress cut off military aid in response to human rights violations, but the Nixon and Ford administrations secured significant levels of economic aid for the country, mainly through using a large percentage of discretionary P.L. 480 (Food for Peace) funds. This economic aid was then suspended during the Carter administration and remained low during the Pinochet government (see figure 3).

Guatemala and El Salvador reveal quite a different pattern. During the period 1954–76, Guatemala was a major recipient of U.S. military and economic assistance, including substantial training and equipment for military and police officers.[48] Congress cut off military aid and limited economic aid in 1977 in response to human rights violations. The Reagan administration attempted to reinstate aid but met with resistance from the Congress. Guatemala was receiving no U.S. military aid and only low levels of economic aid during the peak of human rights violations in 1981 and 1982. Some significant commercial sales were made during this period that had implications

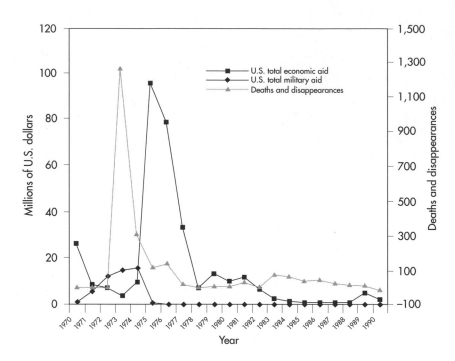

Figure 3. Chile: Deaths, Disappearances, and U.S. Aid

for repression, but there was very little concessional aid. Some aid was simply rerouted. For instance, the United States provided extensive aid to Israel, and Israel in turn supplied substantial aid to Guatemala in this period. But the Israeli assistance was not high enough to alter the overall picture of low levels of U.S. aid to Guatemala during the highest period of repression (see figure 4).

In contrast, El Salvador received very high and constantly increasing levels of military and economic aid during the period under study. High levels of aid coincided with high levels of human rights violations, as charged by critics of U.S. policy. But human rights violations declined as military and economic aid increased, so it is difficult to establish an obvious link between levels of aid and levels of human rights violations, especially when we compare the case of El Salvador with that of Guatemala (see figure 5).

I want to suggest that to focus mainly on decisions about military and economic aid misses the overall normative and institutional context within which repression occurred in Latin America. Decisions about military and economic aid are cues or signals given by one country to another. Policy makers use these

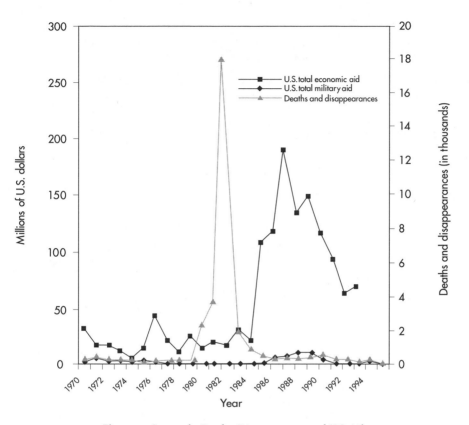

Figure 4. Guatemala: Deaths, Disappearances, and U.S. Aid

cues to make sense of the relationship between two countries. Making sense involves interpreting these cues by linking them to existing, well-learned cognitive structures, such as dominant foreign policy frameworks and perceptions of state identity.[49]

In the normative context of the early 1970s and early 1980s, Latin American policy makers linked cues about aid to an existing policy framework in which repression figured as a necessary component of the struggle against communism. This framework also supported the military's identity as a defender of the nation against the communist threat. Policy makers were confused by and resistant to contradictory cues, especially those that challenged the dominant framework and called into question their identity. On the one hand, the U.S. Congress was cutting off military aid because of human rights practices, and on the other, many U.S. diplomats continued to stress the familiar messages of national security doctrine. Latin American leaders had to make sense

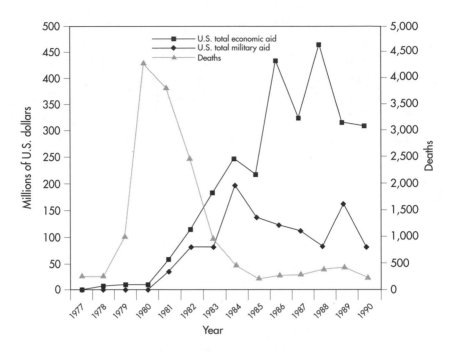

Figure 5. El Salvador: Deaths and U.S. Aid

of these mixed signals. They chose to think about human rights policy as a temporary enthusiasm that would not become a dominant theme in U.S. foreign policy. Messages sent by top-level U.S. policy makers often reinforced this interpretation.

In the last fifteen years, comprehensive documents detailing the scope and nature of repression have been produced in Latin America. A comparative analysis of these documents suggests a puzzling trend of repression in Latin America—the highest peaks of repression in the twentieth century occurred in dissimilar countries within a single decade, 1973–82. When charted against U.S. economic and military aid during the same period, no obvious relation is discernible between levels of military or economic aid and the patterns of repression.

Nevertheless, the similarities among the trends of repression suggest that the causes of repression are not purely domestic and that some international or regional factors may be at work. We need to consider aspects of U.S. policy besides direct military and economic aid. I will argue that the overarching signals or messages conveyed by top-level policy makers about the worldviews that conditioned bilateral relations were the most important international factor influencing internal decisions about repression. The following chapters examine U.S. policy in detail during the period 1976–2000 in order to understand the international and domestic factors that contributed to or undermined human rights in the four case countries.

CHAPTER FIVE

U.S. Human Rights Policy during the Nixon and Ford Administrations

The initial human rights legislation, passed in the U.S. Congress in 1974 and 1975, called on the State Department to produce human rights reports and tied U.S. security assistance to recipients' records on human rights. But the early legislation merely expressed a "sense of the Congress" and thus was not binding on the executive branch. During the Nixon and Ford administrations, the executive sharply opposed the human rights legislation and resisted enforcing measures passed by Congress. This resistance led Congress gradually to reduce the executive's freedom of action by moving away from "sense of the Congress" resolutions and general legislation toward binding, country-specific measures. According to one official who served in the Congressional Office at the State Department during this period, "Kissinger is responsible for the [congressional] requirement for Human Rights reports because he was so adamant about not playing ball at all."[1]

Congress began to implement a human rights policy that brought it into conflict with Kissinger's policy of anticommunism at any cost. In particular, Congress mandated a series of country-specific aid cutoffs to Argentina, Chile, and Uruguay. Senator Edward Kennedy had worked for a number of years trying to limit economic and military aid to the repressive Chilean regime. Congress succeeded in blocking military aid, but its attempts to put a ceiling on economic aid were undermined by the Nixon and Ford administrations.[2]

Because the Nixon and Ford administrations did not initiate or support human rights legislation, it may seem odd to devote a chapter to their human rights policy. Nevertheless, by the mid-1970s, the human rights legislation mandated a change in U.S. foreign policy. This chapter examines how the Nixon and Ford administrations responded to the new congressional human rights policy initiative in two key cases, Chile and Argentina.

The peaks in human rights violations in both Argentina and in Chile came during these administrations. In both cases, there is evidence that top-level U.S. policy makers gave verbal assurances that were understood as giving a green light to human rights violations. Recently declassified diplomatic cables reveal that Secretary of State Kissinger led Chilean and Argentine military officers to believe that the United States would not protest human rights violations. Indeed, human rights policy was portrayed as a concern merely of a few congressmen. These verbal green lights were part of a larger normative context in which the struggle against subversion was seen as essential and human rights violations were acceptable, and indeed even necessary, in the struggle against communist subversion and terrorism. When Latin American policy makers weighed the costs and benefits of repression, they concluded that they would incur little or no cost in their relation with the United States.

Nevertheless, other policy makers during this period, such as Robert Hill, ambassador to Argentina, did attempt to implement human rights policy. Hill raised human rights issues frequently in his conversations with the Argentine military. He pointed explicitly to congressional human rights legislation and warned the military of the possibility of future aid cuts. So the Ford and Nixon administrations were not monolithic in their rejection of human rights policy, although the policy associated with Kissinger prevailed. U.S. policy toward Chile and Argentina illustrates the presence of sensemaking in interactions between Latin American and U.S. policy makers, in a context where national security doctrine was the main interpretive framework.

Chile

U.S. human rights policies were not yet formulated when the bulk of repression happened in Chile. Rather, Chile was one of the key cases that led individuals to question existing policy and to advocate a new human rights policy.

Before the coup against President Allende in 1973, Chile had the longest tradition of democracy in the hemisphere, a well-institutionalized party system, and relatively high levels of economic development, urbanization, and industrialization. The 1925 constitution included significant human rights guarantees, which an independent judiciary helped enforce.[3] The political system prior to 1973 combined a democratic political regime with substantive democratization, in which marginalized groups were gradually incorporated into the political system and Chileans saw their standard of living improve.[4]

The 1973 coup followed a period of intense mobilization and polarization in Chilean politics after SalvadorAllende began to implement his program for a peaceful road to socialism. Allende's decision to implement far-reaching economic and political reforms, despite receiving only a slim plurality of the votes, provoked strong national and international reactions and domestic polarization. Though a time of turmoil and hardship, the Allende period was not marred by any accusations of torture, execution, or political imprisonment. This changed dramatically with the coup.

After General Pinochet, commander in chief of the armed forces, took over as president of the republic after the coup of 1973, he concentrated power in his person in a manner never before seen in Chilean history. A group of mainly army officers connected to the National Intelligence Directorate (DINA) was deeply implicated in much of the repression in Chile, which was unprecedented in degree and cruelty. Thousands of individuals were arrested and detained without charge. Torture was common, and many prisoners were disappeared and later executed. Over half of the almost three thousand documented cases of death and disappearance during the seventeen years of the Pinochet regime took place in 1973 and 1974.[5]

Chile caught world attention because people had been watching President Allende's experiment with an electoral route to socialism. The particularly brutal and public way the military carried out the coup, with the bombings of the presidential palace and the death (later confirmed as a suicide, but at the time widely believed to be murder) of President Allende, galvanized regional and international attention. The military carried out the repression publicly, rounding up large numbers of their political opponents and imprisoning them in the national stadium, carrying out executions, and confining key leaders of the Unidad Popular government in harsh prison camps.

Large numbers of dissidents took refuge in the embassies of sympathetic European and LatinAmerican governments. As thousands of these dissidents went into exile, they used their considerable political contacts and lobbying skills to arouse international solidarity and sympathy. International NGOs and Chilean exiles mobilized immediately after the coup to bring human rights violations in Chile to international attention. These exiles were often highly educated and well-connected political party activists. After the coup, they rapidly mobilized existing nongovernmental networks or built new ones to protest the repressive policies of the regime. The Catholic Church in Chile took an activist stance, providing an umbrella of protection under which a sophisticated array of domestic human rights organizations arose, led by the flagship human rights organization, the Church's Vicaría de Solidaridad.[6] Domestic human rights groups in Chile provided constant information to international contacts, which in turn made this information available to policy makers. The reports of international human rights organizations, given publicity through lobbying and the media, were used to justify cuts in military and economic assistance to the Chilean government.[7]

Yet Nixon and Ford administration policy makers were unmoved. At the height of repression in Chile in 1974, only one week after 104 members of the House and Senate wrote Kissinger expressing their opposition to continued military assistance to repressive regimes, Kissinger rebuked David Popper, U.S. ambassador to Chile, for raising human rights issues with the Chilean military. A *New York Times* story reported that sources in the State Department had leaked a memo revealing that Kissinger had criticized Ambassador Popper after he had discussed torture and other human rights issues during a meeting on military aid with Chilean officials. According to the State Department sources, Kissinger had written, "Tell Popper to cut out the political science lectures," in the margins of a diplomatic cable, which led the State Department to issue a formal complaint to Mr. Popper.[8] The complaint created a major dispute in the State Department, with some sources unusually willing to leak information to the press to explain their points of view.

The State Department spokesperson told reporters that Kissinger "considers it a disgrace to the Foreign Service when members of the Foreign Service leak classified information."[9] This story suggests that during the Nixon and Ford administrations, even private diplomacy on human rights issues was considered inappropriate, and efforts to raise human rights could hurt careers. But it also suggests that there was sufficient opposition to this policy under Kissinger that some sources felt they *had* to leak the information to the press. In other words, the department was not monolithic in its opposition to a human rights policy.

Congressman Fraser wrote the State Department requesting a meeting to clarify the report. The department denied the stories but refused to meet with Fraser or show Congress the documents to support their position.[10] State Department sources who had leaked the information specifically referred to their obligations under existing legislation to take human rights into account in foreign policy decisions.

Two years later, Kissinger had changed his tune in public but not in private meetings. In June 1976, he traveled to an OAS meeting in Santiago, Chile, where he made a speech with a strong public statement on human rights. In private meetings at the same time, however, he sent a very different message.

Kissinger met with General Pinochet while in Santiago and, according to a memorandum of that meeting, reassured Pinochet that Washington supported his government and that human rights concerns were "confined to some sectors of Congress and were not shared by the Ford Administration." When Pinochet complained about the lobbying efforts of Allende's exiled defense minister, Orlando Letelier, to cut off U.S. support for his government, Kissinger noted the existence of a "world-wide propaganda campaign by the Communists."[11] Here Kissinger issued a series of clear diplomatic cues to a Chilean military regime avid to hear them. He told Pinochet that human rights policy was not the policy of the Ford administration, and he appeared to suggest that the U.S. government considered Letelier an enemy.

In September 1976, a car bomb exploded in downtown Washington, killing Orlando Letelier and his U.S. associate Ronnie Moffit. Although it would take over a year to confirm the Chilean government's involvement, many people immediately believed the bombing to be the work of the notorious Chilean intelligence agency, the DINA. The murder of Letelier and Moffit became a symbol of the impunity of repressive regimes in Latin America. The Chileans were apparently so certain of U.S. support that they dared to murder their opponents in a terrorist bombing in the streets of Washington, D.C., without fear of retribution or rebuke.

The story of Kissinger's support for the coup in Chile has been told at length elsewhere, including in the reports of the Church committee of the Senate.[12] New research making use of declassified U.S. government documents demonstrates that Kissinger sent clear signals of support for Pinochet. For example, speaking confidentially to Pinochet, Kissinger said, "In the United States, as you know, we are sympathetic with what you are trying to do here. . . .We want to help, not undermine you."[13] Newly released cables reveal that despite the vocal criticism of his policy toward Chile, Secretary Kissinger issued similar green lights for repression to the military junta in Argentina two years later, often in virtually identical language.

Argentina

The military coup that brought General Jorge Videla to power in March 1976 was preceded by an upsurge in activities by right-wing death squads and by left-wing guerrilla movements. The death squads carried out over two hundred disappearances before the military coup. High levels of violence and chaos during the government of Isabel Perón had led large sectors of the population to welcome the military decision to step in and stabilize the country, as they had done in the past. Only later did people learn that this coup was different. The military would stay longer in power and engage in human rights violations at levels previously unknown in Argentine history, in order to support what they called a "war on terrorism" against armed leftist insurgents, alternatively called subversives or terrorists. Two important guerrilla groups operated in Argentina in the early 1970s, the Montoneros and the Revolutionary Army of the People, the ERP. Although neither group had large numbers of combatants, their bombings, assassinations, bank robberies, and kidnappings of the wealthy for ransom produced widespread panic and fear.[14]

The war on these insurgents included brutal repression of the opposition, mass kidnappings, torture, murder, and imprisonment without charge. Most of the disappeared were eventually murdered and their bodies incinerated, buried in unmarked mass graves, or thrown into the sea.[15] Although disappearances and repression began before the coup, there is reason to believe that if the military coup had been prevented, the repression never would have reached these levels.

Unlike the case of Guatemala in 1954 and Chile in 1973, there is no evidence that the U.S. government either directed or promoted the Argentine coup, though it certainly did not oppose it.[16] But the Argentine military believed they could depend on the United States to support their war against internal armed guerrilla groups.

The new military government was controlled by a junta of three military officers, the commanders of the army, navy, and air force. The junta member from the army, General Jorge Videla, was the new president of the country. Videla appeared mild and serious, and many were initially reassured and impressed by his moderate demeanor. The three branches of the military divided up the bureaucracy among them. The navy took over the foreign ministry and placed Admiral César Guzzetti at its head. Diplomats who challenged the new leaders or any new policy found themselves in trouble. Within two months, Guzzetti and his navy staff dismissed thirty ambassadors and fifty career foreign service officers and replaced them with navy officers. All levels and branches of the military were deeply involved in repression during the dictatorship, but the navy was the most infamous for its detention center, or concentration camp, located in the Navy Mechanical School. There were even reports of personnel from the foreign ministry's press office who would come and go between the ministry and the camp, and who would take part in kidnapping and torture.[17]

Ambassador Hill was a veteran hand in Latin American affairs, having served as U.S. ambassador to Costa Rica, El Salvador, and Mexico. He had served in Argentina since 1973 and had greeted the 1976 coup as one of the best-executed coups in Argentine history. But shortly after the coup, Hill began to worry about repression under the new regime. Declassified U.S. documents reveal that Hill made human rights issues a priority in his conversations with the new military government. Yet these messages were contradicted by more powerful messages from higher levels.

Ambassador Hill was troubled by a series of events in May 1976: the apparently politically motivated murder of two Uruguayan congressmen exiled in Argentina, Zelmar Michellini and Héctor Gutiérrez Ruíz; and the kidnapping of several Argentines working with U.S. universities, Ford Foundation grantees, and at least two U.S. citizens. He raised his concern for the human rights situation in a meeting with the undersecretary of the presidency, Ricardo Yofre, on May 25, two months after the coup. Yofre promised a number of specific reforms but argued that the country "is in an all-out war against subversion. . . . In the heat of battle there will inevitably be some violation of human rights." Yofre warned that the government was planning to drastically step up its campaign against the terrorists very shortly. At the same time as he issued this chilling justification of abuses and prediction of more to come, Yofre also claimed that there were other hard-liners operating that were not under Videla's control and suggested that these groups were responsible for the kidnapping and murder of Michellini and Gutiérrez Ruíz.[18] The very day of the meeting, the embassy learned that the Fulbright Program coordinator had been kidnapped. Ambassador Hill immediately sent a cable to Washington requesting permission to launch a demarche on human rights "at the highest level." Hill received permission and three days later met with Guzzetti, the foreign minister. Hill said to Guzzetti:

> The US very much sympathizes with the moderate policies announced by President Videla and had hoped to be helpful to Argentina in her process of national reconstruction and reconciliation. We fully understand that Argentina is involved in an all out struggle against subversion. There are, however, some norms which can never be put aside by governments dedicated to the rule of law. Human rights are one of them. The continued activities of . . . death squads which have recently murdered Michellini, Gutiérrez Ruíz and dozens of others and have just kidnapped a member of the Fulbright Commission, Miss Elida Messina, are damaging the GOA's [Government of Argentina's] generally good image abroad. These groups seem to operate with immunity and are generally believed to be connected with the Argentine security forces.[19]

Coming from the U.S. foreign service at this time, this was a strong and courageous statement on human rights. The coup just two months earlier had been welcomed by large numbers of the Argentine public. Videla was still viewed as a moderate by many in the diplomatic community.

Secretary of State Kissinger and other high-level members of the Ford administration, however, completely undermined Hill's expressions of concern about human rights. Kissinger, Vice President Rockefeller, and other top officials gave a clear green light to repression in Argentina, urging military leaders to continue, and in fact accelerate, the war against "terrorism." They made no explicit mention of the methods they surely knew the military was using: torture, disappearance, and summary executions.

What do I mean by "green light?" The chronology here is key, especially in identifying a "critical juncture." On June 10, 1976, Guzzetti traveled to Santiago de Chile for a meeting of the Organization of American States (OAS). In his public remarks at the meeting, Secretary of State Kissinger spoke of the importance of human rights. Kissinger was no stranger to this theme, as he had left Nazi Germany with his parents when he was fifteen to escape persecution. At least thirteen of his close relatives were sent to the gas chambers or died in concentration camps. These childhood experiences apparently instilled in Kissinger a concern with the need to preserve *order* at all costs. His studies turned him into a proponent of "realist" foreign policy, focused on the need to safeguard order through maintaining a balance of power in the world. By the time he was appointed secretary of state in 1975, Kissinger was "the most admired person in America," according to a Gallup Poll.[20] Kissinger saw the authoritarian regimes of the Southern Cone of South America not as gross violators of human rights but as bulwarks against disorder in countries that were "under violent attack from radical, antidemocratic, and antimarket forces."[21] He believed that the Cold War reality impelled the United States to maintain a "constructive" relationship with authoritarian regimes of South America.

By September 1976, however, Kissinger and his foreign policy were under attack by critics in Congress and by presidential candidate Jimmy Carter. Perhaps because Kissinger's concern with human rights was motivated more by his strategic calculus of what was important in U.S. electoral debates than by his belief that human rights should be a key part of foreign policy, he stressed human rights in his public remarks but not in his private meetings with either Pinochet or Guzzetti in Santiago.

On June 8, 1976, Kissinger gave an entire speech focused on the theme of human rights. He said, "No government can ignore terrorism and survive, but it is equally true that a government that tramples on the rights of its citizens denies the purpose of its existence." He went on to state that "there are standards below which no government can fall without offending fundamental values—such as genocide, officially tolerated torture, mass imprisonment or murder, or comprehensive denials of basic rights to racial, religious, political, or ethnic groups. Any government engaging in such practices must face adverse international judgment."[22]

But in his private meeting with Guzzetti in Santiago, Kissinger apparently did not raise human rights issues. We do not have documents from that meeting, but we can piece together what happened from subsequent cables that the embassy sent to Washington, in which Argentine officials are quoted making frequent references to the Kissinger-Guzzetti meeting in Santiago. These cables indicate that Kissinger did not offer Guzzetti specific instructions or guidelines. Rather, he is reported to have said that he "hoped the Argentine government would get the terrorism problem under control as quickly as possible."

Guzzetti later told Ambassador Hill that he had reported his conversation with Kissinger to President Videla and to the cabinet and "that their impression had been that USG's overriding concern was not with human rights but rather that the GOA 'get it over quickly.'"[23] Just one week after Guzzetti's meeting with Kissinger on June 16, 1976, Max Chaplin, the deputy chief of mission at the embassy in Buenos Aires, met with the top civilian official of the Argentine foreign ministry. When Chaplin expressed his concern about human rights, the Argentine official responded by expressing his satisfaction that Secretary Kissinger was "realistic and understood the GOA's problems." Chaplin, in a cable summarizing the meeting, reported that the official was "not disposed to give one inch on the issue of human rights."[24]

One month later Chaplin sent a cable to the State Department Bureau of Intelligence and Research disagreeing with two points in a recent report they had issued. First, Chaplin wrote that the intelligence unit had underestimated the cooperation between Southern Cone countries, as evidenced by the presence of Uruguayan and Chilean forces operating with Argentine security units. Second, Chaplin clarified that "there appears also to be a misunderstanding, to which we may have contributed, as to the composition of the various forces engaged in battle in Argentina." He argued that the conflict in Argentina was no longer a "tri-corner battle among security personnel, leftists, and right-wing assassins. . . . In our best judgment, the only 'right-wing assassins' operating in Argentina at this point, however, are members of the GOA security forces. . . . Only real question is degree to which security forces personnel may be operating out of GOA control." Because this cable was written to an intelligence bureau, it was not available to all members of the foreign service. Secretary of State Kissinger and other top level officials nonetheless naturally would have had access to it before their meetings with Guzzetti in October.

In September 1976, Ambassador Hill met with President Videla and again expressed his concern about the human rights situation. Hill reported telling Videla that in the United States there was "great sympathy for his government, which had taken over under difficult circumstances and which all understood to be involved in struggle to the death with left-wing subversion. However, such things as the murder of the priests and the mass murder at Pilar were seriously damaging Argentina's image in the U.S." Hill continued, "I suggested that in the final analysis, the best way to proceed against terrorists was within law." Videla responded that he had been "gratified" when Guzzetti reported that Kissinger understood their problem and had the impression that "senior officers of the U.S. government understand the situation his government faces but junior bureaucrats do not." Here, Videla appears to be categorizing the ambassador as a junior bureaucrat who doesn't understand him while indicating that the secretary of state and others do. Ambassador Hill assured him that this was not the case: "We all hope Argentina can get terrorism under control quickly—but do so in such a way as to do minimum damage to its image and to its relations with other governments. If security forces continue to kill people to the tune of brass band, I concluded, this will not be possible. I told him the Secretary of State had told me when I was in U.S. that he wanted to avoid human rights problems in Argentina."[25]

Nevertheless, when Guzzetti traveled to Washington and New York to meet with top-level U.S. officials in October, he was once again persuaded that the top levels of the U.S. government were not concerned about the human rights practices of his government. In a meeting at the State Department, Guzzetti explained that one of the most important issues facing the Argentine government was "the capacity of international terrorist groups to support the Argentine terrorists through propaganda and funds."[26]

Acting U.S. Secretary of State Charles W. Robinson responded that "during this initial period the situation may seem to call for measures that are not acceptable in the long term." He emphasized that the real question is "knowing how long to continue these tough measures." Robinson continued by explaining U.S. human rights policy. He pointed clearly to the role of U.S. national identity in human rights policy but indicated, in so many words, that the executive branch was not committed to the policy. Instead, it had to cope with human rights due to Congress and public opinion:

> The problem is that the United States is an idealistic and moral country and its citizens have great difficulty in comprehending the kinds of problems faced by Argentina today. There is a tendency to apply our moral standards abroad and Argentina must understand the reaction of Con-

gress with regard to loans and military assistance. The American people, right or wrong, have the perception that today there exists in Argentina a pattern of gross violations of human rights. . . . There are many well-meaning people in the United States, though perhaps somewhat naïve, who indiscriminately take the side of those imprisoned in Argentina.[27]

Robinson then urged Guzzetti to reduce the "tough measures" by reminding him that the U.S. Congress returned in January. If the Argentines reduced "the intensity of the measures" by then, the charge that there is a consistent pattern of gross violations of human rights would be invalidated, reducing the possibility of Congress's cutting off aid to Argentina.

This mild and arms-length position on human rights policy was nevertheless undermined by Kissinger, who met with Guzzetti the next day in New York. Using language virtually identical to the language he had used years earlier with Pinochet, Kissinger said "Look, our basic attitude is that we would like you to succeed. I have an old-fashioned attitude that friends ought to be supported. . . . We won't cause you unnecessary difficulties."[28]

When Guzzetti returned from his visit, he met immediately with Hill. Hill reported that Guzzetti appeared "euphoric" with the "success" of his visit. The visit was a "success" for Guzzetti because it confirmed that the Ford administration would not criticize or sanction the Argentine military for its campaign of mass murder against its own population. Instead, the top leaders of the Ford administration accepted the Argentine government's portrayal of the situation as a war against terrorism in which any means were apparently acceptable.

Hill described his meeting with Guzzetti: "He bounced into the room and greeted me effusively with an abrazo [hug] which is not typical of him. He took me into his private office where for 35 minutes he enthusiastically told me of the success of his visit." Guzzetti was "almost ecstatic" in describing his meeting with Vice President Rockefeller. Rockefeller had urged him to advise President Videla to "diminish the terrorist problem quickly." In his meeting with Kissinger, the Secretary of State told Guzzetti that "if the terrorist problem was over by December or January, he believed serious problems could be avoided in the U.S." Guzzetti said that Kissinger had assured him that the U.S. "wants to help Argentina."

After his meeting with Guzzetti, Hill cabled a protest to Kissinger that the Argentine military had not received a strong disapproval signal from Washington for their human rights violations. As the cable noted, Guzzetti's remarks were "not those of a man who has been impressed with the gravity of the human rights problem as seen from the U.S. Guzzetti went to the U.S. fully expecting to hear some strong, firm, direct warning of his government's human rights practices. Rather than that, he has returned in a state of jubilation convinced that there is no real problem with the U.S. government over this issue." At the end of the cable, Ambassador Hill concluded that it was "unrealistic" for him to continue to pressure the Argentine government on human rights: "Based on what Guzzetti is doubtlessly reporting to the GOA, it must now believe that if it has any problems with the U.S. over human rights, they are confined to certain elements of Congress and what it regards as [unclear] and/or uninformed minor segments of public opinion. While that conviction lasts it will be unrealistic and unbelievable for this embassy to press representatives to the GOA over human rights violations."[29]

To defuse Hill's frustration, Harry Shlaudeman, assistant secretary of state, wrote back to him saying that Guzzetti may have misunderstood the message because of his "poor grasp of English" or his desire to hear "only what he wanted to hear." Shlaudeman claimed that Guzzetti "was told in detail how strongly opinion in this country has reacted against reports of abuses by the security forces in Argentina, and the nature of threat this poses to Argentine interests."[30] But Shlaudeman did not offer an alternative interpretation of the meetings, nor did he ask Hill to correct any misunderstanding. Instead, he agreed with Hill's decision that it would be unrealistic to continue to put pressure on human rights. "Argentines," he said, "will have to make their own decision, and further exhortations or generalized lectures from us would not be useful at this point."[31]

The recently released memorandum of conversations between Guzzetti and Kissinger and Guzzetti and Robinson reveal that Guzzetti's hearing and grasp of English were fine. He reported relatively accurately about what he had heard from Kissinger. He did not mention the concerns U.S. policy makers expressed about U.S. public opinion or the U.S. Congress, perhaps because executive policy makers gave the impression that they sided with the Argentines and would try to block efforts to cut aid. Shlaudeman, in other words, by saying that Guzzetti "may have misunderstood," appears to be misrepresenting the situation to Hill, his own ambassador.

One month later, Jimmy Carter won the presidential election. Shortly after taking office in January 1977, he pledged to make human rights issues a cornerstone of his foreign policy. The Carter administration decided to make Argentina one of the priority countries for its new human rights policy. On January 29, 1977, a State Department official had a conversation with the Argentine political counselor in Washington, Mr. Beauge. The State Department official explained that "human rights concerns are not the preoccupation of a few in Congress *but represent basic political forces at work in United States*" (emphasis added). The U.S. official once again stressed that human rights policy was a reflection of U.S. identity, but here the official took ownership of the policy. He stressed that "it would be desirable for rule of law to operate again in Argentina so that when people are arrested, their arrest is acknowledged and their defense is permitted. . . . While we recognize the terribly difficult problem GOA faces in dealing with terrorism, we cannot accept that people with different views are persecuted, tortured, and murdered." Beauge asked if the U.S. embassy in Buenos Aires had made these same points and stressed that "it is essential for your same message to come from all channels. This did not happen in the past."[32] In other words, even representatives of the Argentine military regime were aware of the kinds of mixed signals that were sent by the U.S. government and advised the United States to be more consistent.

I deal with this period at length because of its unique characteristics. First, the reliable data from the Argentine truth commission make clear that this is exactly the critical juncture in human rights policy in Argentina. Second, the collection of recently declassified U.S. cables and memoranda gives us an unusually complete view of the bilateral conversations between Argentina and the United States at this critical juncture. We can see precisely what U.S. policy makers said to Argentine policy makers. The conclusion must be sobering.

The report of the National Commission on Disappearances (CONADEP) in Argentina shows that the number of deaths and disappearances peaked between June 1976 and January 1977. The National Commission was set up by President Raúl Alfonsín in 1983 after redemocratization in Argentina. Commission members took ample testimony about human rights abuses, and their data on human rights violations are based on individual complaints they received and investigated. They estimate a total of 8,960 deaths and disappearances in Argentina during the 1975 – 83 period. In mid-1976 many Argentines, under the influence of a controlled press, continued to deny that any government repression was happening at all. As we see from the cables, however, Hill and Chaplin were confident by July 1976 that the right-wing death squads were part of the government security forces and were responsible for many disappearances and murders. They communicated this conclusion to members of the Argentine government, and to the U.S. government in their cables.

The number of deaths and disappearances peaked at precisely the time of Kissinger's "green light," between June 1976 and January 1977. That is, the most intense repression in Argentina coincides in a ghastly manner with the period in which senior U.S. officials were downplaying human rights and stressing the need to fight terrorism quickly. Although it is difficult to find "smoking guns" with respect to U.S human rights policy, this is the closest we can come to saying that U.S. policy makers bear an important responsibility for the peak of repression in Argentina.

From the analysis of U.S. practices in Chile and Argentina, we can conclude that the content and tone of policy discussion matters. Senior official statements, verbal signals, and tacit cues are all of central importance. Cutting aid and other forms of sanctions and conditionalities are also important, but principally as an extension of forceful verbal signals. The actual words used by Kissinger may seem innocuous. These were simple words about fighting terrorism and supporting friends. How could we possibly link these simple words to a pattern of vicious repression? But it is key to remember that these cues were given to a particular audience in a particular historical period.

First, the audience consisted of military leaders who had been socialized into a particular military doctrine and set of practices that made repression more likely. National security doctrine refocused military attention to an internal enemy—guerrillas, subversives, or terrorists, as they were alternately labeled—and made the destruction of this internal enemy the primary goal of military institutions. The tactical tools for fighting the internal enemy were those of counterinsurgency doctrine, which was inattentive to the human rights implications of declaring an irregular war against citizens. U.S. training, especially through the School of the Americas, had contributed to this socialization process, and U.S. policy was strongly associated with anticommunism and the national security doctrine.

Because these military leaders had been socialized to national security doctrine, and since U.S. policy supported and reinforced that doctrine, when Kissinger told them to "fight terrorism" quickly, they interpreted this instruction within the shared framework of the national security ideology. Kissinger told the military rulers that he "understood" their situation, that he considered them "friends" that needed support, and that he would not create difficulties for them. We must believe that the Argentine military assumed Kissinger knew that massive human rights violations were being carried out by the Argentine government. After all, Hill and Chaplin knew, so Kissinger must have known. So, when Kissinger proclaimed that he "understood" and supported them, they heard him say that he supported their practices of disappearances and execution.

It is important to note that what was *not said* is just as significant as that which was expressly stated. Kissinger did *not* discuss democracy or the rule of law. He did *not* mention the alternative of putting guerrillas or "terrorists" on trial and then in prison. He did *not* mention the negatively charged words "kidnapping," "execution," or "torture." He furthermore did *not* mention a single name of a victim, express concern about the disappeared, or inquire about those suffering repression. Indeed, even though Argentine security forces had recently executed two top-level Uruguayan congressmen in exile, no one in Washington even bothered to mention their names. Clearly, the Argentine military also heard all that *wasn't* said and drew their conclusions.

The listener uses cues to make sense of the situation. Diplomatic cables give little doubt that Guzzetti and the Argentine military made sense of Kissinger's cues (spoken or not) as tacit support for a policy of mass murder. This is why Guzzetti was euphoric upon his return from Washington.

At the same time, the Argentine military had trouble hearing what Hill was saying to them about human rights policy. Such policy was new to them, and they doubted its sincerity and longevity. Hill was a "lower-level" policy maker making a novel and painful point. To hear Hill would have called into question their worldview and their identity. The U.S. government gave contradictory cues, but Argentine policy makers, not surprisingly, decided to "hear" those cues from topmost policy makers (Kissinger and Rockefeller) that fit with their national security worldview and that reinforced their identity as defenders of the nation against communism.

This event of a generation ago, emblematic of some of the errors the United States made repeatedly during the Cold War, has key implications for policy makers today. Even apparently vague and subtle cues are interpreted within existing frameworks of meaning. Human rights cues may be hard to hear because they call into question a person's positive identity. It would take a very forceful policy to change the overarching framework and make it possible to hear the human rights messages in Latin America. Ambassador Hill did not live to see such a policy implemented. From behind bulletproof windows, Hill once watched his residence in Buenos Aires being machine-gunned. The tension of living under such unstable conditions undermined Hill's health. He resigned from his post in 1977 and returned to his home in New Hampshire, where he died in 1978.[33]

CHAPTER SIX

The Carter Administration and Human Rights Policy toward Latin America

Patricia Derian and F. Allan "Tex" Harris shared an obsession with human rights in Argentina. Both were active players in the unfolding drama of U.S.–Argentine relations and human rights during the Carter administration. President Carter had named Derian coordinator of human rights in the State Department. The job wasn't at the level of assistant secretary because Kissinger hadn't wanted it at that level. Shortly after Derian took office, Congressman Fraser came to visit her, and told her that they were going to change the title to make sure she was an assistant secretary of state. The change in title gave Derian bureaucratic power she wouldn't have had as coordinator, and she intended to use it. She held a meeting with the other assistant secretaries and told them that she intended to try to implement the human rights legislation. Derian recalled that at the meeting, "All these men, every one very embarrassed, looked at the walls," as she told them that she had surveyed the legislation and she intended to do what it said.[1]

The head of the bureau responsible for Latin America suggested that she travel to Argentina. Given the current hostility in the State Department to incorporating human rights into U.S. foreign policy, Derian understood that the invitation was a challenge. Other officials found her approach to human rights naïve. They thought that if only Derian traveled to Argentina and had conditions explained to her, she would come to understand why it was difficult to implement human rights policy. Instead, Derian's three trips to Argentina over the next few years reinforced her commitment to human rights policy. She met with family members of the disappeared and with representatives of human rights organizations. She never forgot the stories and those who told them: a trembling young man who had been drafted into the military and forced to witness torture; the parents of two boys, twelve and thirteen, who had been disappeared on the streets of Buenos Aires in broad daylight; a woman whose daughter's body had been returned with a rat sewn up in her vagina.[2]

Derian recalls fighting against racism when she was a nursing student at the University of Virginia. Later, as a mother of small children in Mississippi, she worked on voting rights and opened a local chapter of the American Civil Liberties Union. She and her husband, Hodding Carter, were friends and political allies of Jimmy Carter, and Carter gave both of them important positions in his administration. "Tex" Harris would become Derian's right-hand man in the U.S. embassy in Argentina. Harris and Derian, both Southerners, first encountered human rights concerns in civil rights work in the United States. A self-described "Texas liberal," Harris had been the head of a group of law students working for civil rights at the University of Texas law school.[3]

Carter Administration Human Rights Policy

When Derian took over as the head of the new Bureau of Human Rights and Humanitarian Affairs (HA) she had little experience in international affairs and none in bureaucracies. Having grown up and fought for civil rights in a segregated South, she was no stranger to political conflict however. At first apprehensive about the foreign policy bureaucracy, she relaxed when she came to realize that it was "just like Mississippi politics."[4] Under Derian's leadership, HA grew into an active participant in foreign policy making. Derian's main deputy was Mark Schneider, Senator Edward Kennedy's staff person working on human rights and Latin America. John Salzberg also went to work in the bureau after Donald Fraser lost his Senate bid in 1978. Through these appointments, the State Department gained human rights expertise and contacts from both houses of Congress. The vision of the Bureau of Human Rights, however, was hotly contested by other parts of the State Department, especially the regional bureaus, and by the executive. Diplomats in the Latin America Bureau, officially called the American Republics Region Bureau, or ARA, were "absolutely fixed" in their conviction that human rights policy was deeply flawed because it interfered with the good relations they believed the United States needed to maintain with the military.[5]

Many analysts and activists have criticized the Carter administration human rights policy as ineffective, inconsistent, or even counterproductive to U.S. interests.[6] Others, including some victims of repression released from their prisons as a result of Carter's policies, claim it saved many lives.[7] Some of these evaluations of Carter's human rights policies were made during or shortly after the end of his administration, without the benefit of a longer time frame, exhaustive studies, numerous truth commissions, and recently declassified documents.[8] Although the short-term impact of a human rights policy is important, it is equally essential to evaluate the longer-term impact of human rights policies, especially the impact on democratization. In light of the new information and the passage of time, the effectiveness of the Carter human rights policy deserves reevaluation.[9] In this chapter I assess the effect of human rights policy on human rights practices and democratization in Argentina, Chile, El Salvador, Guatemala, and Uruguay. I conclude that Carter's human rights policy was partially effective in both the short and long term in Argentina, Chile, and Uruguay. The policy directly limited the incidence of human rights abuse, and it indirectly contributed to democracy by withdrawing U.S. symbolic and material support for these authoritarian regimes.

We can identify two broad phases of the Carter administration's human rights policy: an active phase in 1977 and 1978 and a "disenchantment" phase in 1979 and 1980.[10] During the active phase, administration members with a greater commitment to the human rights agenda—including Derian and Secretary of State Cyrus Vance—had considerable influence on policy. During this period Congress passed some of its most forceful human rights legislation, and the State Department developed tools at the executive level for implementing human rights policy. Relations between members of Congress pressing the human rights agenda and the executive were relatively cordial and collaborative.

During this active phase, however, the U.S. government did not act with complete consistency in making and carrying out human rights policy. Derian encountered significant resistance to backing up traditional diplomacy with actual cutoffs of U.S. assistance.[11] Early in the Carter administration, a special committee was created under the leadership of Warren Christopher, deputy secretary of state, to decide on specific human rights issues, such as whether to approve loans from multilateral development banks. While Derian argued strongly in favor of taking human rights considerations into account, members of the Interagency Committee on Human Rights and Foreign Assistance (more commonly known as the Christopher committee) and representatives from the Treasury Department, Commerce Department, Agency for International Development, and regional bureaus within the State Department tended to resist such "politicization" of their work. In the disputes between Derian's bureau and the more powerful ARA, the outcome of policy often depended on which side won out in a particular internal debate. These struggles were fought, issue by issue, within the foreign policy bureaucracy.

By mid-1979 a period of "disenchantment" began in human rights policy. A combination of factors contributed to this change. The president was increasingly preoccupied with domestic issues, especially the economy and the preparations for the 1980 election campaign. In the international realm, a series of foreign policy setbacks undermined administration officials' confidence in their policy and emboldened the opposition to human rights. These events included the July 1979 victory of the Sandinistas against the Somoza regime in Nicaragua, the successful overthrow of the Shah of Iran, the militants' seizure of U.S. hostages at the embassy in Tehran in November 1979, and the Soviet invasion of Afghanistan in December 1979.[12] The crisis atmosphere led Derian to comment that she would label the period the "panic phase" of the Carter administration rather than the "disenchantment phase."[13] These events effectively sidelined or stalled human rights initiatives, especially in countries like Guatemala and El Salvador with increasingly significant insurgent movements.

The implementation and effectiveness of human rights policy during the Carter administration varied depending on the country. In the three Southern Cone countries, the peak of human rights violations preceded or coincided with the active phase of human rights policy, thus permitting a forceful and consistent policy response. High-level officials were involved in decision making about policy, and they communicated the seriousness with which the administration viewed the human rights situation through frequent meetings and human rights policy initiatives. The governments in Argentina, Chile, and Uruguay received sufficiently clear messages that they could not misinterpret or fail to hear.

In Guatemala and El Salvador, where the peak in repression coincided with or followed the disenchantment phase and occurred in the context of increasing insurgency, national security predominated over human rights policy. Ambassadors with insufficient commitment to the human rights goals of the administration carried out foreign policy with these authoritarian regimes. It was not until late 1979 that the crisis in El Salvador attracted the attention of high-level Carter officials, and by then the disenchantment phase of human rights policy was in full swing.

Just as the U.S. policy makers were divided in their policy, so the authoritarian regimes that were the target of human rights policy were divided in their positions on repression and human rights. Military leaders had to negotiate with other branches of the armed forces, as well as with hard-liners or soft-liners within their own force. The concerns of some interest groups, such as business organizations, also influenced policy in some military regimes. The outcome of human rights policy depended on how external pressures affected internal negotiations within the regime. This led to a very complicated two-level negotiation "game" over human rights, as the (divided) U.S. government interacted with different factions in the regime.[14]

To further complicate the picture, U.S. human rights policies were only one part of a broader process of international human rights pressures involving international and regional organizations, nongovernmental organizations, and governments. U.S. policy was most effective when it worked with other governments and with multilateral human rights organizations.

Chile

By the time the Carter administration took office, Congress had set the broad parameters of U.S. human rights policy toward Chile. A number of hearings and a series of sanctions had been enacted before Carter was elected in late 1976. Earlier that year, Congress had voted to suspend military aid and arms sales to Chile and to limit economic aid pending substantial progress in improving human rights. After 1977, Chile received no U.S. military aid or sales, and economic aid declined significantly.

If Congress had set the parameters of human rights policy toward Chile, the Carter administration gave it a higher profile and greater force. Carter mentioned Chile frequently during his campaign speeches, and the Democratic Party platform specifically criticized Republican support for that dictatorship.[15]

It is impossible to make a clear causal connection between the numbers of human rights violations and U.S. government policy. Nevertheless, there was an improvement in human rights practices in Chile after Carter's election in 1976, although human rights abuses continued throughout his administration. For example, in November 1976, just after Carter's election, Chile released more than three hundred political prisoners and closed two detention centers.[16] The figures on deaths and disappearances from the official Rettig Commission report show that the Carter presidency was the period of least deaths and disappearances for any four-year period of the Chilean authoritarian regime of 1973–90. There were 62 deaths and disappearances in Chile during the years of the Carter administration, as compared to 1,828 during the Nixon/Ford administration, 210 during Reagan's first term, and 161 during Reagan's second term.[17] The pattern is indeed indicative. In other cases, human rights violations tend to have a more normal distribution, peaking and then diminishing in a consistent fashion. That the violations should have declined significantly under Carter, to then increase and stay higher during the Reagan administration, suggests that a clear and outspoken U.S. policy had the effect of diminishing deaths and disappearances. A Chilean human rights lawyer argued that "when Carter took the presidency and announced his policy, we began seeing a quantitative decline in the number of violations in Chile."[18]

Perhaps the most crucial Carter contribution was the Pinochet government's decision to disband the main repression organ, the National Intelligence Directorate (DINA), a secret police agency, and replace it with the National Information Center (CNI). At the time, the policy change was often interpreted as cosmetic, designed to deflect international criticism without having to dismantle the repressive apparatus. New scholarship contends that the end of DINA instead marked a power shift within the Chilean government, weakening the influence of the hard-liners and leading to improved human rights practices.[19]

The timing of the announcement of the dissolution of DINA reveals the role that U.S. and international pressures played. The pressures on Chile occurred during the early "active" phase of the human rights policy, when both Congress and the administration were putting heavy pressure on Chile. In June 1977 Secretary of State Vance had met with Admiral Patricio Carvajal to press for the dissolution of DINA and the lifting of the state of siege. Pinochet announced the dissolution of DINA during the August 1977 visit to Santiago by Terrence Toddman, assistant secretary of state, and in advance of his trip to Washington for the signing of the Panama Canal Treaty. During his trip to Washington, Pinochet was pressured publicly by the press and privately by Carter. Returning in November of 1977, he took another key action by removing the former DINA director Manuel Contreras, who had continued as director of the new CNI.

After Carter took office in 1977, both the United States and the USSR could agree that international sanctions were desirable in Chile. This opened up the way for active UN involvement as well as for effective network activities and pressures within the United Nations. The United States supported an on-site investigation by the UN Human Rights Commission in 1978 and endorsed the appointment of a UN special rapporteur on Chile. The Human Rights Bureau in the State Department supported these initiatives, often in disagreement with both ARA and the U.S. embassy in Chile.[20] Chile initially cooperated with international human rights monitors, but once it saw the negative reports the monitors produced, it suspended cooperation.

Even during the "active phase," U.S. policy makers gave divided and often contradictory messages about human rights in Chile. When Assistant Secretary Toddman visited Santiago in August 1977, he made statements suggesting "that the situation in Chile was far better than that projected by the world press and that Chile was moving in the right direction in the human rights field." Shortly after Toddman's visit, a group of conservative (Democrat and Republican) members of the House International Relations Committee visited Chile. U.S. embassy staff in Santiago felt that positive developments in Chile were being "overlooked in the United States," they reported. "Embassy officials told the delegation that the majority of the Chilean people was behind the present government."[21]

In 1977 embassy staff, a high-level administration official, and some congressmen were all willing to defend the Pinochet government against the allegedly "unfair" treatment from the U.S. Congress and from the press. Nevertheless, because Chilean human rights violations continued to receive attention from both Congress and the top levels of the administration, it was difficult for the Pinochet government to misinterpret the Carter administration's cues on human rights.

Progress on human rights in Chile stalled after the plebiscite of 1980, which was designed to consolidate the legitimacy and authority of the military regime. The plebiscite results indicated public support for a constitutional change permitting continued military rule, although allegations of fraud were widespread.[22] Bolstered by this support, Pinochet held a press conference after the plebiscite in which he explicitly criticized U.S. policy toward Chile.

Although Carter administration policy didn't contribute to a process of *redemocratization* in Chile, the efficacy of international pressures is evident in the minutes of the meetings of the Chilean juntas. In his review of these minutes, Darren Hawkins reports that "Junta records are filled with debate on how to counter international critics of its human rights policies."[23] In a speech to the Army Corps of Generals in 1977, Pinochet said, "Well we know that the action of our internal adversaries is connected with important political and economic centers in the international world[,] which complicates even further the situation just described."[24] Junta members thus attempted to block the connections between domestic groups and their international allies, but they feared they would prompt international protests if they cut off international contacts or dismantled prominent domestic groups.

Uruguay

Before Carter took office, U.S. policy toward Uruguay sent mixed messages because of differences between Congress and the executive branch.[25] While Congress cut off military aid through the so-called Koch amendment, the State

Department maintained cordial relations with the Uruguayan government. When Carter took office, repression in Uruguay had already peaked and aroused considerable awareness in U.S. policy circles, mainly due to the efforts of Amnesty International and other human rights organizations. The high level of repression in Uruguay created conditions for a forceful response. In early 1977 Secretary Vance announced that the United States would reduce economic aid to Uruguay, making it a test case of the new administration's commitment to take human rights into consideration in the granting of economic aid. The United States also opposed twelve of thirteen loan requests by Uruguay to international financial institutions during the period 1977–80.[26] In February 1977 the OAS ambassador, Robert White, addressed the opening session of the seventh meeting of the Inter-American Council on Education, Science and Culture in Montevideo, calling on states to protect the right of assembly, freedom of expression, and protection against arbitrary arrest and punishment. The military denounced White's speech as a "veiled but direct attack on the country," banned further diffusion of the speech, and prohibited journalists from either commenting on the text or interviewing White.[27]

That same month, a joint commission of Uruguayan opposition party leaders called upon the Carter administration to show concern for human rights in Uruguay by withdrawing Ambassador Siracusa. Derian traveled to Uruguay at Siracusa's insistence in early 1977. She described Siracusa later as someone who was "great pals with leading people in the dictatorship," but who "didn't make excuses for them, and wanted me to talk about human rights problems in my meetings with Uruguayan officials."[28] Carter officials assured Congressman Koch that Siracusa was retiring, and that the new ambassador "possesses the deepest respect for human rights."[29]

Under the new ambassador Lawrence Pezzullo, U.S. human rights policy toward Uruguay from 1977 to 1980 was indeed one of the most coherent and consistent of all U.S. bilateral human rights policies, particularly on the problem of political prisoners.[30] In the two years of most intense human rights pressures, 1977 and 1979, the number of political prisoners dropped from 4,300–5,000 to 1,000–2,500.[31] It is, of course, difficult to know the exact causes of these releases. Even critics of Carter administration human rights policy, however, admitted that Pezzullo had some influence on the human rights situation. The minister of economics at the time, Alejandro Vegh Villegas, claimed "little sympathy" for Carter's policy. While the military viewed it with "enormous hostility," he admitted that Pezzullo undoubtedly made people be "more prudent in the antisubversive struggle. People felt obligated to produce outcomes to improve the situation. There was an atmosphere of pressure, and there was always the need to move toward normalization and democracy."[32]

U.S. policy worked in interaction with multilateral human rights bodies, including the OAS, the IACHR, and the UN Human Rights Committee. The IACHR issued reports in 1978, 1979, and 1980 outlining abuses of human rights in Uruguay, reports that were later adopted by the OAS General Assembly. As a result of this human rights record, together with U.S. and Venezuelan lobbying, the OAS rejected the Uruguayan offer to host the meeting of the General Assembly in 1978.[33] At the same time, the UN Human Rights Committee, generally considered the most forceful of the UN human rights machinery, made numerous decisions on Uruguayan human rights cases.

The Uruguayan government's decision to adopt a *cronograma* (timetable) for returning to democracy was in part the result of pressures from the Carter administration.[34] External pressures influenced the internal negotiations, strengthening the position of the soft-liners within the military. "Partly as a result of pressure from the Carter Administration, the power struggle in the army resulted in a complex victory for the proponents of what was called the cronograma."[35] A crucial step in the timetable was the call for a plebiscite on a military draft constitution. Early in 1980, the Carter administration approved the sale of three search-and-rescue aircraft, apparently as a means of encouraging the move toward the plebiscite that year.

Contrary to the case in Chile, the Uruguayan public soundly defeated the military's proposed constitution, paving the way for an eventual transition to democracy. Unlike their Chilean counterparts, military leaders in Uruguay had left the pre-coup electoral registers intact, allowing fewer possibilities for fraud. Exiles like Wilson Ferreira worked to defeat the plebiscite from abroad, smuggling in taped messages that encouraged Blanco Party members to vote No to the new constitution. People were afraid to speak out against the plebiscite but used subtle means to convey their opposition. Some turned on their windshield wipers when it wasn't raining: the back-and-forth movement symbolized a finger shaking No. Others mumbled the words of the national anthem until they got to the words "Tyrants tremble" and then sang those words as loudly as possible. But fear was so pervasive that some people went to the polls wearing gloves so that the military couldn't find their fingerprints on the ballots.

Uruguayans went to the polls believing the opposition to be a minority, only to find out the next day that they were part of a democratic majority. After the 1980 plebiscite, internal groups became the main protagonists for redemocratization. But during the repressive 1976–79 period, internal political groups were barely permitted to function, and external pressures were central to the initial process of redemocratization. A stronger democratic tradition existed in the Uruguayan military than in the other militaries of the Southern Cone. More military officers in Uruguay were forced to retire early because of their apparent support for political opening than in either Argentina or Guatemala. In 1977 alone, over seventy-five Uruguayan officers were forced into retirement.[36] Yet the purges themselves indicate that the prodemocracy officers were a minority and the hard-liners continued to hold the upper hand. In this situation, international pressures helped throw new weight behind the arguments of the soft-liners. One of the most important aspects of U.S. human rights policy was the withdrawal of symbolic support for the military regime, which helped delegitimize it.

The role of internal human rights organizations was minimal in Uruguay as compared to Argentina. Until 1981, when a Uruguayan branch of the Latin American and faith-based human rights organ SERPAJ (Servicio Paz y Justicia) was set up, no human rights organization existed in Uruguay. As a result, the limited human rights documentation work in Uruguay was done by people connected to political parties like Wilson Ferreira's faction of the Blanco Party, or the left coalition the Broad Front. Internationally, however, quite a number of groups devoted their energy to the cause of human rights in Uruguay. Of these, Amnesty International played the most crucial role throughout the period of the dictatorship, documenting and denouncing human rights violations.

In Uruguay, the Carter human rights policy permitted the reestablishment of closer relationships between the political opposition and U.S. policy makers. To do so, the embassy invited opposition politicians to receptions and dinners for visiting U.S. policy makers. This practice so annoyed the military that they once snubbed a U.S. visitor by not attending a dinner, to protest his decision to meet with opposition politicians. Although it alienated the military, the receptions and dinners helped maintain positive relations between the U.S. government and opposition politicians.

Argentina

As we saw in the previous chapter, Secretary of State Kissinger undermined Ambassador Hill's attempts to implement a human rights policy in Argentina before the beginning of the Carter administration. A State Department report released at the end of 1976 admitted that human rights abuses were taking place in Argentina but argued that continuation of security assistance, including $48.4 million in military sales credits, would be in the national interest.[37]

In contrast, human rights concerns dominated the diplomatic agenda of the Carter administration toward Argentina. Early in the administration, Argentina was chosen as one of three human rights target countries, along with Ethiopia and Uruguay. According to one State Department official, no human rights situation created greater concern in Washington than that of Argentina in the 1970s.[38]

During her second visit to Argentina in 1977, Derian questioned Admiral Emilio Massera, the head of the navy and a member of the ruling military junta, about the navy's use of torture. When Massera denied such practices, Derian told him that she had seen a rudimentary map of a secret detention center in the Navy Mechanical School, where she and Massera were meeting. She asked him whether it was possible that, right under their feet, someone was being tortured. "Massera smiled at me and said, 'Do you know what happened to Pontius Pilate?'"[39] This was not the stuff of typical diplomacy, and the Argentine military were outraged at Derian's audacity. Derian later described her technique: "You have to be guileless in your discussion until you get to your point, and then you have to be very firm."[40]

On February 24, 1977, Secretary of State Vance announced that the administration was reducing the planned level of military aid for Argentina from the $32 million requested in the Ford administration's budget for the next fiscal year to $15 million, due to human rights abuses. Argentina reacted angrily, claiming that this action was undue interference in its internal affairs, and rejected the remaining U.S. military aid.[41]

When Tex Harris arrived at the U.S. embassy in Buenos Aires in July 1977, his boss asked him to be the new human rights officer. Until that time, the embassy had a policy that the human rights officer could not collect testimony at the embassy from victims of human rights violations. Harris said that he would serve as the human rights officer, but he insisted that to do his job, he had to be able to take testimony at the embassy from the families of victims of human rights abuses. Harris began to receive testimony from hundreds and eventually thousands of family members of the disappeared, who waited in long lines to see him. Harris and his assistant recorded each case on a five-by-eight card and later sent copies of the card files as reports back to Washington. For the first time the information on human rights problems was coming directly from an embassy source, not from local human rights organizations that might have less credibility in the State Department. Derian found that her hand was strengthened in debates in the State Department when she had reliable current information about the human rights situation at her fingertips. When Vance led a delegation to Argentina, he carried with him a list of approximately seven thousand disappeared people in Argentina, which was presented to Argentine authorities.[42]

Although the Carter administration had already reduced aid to Argentina, it lobbied actively against a total aid cutoff, arguing that such a measure would tie its hands in negotiations over human rights.[43] Taking this into account, in July 1977 Congress passed a bill eliminating all military assistance to Argentina, to go into effect on September 30, 1978, which allowed the administration one year in which to supply Congress with evidence of improvement in the human rights situation in Argentina before arms sales were ended.[44]

As a result, Harris's human rights reporting began to provoke conflict in the U.S. embassy. At first the new U.S. ambassador, Raul Castro, was pleased with the human rights reporting. But the Carter administration now wanted to show improvement in the human rights situation to prevent the congressional aid cutoff. The Argentine military government claimed that it was improving its human rights practices. But Harris was sending reports that showed that disappearances were continuing. His superior, Max Chaplin, began to try to limit and control his cables so as to lessen their impact on policy. This was the same Max Chaplin who had served under Ambassador Hill, and who had written a cable almost two years earlier that had said, "In our best judgment, the only 'right-wing assassins' operating in Argentina at this point, however, are members of the GOA security forces." Harris didn't know about this previous cable of Chaplin's. But he knew that Chaplin was now adjusting the human rights messages he was sending back to Washington to fit the needs of administration policy. Harris later explained it like this: "You have embassies painting pictures through their reporting which supports the vision of the relationship that they wish to see implemented between the United States and Country X. Now the problem is, where is truth?"[45]

But, contrary to the case of Ambassador Hill who was simply trumped by Kissinger and had to give up, Harris was operating in a very different bureaucratic and political context. He was part of an administration that had publicly committed itself to a human rights policy, and he had the support of an assistant secretary of state for human rights.

The embassy was not able to make a persuasive case for human rights improvement in Argentina by September 1978, and an indefinite embargo on arms sales went into effect. Argentina rushed to purchase military equipment during the yearlong grace period, but on September 30, the last day of fiscal year 1978, Argentine military attachés were called to the Pentagon and told that the State Department had denied pending requests for licenses for nearly $100 million dollars of U.S. military equipment.[46]

The cutoff of security assistance itself did not provide sufficient leverage to gain changes in human rights practices. In the Argentine case, it was the convergence of multiple forceful human rights pressures that led to a successful outcome. Ongoing diplomatic pressures reinforced the perception that the U.S. government was committed to pursuing human rights issues. Harris discussed both general human rights policy and specific cases of disappearances regularly with the Argentine government. Higher-level officials, including the secretary of state and the president, discussed human rights issues in their meetings with the Argentine government, bringing up specific cases and pressing the government to allow visits by nongovernmental organizations.[47] In the multilateral financial institutions, the United States voted against approximately twenty-five Argentine loan applications, although none of these votes actually led to loans being denied.

The most successful attempt to increase pressure on the junta occurred during the summer of 1978. Derian used information from Harris to help carry the day in an important meeting about an Export-Import Bank loan to Argentina. She convinced the U.S. government to withhold a $270 million Export-Import Bank loan for a plant to construct turbines for the hydroelectric plant on the Yacyretá River. This was the first time that human rights had been used to inhibit nonmilitary trade. The U.S. business community, led by the Allis-Chalmers corporation, which was to supply the parts for this plant, launched a major lobbying effort to approve the loan to Argentina and to change the legislation that attached human rights conditions to Export-Import Bank loans.

Within the administration, Secretary of Commerce Juanita Kreps argued against the decision to block the Export-Import Bank loan to Argentina. Members of Congress who had supported the termination of military aid to Argentina worried that the extension of sanctions to nonmilitary items could prove extremely costly to U.S. trade at a time when the trade deficit was increasingly troublesome. It seemed likely that Congress would overturn the Export-Import Bank decision. When denial was imminent, however, Vice President Mondale met with President Videla and agreed to release Export-Import Bank funds if Argentina invited the Inter-American Commission on Human Rights to visit the country.[48] In December 1978 the Argentine government invited the IACHR to conduct an on-site investigation.

At the time, human rights activists strongly criticized the administration's decision to approve the Export-Import Bank loan. They believed that the administration was backing away from its commitment to human rights and caving into business pressures. In retrospect, the agreement to invite the IACHR to Argentina was an important turning point in the human rights situation there. In 1978, in expectation of the IACHR visit, the junta took steps to improve human rights conditions. The IACHR report provided the most in-depth, well-researched information on the human rights situation in Argentina, documenting that the Argentine government had engaged in a systematic government campaign of gross abuses of human rights. The report concluded: "It

appears evident that the decision to form the command units, that were involved in the disappearance and possible extermination of these thousands of
persons, was adopted at the highest level of the Armed Forces."[49]

Just as in the case of Chile, the U.S. government spoke with a mixed voice
on human rights in Argentina. A delegation of members of the House International Relations Committee that visited Argentina in mid-1977 reported that
"the Argentine military finds U.S. signals are mixed. . . . They feel Argentina
is carrying out a war against Communist subversion and they are perplexed to
find themselves at odds with the United States."[50] Ambassador Castro and Max
Chaplin were known for their ambivalence about Carter's human rights policy. As opposed to the way Kissinger treated Ambassador Hill, however, top-level
Carter officials devoted considerable attention to Argentina and communicated
clearly the administration's concern with human rights.

A number of European countries were also raising the issue of human rights
with the Argentine government, but they were less forceful in their policy than
the United States. The Europeans were not yet committed to a policy of human rights sanctions, and as a result, their pressures were more moderate. The
minister of economics during the Videla government, Dr. Martinez de Hoz, recalled that "in Europe, they spoke much less of human rights. Always a little
word in passing. They fought with each other to grant us credits. It was not the
constant pressure of Carter."[51]

During 1980 Carter policy toward Argentina was complicated by efforts to
gain its cooperation in imposing a grain embargo on the Soviet Union. During
the disenchantment phase, pressure on the human rights front seems to have
been relaxed, although the ban on arms sales continued. Two key international
events served to keep the case of Argentine human rights in the minds of U.S.
policy makers. First, in 1979 the Argentine authorities released the noted journalist Jacobo Timerman. The publication of his powerful memoir detailing his
disappearance and torture by the Argentine military—which Timerman described as fascist and viciously anti-Semitic—had an important impact on U.S.
policy circles.[52] Timerman attributed his release to international pressure and
pointed especially to the role of Derian, who had met him during her first visit
(before his disappearance) and inquired about him explicitly during her following visits. Second, in 1980 the Nobel Peace Prize was awarded to the Argentine human rights activist Adolfo Perez Esquivel, who used his public
position to speak out against the continuing human rights abuses in Argentina.

There is evidence that the decline in the government's practice of disappearing its opponents followed a period of intense international scrutiny and
the convergence of strong U.S. pressures on the Argentine regime.[53] The decline in the practice of disappearance is particularly noticeable in the period

following September 1978. At this point, the congressional arms embargo went into effect, and the Export-Import Bank loan to Argentina was still being withheld. In high-level meetings U.S. officials stressed that the Argentine government needed to improve human rights practices and invite the IACHR as a precondition for improved bilateral relations.[54] In the period that followed the decision to invite the IACHR the human rights situation in Argentina improved significantly. This analysis of the impact of U.S. policy is reinforced by the testimony of victims and interviews with Argentine policy makers during the military regime.[55]

The counterfactual argument that one has to confront here is that the changes in levels of repression were due to an internal dynamic in Argentina that happened to coincide with external pressure but was not caused by it. What this argument fails to take into account are the divisions within the Argentine military about the definitions of "the enemy" and the necessary extent of the "dirty war." One faction was led by Admiral Massera, another by General Carlos Suarez Mason and General Luciano Menéndez, who supported an indefinite military dictatorship and an unrelenting war against the left, and a third, led by General Videla and General Roberto Viola, who hoped for eventual political liberalization under a military president.[56]

Which of these factions prevailed is of crucial importance, as is the way in which international pressures influenced the internal negotiating process within the Argentine military. The only significant civilian allies of the Argentine government whose opinions could have contributed to military decision making were the civilian technocrats, especially the economic policy makers, and key business groups. But neither the economic policy team nor domestic entrepreneurs advocated changing human rights practices, in part because the topic of the repression was perceived as "taboo" by civilian allies of the military.[57] Moreover, because businessmen and members of the economic team had been targets of left-wing kidnapping and assassination attempts, they tended to support military measures.[58] By 1978, when the Videla-Viola faction had emerged supreme within the junta, U.S.–Argentine relations, and to a lesser extent Argentine relations with European countries, had deteriorated over the human rights issue. Meanwhile, the conflict with Chile over the Beagle Canal had intensified in mid-1978, while relations with Brazil remained troubled.[59]

Videla and Viola understood that in order to improve their international image, as part of the process of military-led political liberalization they were advocating, some kind of explanation of past repression would have to be provided. It appears that they saw the visit of the IACHR and its report as a potential means of whitewashing or drawing a curtain on the past, by providing a minimal explanation of abuses while emphasizing the limited liberalization they were initiating.[60] Thus the international pressures played into the internal conflicts within the Argentine military, adding strength to the argument that something had to be done to change repressive patterns and improve external relations.[61]

One factor that contributed to the effectiveness of U.S. human rights policy toward Argentina was the endeavor by Carter administration officials to coordinate U.S. bilateral policy initiatives with multilateral human rights institutions. In a well-documented book on the role of the United Nations on human rights in Argentina, Iain Guest shows "how, after seizing power in 1976, Argentina's military rulers set out to cripple the U.N.'s human rights machinery in an effort to muzzle international protest, and how—with the support and encouragement from the Carter Administration—the U.N. fought back. This fight rejuvenated the U.N.'s ponderous human rights machinery."[62] The very able diplomacy of the Argentine foreign service, with the support of the Soviet Union, with which the Argentine military regime had developed a close trading relationship, initially blocked consideration of the Argentine human rights situation in the United Nations. The UN Working Group on Disappearances, created in 1980 with strong U.S. support, allowed the United Nations a less politicized forum to draw attention to the practice of disappearances in Argentina and elsewhere in the world. Jerome Shestack, Carter's delegate to the UN Human Rights Commission's 1980 session, and former president of the International League for Human Rights, played a central role in the creation of the Working Group on Disappearances.

During the Carter administration, the Argentine military government thus moved from an initial refusal of international human rights interventions to a cosmetic cooperation with human rights pressures, and eventually to an improvement in its human rights practices. Once it had invited the Inter-American Commission and discovered that it could not be co-opted or confused, the government moved to end the practice of disappearance, released political prisoners, and restored some semblance of political participation. Full restoration of human rights in Argentina did not come until after the Malvinas War and the transition to democracy in 1983, but after 1980 the worst abuses had been curtailed. This transformation is consistent with the spiral model of human rights change discussed in chapter 3.

In 1985, after democratization, Argentina brought the top military leaders of the juntas to trial for human rights abuses. Derian was asked to testify at the trials, and her appearance in the courtroom provoked the military defendants to leave the room, the only time in the entire trials when this took place. This is an interesting testimony to the irritation that Carter policy provoked among

the military. The military commanders had confronted weeks and weeks of testimony of victims of human rights abuses, as well as representatives of domestic and international NGOs and intergovernmental organizations. It is likely
the military left because Derian symbolized the Carter human rights policy in
Argentina, a policy that for the military was an inexplicable betrayal and an
about-face on the part of the United States, which the military had tradition-
ally considered a source of support.

Guatemala

Carter administration human rights policy toward Guatemala was less comprehensive and forceful than its policy toward Chile or Argentina. General
Kjell Laugerud, president of Guatemala from 1974 to 1978, had taken some
steps to moderate the level of human rights abuses. Kidnapping and other violations continued at a somewhat lower level. A quantitative analysis of human
rights violations in Guatemala reveals that deaths and disappearances during
the Laugerud regime were lower than during any other regime in the 1970–
91 period.[63] The reforms of the Laugerud government, "so modest in another
setting, yet uncharacteristic of post-1954 Guatemala—afforded hope to elements of the political center and moderate left of an incipient opening."[64] This
hope of an opening may have led U.S. policy makers to exert fewer human
rights pressures on the Laugerud administration. For instance, Congress held
no hearings specifically on Guatemala from 1976 to 1981. The president never
engaged in the kind of high-level arm-twisting that he, Vance, and Derian used
in Argentina. The State Department did release a report noting human rights
abuses in Guatemala in March 1977 but also stated that President Laugerud appeared to be improving the situation. In June 1977 the Guatemalan government, angered by the report, rejected U.S. military aid. In response to the
human rights situation and the government's rejection of aid, the U.S. Congress reduced military assistance that year and terminated military aid to Guatemala in 1978.[65]

Guatemala is one case where the period following the cutoff of U.S. assistance witnessed not a decline in human rights abuses but an escalation in out-
right killings and disappearances. The most serious escalation of repression
occurred in 1980–83, once Reagan had entered office. Yet the repression had
begun to soar in late 1979, after the Lucas García government took office in
July 1978 and while Carter was still president.[66] Amnesty International described disappearances as "epidemic" and reported over two thousand people
killed between mid-1978 and early 1980. The Guatemalan press contained re-

ports of 3,252 disappearances in the first ten months of 1979.[67] The 1979 murders of prominent reformist politicians Alberto Fuentes Mohr and Manuel Colom Argueta made clear that no one in Guatemala was protected from repression. President Lucas García refused to meet with other administration officials, and the United States did not send many representatives to the country. William Bowdler, assistant secretary of state, visited in September 1979 but was not able to meet with Guatemalan officials. Overall, what limited attempts the United States made to engage Guatemala in negotiations on human rights issues were failures.

The Guatemalan government was undoubtedly engaged in a concerted repressive policy of murdering its political opposition. Evidence surfaced in 1980 of a specialized agency that coordinated the actions of various "private" death squads and regular army and policy units, an agency under the control of President Lucas García and located in an annex to the National Palace.[68] Repression became so severe that no effective local human rights NGOs could operate in Guatemala.[69] Even foreign NGOs closed down their Guatemala City offices, and Guatemala was isolated from even an international presence during the height of repression.[70]

Carter administration human rights policy was further hampered by the appointment of Frank Ortiz as ambassador to Guatemala in July 1979 during a period of increasing human rights abuses. Ortiz, widely seen as a conservative without a strong commitment to human rights issues, developed close relations with the Lucas García government and claimed that government-condoned violence was abating. He approved the March 1980 visit of a U.S. destroyer to a Guatemalan port, apparently without prior State Department knowledge, which many observers took as a sign of U.S. support for the repressive Guatemalan government.[71] Pressures from human rights organizations and Congress contributed to the decision to replace Ortiz less than a year after he took office, but by that point the Carter administration had missed an opportunity to respond effectively to the repressive spiral already under way in Guatemala.

The revolutionary forces had been gaining strength during the 1975–80 period. It is estimated that by 1979 the guerrillas had at least 1,800 armed men and substantial civilian support.[72] The upsurge in the rural insurgency in Guatemala in the late 1970s further unified the military ideologically in its task of counterinsurgency. In this juncture, the military viewed U.S. human rights policy as interventionist, divisive of the military, and an interference in the strategy of counterinsurgency. The military was also able to manipulate the domestic perception of international human rights pressure and provoke a nationalist backlash. It created an image of Guatemala as a country able to sustain itself without outside support, an image that found acceptance in certain segments of society. After U.S. military aid was terminated, Chief of Staff Lobos Zamora declared that "we Guatemalans can feel satisfied at being the first country in the world that has managed to inflict a substantial defeat on subversion by means of our own eminently nationalistic strategy and tactics, without outside assistance."

The efforts of regional and international human rights organizations likewise were rebuffed. During the 1970s and early 1980s, the Guatemalan government refused to permit an on-site visit by the Inter-American Commission on Human Rights or to cooperate with any international or regional human rights organization.[73] During this period the Guatemalan government also avoided UN investigation. Fewer human rights groups were actively engaged in Guatemala than in Argentina and Uruguay and less information was available on the immensity of human rights violations there.

Although Congress eliminated all military aid to Guatemala from 1978 until 1983, military supplies already in the pipeline continued to flow. For instance, the administration continued shipments of some military supplies by reclassifying them as nonmilitary items.[74] Guatemala primarily used the route of commercial sales, made by U.S. companies to the Guatemalan government and private businesses and licensed by the U.S. government, to obtain military equipment and technology from the United States. The State Department disapproved some of these export licenses in the period from 1980 to 1983.[75] However, neither the administration nor Congress took any steps toward cutting economic aid or imposing trade sanctions as they did on Argentina and Uruguay. The United States opposed two multilateral development bank loans to Guatemala on human rights grounds, but approved five others during this period.

The Guatemalan military identified U.S. human rights pressures solely with Jimmy Carter. Guatemalan government and private enterprise lobbies thus devoted considerable money and energy to wooing Republican politicians even before the Reagan administration took office, as they were convinced that under the Reagan administration the human rights pressures would disappear. One Guatemalan lobby, Amigos del País, hired the Washington public relations firm Deaver and Hannaford to improve Guatemala's international image and divert attention from its human rights record.[76] The anticipation of Reagan entering office allowed the Lucas García government to resist U.S. human rights pressures during the last year of the Carter administration, pressures that were already weakened in the wake of the Nicaraguan revolution and the general U.S. disenchantment with human rights policy.

El Salvador

El Salvador had been under "institutionalized military rule" for thirty years since a military coup in 1948.[77] The military selected one of their own to rule, who was then endorsed by the official political party and legitimized through increasingly fraudulent elections. When the opposition finally gained the strength to win elections in 1972 and 1977, the military carried out massive fraud to stay in power. With their electoral options blocked by fraud, opposition political parties became increasingly radicalized, and society polarized. The government of President Carlos Humberto Romero (1977–79) responded with increasing repression, and his regime began to resemble the authoritarian regimes of the Southern Cone of South America more than it did the previous Salvadoran regimes. While the previous regimes had tried to maintain an uneasy balance between reform and repression, the Romero administration put aside any reformist pretensions and engaged in direct repression and confrontation with the opposition.[78]

U.S. policy makers accorded low priority to human rights in El Salvador until late 1979. After Romero was elected president in fraudulent elections in February 1977, Congressman Fraser held hearings on the elections and on human rights in his subcommittee. Significant human rights violations occurred in particular between the time that Romero was elected and when he took office in July 1977, prompting various responses by the U.S. government. During this period the Carter administration called their ambassador back to Washington for "consultations" as a rebuke to the Salvadoran government for human rights violations, while the State Department published a human rights country report critical of El Salvador and announced that it would cut aid to countries engaged in gross patterns of human rights violations.[79] The Salvadoran government responded by preemptively renouncing all aid. At the same time, the U.S. government threatened to vote against an Inter-American Development Bank loan to El Salvador for human rights reasons.

President Romero took power in an atmosphere of international scrutiny of human rights that led to a moderation of human rights violations. Assistant Secretary Derian had traveled to meet with President-elect Romero and members of the Salvadoran government in 1977. Shortly before her visit, the right-wing death squad "White Warriors' Union" had threatened to kill all Jesuits active in El Salvador unless they left the country by a set deadline. When Derian raised the issue with President Romero, he denied that the White Warriors' Union existed but promised to look into the issue. During the same visit, Derian met with Archbishop Oscar Romero, who discussed the Church's frustration with the failure of the Salvadoran oligarchy to make reforms and his commitment to working with the poor.[80]

Shortly after taking office, President Romero denounced the threats against the Jesuits, visited them, and provided armed guards for their homes. Furthermore, "the intensity and kind of violence changed abruptly" and Romero suppressed the types of violence that would attract international attention, such as urban assassinations and shooting of demonstrators.[81] But aside from the meeting between Derian and President Romero, El Salvador received relatively little high-profile attention during this period. As a result, most aspects of bilateral relations were handled by the new ambassador, the professional diplomat Frank Devine, who was "personally hostile" to human rights policy.[82] When Romero passed a new public order law that one academic characterized as "practically a license to kill,"[83] Devine argued that "any government has the full right and obligation to use all legal means at its disposal to combat terrorism." Devine's remark is another example of a verbal cue that apparently was interpreted by the Salvadoran military as a green light for repression. "Romero read this remark as a signal that the United States would now tolerate repressive measures, whether legal or not,"[84] and the imposition of the public order law was followed by a significant increase in acts of violence against the opposition.

The perpetrators of repression in El Salvador were the armed forces themselves and paramilitary groups with connection to the military and the executive. The most infamous of these was the "official" paramilitary group, ORDEN, formed in 1966 and staffed by army reserve and retired military officers. Other paramilitary groups like the White Warriors' Union also emerged in the mid-1970s. Reliable data on human rights violations in El Salvador during this period are difficult to find. Authors estimate that from 1972 to 1977 the government was responsible for 37 assassinations and 69 disappearances, while during the short-lived Romero administration (1977–79) the government was responsible for 461 assassinations and 131 disappearances.[85]

El Salvador is the most glaring failure of the Carter administration's human rights policy. The symbol of that failure came in early 1980, when gunmen assassinated Archbishop Romero as he celebrated mass. Romero was known as an advocate of the poor and a critic of the regime for its human rights violations and failure to carry out reforms. Observers accused right-wing death squads of the murder. The UN Truth Commission later confirmed that the killing was ordered by Roberto D'Aubuisson, a notorious death squad leader.

Many Salvadorans concluded that if killers could execute the Archbishop of San Salvador in broad daylight with impunity, no one was safe. Their conclusions would prove correct. Although it would intensify in the 1980s, intense repression in El Salvador started during the Carter administration. The UN Truth Commission identified 1980, the last year of the Carter administration, as the most repressive year of the decade, with 4,288 deaths. Historical comparisons thus make 1980 the most repressive year of Salvadoran modern history since the massacres of 1932. Like Guatemala, El Salvador is also a case where there were lower levels of repression during the active phase of the Carter administration's human rights policy, with human rights violations escalating dramatically in its last year, just as human rights policy was under siege at home. The failures of the Carter policy came exactly at the point when the administration backed off human rights—when internal divisions, doubts, and distractions created or exacerbated by the hostage crisis in Iran and the Soviet invasion of Afghanistan led the administration to curtail its implementation of human rights policy. In other words, the failures of the Carter policy came not from the excesses of the human rights policy but from a lack of will to fully implement it.

The Effectiveness of Carter's Human Rights Policy

Carter made a move in the direction of a multilateral human rights policy when, in February of 1978, he transmitted to the U.S. Senate for ratification the Covenant on Civil and Political Rights, the Covenant on Economic, Social, and Cultural Rights, the Convention on the Elimination of All Forms of Racial Discrimination, and the American Convention on Human Rights. They were accompanied by a letter from the State Department suggesting reservations to avoid conflict with U.S. law. The letter quotes the Department of Justice's view that "with these reservations, declarations, and understandings, there are no constitutional or other legal objections to United States ratification of these treaties."[86] Although the Senate would not ratify the Covenant on Civil and Political Rights until almost fifteen years later, this action by the Carter administration suggests that it supported not only a bilateral human rights policy but also a multilateral policy, which depended on Senate ratification of essential human rights treaties. Despite Democratic Party control of the Senate and President Carter's support for ratification, the covenants were not ratified. In speeches and private meetings, Carter had also promised to try to ensure the U.S. ratification of the Genocide Treaty. But once Carter became absorbed in his efforts to get the Senate to ratify the Panama Canal Treaty, he felt that he no longer had the political capital to work for the ratification of the Genocide Treaty as well.

At the end of the Carter administration, the human rights situation in Latin America looked grim. Human rights abuses in El Salvador and Guatemala were escalating alarmingly and full-fledged insurgencies engulfed the countries. Repressive authoritarian regimes in Argentina, Chile, Uruguay, Paraguay, and Brazil still seemed entrenched. A new coup in Bolivia had ushered in the most repressive regime in that country's troubled history. Administration officials could not point to any obvious "success story" as a result of their human rights policy in the region. During the 1980 election campaign, the policy was under attack from the Republican camp. Inspired by foreign policy advisor Jeane Kirkpatrick, Ronald Reagan argued that the human rights policy had backfired. He charged that this policy had alienated traditional authoritarian allies and even contributed to their overthrow, while at the same time failing to be sufficiently critical of abuses in the Soviet block. In relation to the occupation of the U.S. embassy in Iran by student revolutionaries, the charge that U.S. human rights policy had undermined U.S. interests in the world seemed persuasive to a public seeking scapegoats for its insecurity as it helplessly watched television news coverage of the embassy occupation.

The Soviet invasion of Afghanistan also had sidelined U.S. human rights policy. Administration officials did some soul-searching about whether they had misjudged the aggressive character of Soviet communism. The civil wars in Central America were increasingly viewed in the context of renewed fear of Soviet expansion, especially after the Sandinista victory in Nicaragua in 1979.

Human rights organizations, in turn, accused the administration of deserting its human rights ideals as it increased military aid to El Salvador while the repression escalated. These groups criticized the administration's decisions to grant an Export-Import Bank loan to Argentina and to sell helicopters to Guatemala, accusing it of caving in to its conservative critics and making unacceptable compromises to its commitment to human rights.

Meanwhile, Tex Harris was in "deep deep trouble" in the State Department. His boss, Chaplin, had written a bad performance report on him, and he was in the process of being "selected out" or fired from the foreign service. "From his perspective, I was not a team player and a pain in the ass," Harris explained. Harris kept sending in bad human rights news, sometimes through back channels directly to Derian, at a time when the ambassador was trying to deemphasize human rights.[87]

A quarter century later, from greater distance and with the benefit of hindsight, it is possible to form an informed evaluation of the successes and failures of the Carter administration's human rights policies. Such an evaluation leads me to argue that the Carter policy was far more successful than it was given credit for at the time. The Carter administration was successful in taking the human rights policy first pioneered in the Congress and giving it the backing and support of the executive branch. Carter administration officials developed and tested many of the policies that later became the standard repertoire of human rights policies in the United States and elsewhere: aid cutoffs and reductions, No votes on loans in international financial institutions, high-profile missions, arm-twisting to encourage governments to invite the Inter-American Commission, and so on. Because they were pioneers, much of what Carter administration policy makers did was controversial and sometimes clumsy. They did not have the benefit of experience or of a standard operating procedure in this area. They also did not have the benefit of a foreign service with wide knowledge of or commitment to human rights. The Carter administration depended upon senior foreign service officials to carry out its policies, but most of these officials were trained in a foreign service that did not view human rights as an appropriate topic for policy.

Carter compounded these problems by making the simultaneous commitment both to implement an innovative new human rights policy and to promote a more professional foreign service. During the campaign, Carter had promised that diplomatic appointments would be made on merit. He subsequently established the Advisory Board on Ambassadorial Appointments, which succeeded in significantly reducing the number of ambassadors who were political appointees as compared to earlier and later administrations. Raymond Bonner convincingly argues that "what Carter apparently failed to appreciate was that by taking appointments outside of politics he took them outside of his policy—that is, by not making political appointments, he had less control over the ambassadors."[88] Because human rights policies were unprecedented in U.S. foreign policy, very few high-level foreign service officers had any experience with them. All their training and experience mitigated against it. To ensure that his human rights policies were implemented more coherently, Carter would have needed to make more political appointments of ambassadors who shared his commitments.

Despite these failings, I believe that Carter administration human rights policy had a positive effect on human rights in Argentina and Uruguay, and to a lesser degree in Chile. Perhaps nowhere in the world was Carter's human rights policy more forcefully implemented than toward the countries of Latin America's Southern Cone, and it was exactly in those cases where it had the greatest impact. I do not contend that the Carter administration policy itself led directly to changing human rights practices in these countries. Rather, together with other external human rights pressures, Carter's human rights policy influenced internal negotiations within the military governments, lending crucial weight to the positions of soft-liners within these regimes. The single most important impact of human rights policy was to protect domestic political party opponents and human rights activists, and to open up domestic space for their political work. The external influence is necessary but not sufficient to explain the changes, since to function it must coincide with the agendas of internal actors.

In Guatemala and El Salvador, the Carter administration human rights policy did not have a positive impact on repression. In Guatemala, human rights abuses escalated during the final year of the Carter administration, 1980, compared to the previous decade. In El Salvador, the peak in human rights violations occurred during the Carter administration, though high-level abuses continued during the first two years of the Reagan administration.

What is most puzzling about the failure of U.S. human rights policy in Guatemala and El Salvador is that different policies were apparently adopted in both countries, and both policies failed. In the case of Guatemala, military and economic aid was suspended. Despite residual aid in the pipeline, commercial sales, and some proxy aid through Israel, the relatively low levels of U.S. assistance during this period limited U.S. influence and gave wide autonomy to the Guatemalan armed forces. In El Salvador, the United States adopted an alternative policy. Toward the end of the Carter administration, U.S. officials increased levels of economic and military aid to El Salvador significantly and became deeply involved in military and political decisions.

The failure of two such very different policies could indicate that repression would have occurred regardless of U.S. policy. I believe that these two apparently different policies were much more similar than they seemed. In neither case did concern with human rights receive true priority in policy decisions. When it did discuss human rights, the administration spoke with a far more divided voice than in the case of the Southern Cone countries. In other words, Carter administration policy toward both El Salvador and Guatemala lacked a coherent and consistent human rights component.

Perhaps more importantly, both El Salvador and Guatemala were cases of increasingly authoritarian governments confronting substantial military threats from rural insurgents. These military governments embraced an ideology that justified human rights violations against citizens in the name of fighting an internal war. Theories of the causes of human rights abuses suggest that these three conditions: an authoritarian regime, a civil war, and an ends-justify-the-means ideology, are highly correlated with human rights violations.

In four years, an ambiguous Carter administration human rights policy couldn't undo twenty-five years of U.S. support for military regimes and national security doctrine in the region. The Guatemalan military had received substantial U.S. assistance and training for over twenty years. In many ways, past U.S. influence (especially the coup of 1954 and the counterinsurgency campaign of 1966–68) contributed to the structure and beliefs of the Guatemala military that later blocked U.S. human rights pressure. Guatemalan elites, having been the recipients of U.S. anticommunist rhetoric for decades, were skeptical of the U.S. turnaround on human rights. When a U.S. delegation visited with the Guatemalan foreign minister Rafael Castillo in early 1980, during the Carter administration, a member of the delegation admonished Castillo about the Guatemalan government's exaggerated fear of communism. Castillo responded, "Well you know, all the bad things about communists we learned from you Americans. Now that you have changed your minds, you will have to give us time to readjust."[89] While tongue-in-cheek, this comment captures the skepticism of Guatemalan policy makers about U.S. human rights policy in its infancy. Past U.S. policy comes back to haunt us.

Castillo's remark is also an astute observation about how leaders make sense of their situation. New policy cues or signals are interpreted in light of past cues and existing worldviews and identities. After decades of national security doctrine, Latin American policy makers found it hard to hear and make sense of the new human rights policy. It was easier to interpret it as the idiosyncrasies of a single president and hope that it would go away if they simply waited. Mixed signals on human rights from different parts of the U.S. apparatus made it easier to discount the intention of the message.

U.S. human rights policy toward the Southern Cone countries was more effective in part because it was applied in a comprehensive and forceful manner. A clear message was sent through multiple channels that the United States was serious about human rights policy and that bilateral relations would suffer until changes were made. While the United States often sent mixed messages, the human rights messages sent to these countries were somewhat more consistent and forceful than those sent to Central America. In the case of the Southern Cone, U.S. policy worked through both bilateral and multilateral channels; actions from regional and international organizations reinforced bilateral pressures. Moreover, factions within the Argentine and Uruguayan military governments, the so-called soft-liners, decided to use U.S. and international pressures to pursue their own internal liberalization policy. Finally, U.S. human rights policy toward the Southern Cone countries was supported by the work of strong domestic human rights organizations and political parties with commitments to democracy and human rights.

In Central America, many of these conditions were missing. The active phase of Carter's human rights policies coincided with lower levels of human rights violations in Guatemala and in El Salvador. The escalating violations in 1979 and 1980 occurred during an upsurge in the numbers and the success of armed insurgent movements and coincided with the disenchantment phase of human rights policy. The beginnings of a full-fledged civil war in El Salvador and a major rural insurgency in Guatemala meant that U.S. human rights policy toward Guatemala and El Salvador was much less coherent and forceful. The priority of counterinsurgency goals led to the de-emphasis of human rights issues. No powerful group existed within the Guatemalan military that could perceive a tactical advantage in responding to U.S. human rights pressures. In El Salvador, with the failure of the reformist military government in 1979, there were no soft-liners within the regime that could use U.S. pressure to bolster their own liberalization goals.

Although the Latin American military viewed human rights policy as a temporary enthusiasm of the Carter administration, it proved more resilient than anticipated. The human rights message had captured the imagination of an important segment of the U.S public, whose opinion matters in politics. The public even came to the rescue of Tex Harris. When he got back from Argentina, his career was destroyed. But friends in the human rights community convinced Bill Moyers that he should do a show on Harris and his work in Argentina. Moyers went to Argentina and put together a show with extraordinary interviews with some of the people Harris had helped. The State Department received two bags of mail in support of Harris after the program, and his file was reviewed. "They took out the things that should not have been in my file, so I got promoted." Harris went on to have a successful career in the State Department. "My career was resurrected in general at the State Department, but I was still persona non grata in the Latin America bureau. I was not a Latin American hand. I was out of the club . . . and I have proven not to be a team player. . . . I stood up to the team."[90] Much later the American Foreign Service Organization, a union of foreign service officers, named a special award after Harris for officers who have engaged in creative dissent.

Chapter Seven

The Reagan Administration and Human Rights Policy toward Latin America

The Reagan administration came into office determined to reverse and reorient American foreign policy. Nowhere was this determination more evident than in its relations with Latin America. During their first year in office, Reagan officials worked actively to dismantle the Carter human rights policy and to reaffirm positive relations with the authoritarian regimes in Latin America that had been the targets of Carter policy. Some Reagan administration officials claimed that they had not deserted human rights policy but had merely moved from public to private diplomacy when discussing human rights issues with friendly allies.[1] During the first year and a half of the Reagan administration, however, "there was no human rights policy. There was a critique of Carter policy, combined with an instinctive distrust of the phrase, crowd, and community associated with it," according to Elliot Abrams, later assistant secretary of state for human rights during the Reagan administration.[2] A Reagan administration transition team member, furthermore, told Patricia Derian, assistant secretary of state for human rights and humanitarian affairs under Carter, that they were going to shut down the human rights office in the State Department. When she showed him the congressional legislation mandating the office, he replied, "We'll take care of that."[3]

In its first years, the Reagan administration was guided by the strong anti-communism of many key policy makers and by the "Kirkpatrick Doctrine," first elaborated by Jeane Kirkpatrick in her article "Dictatorships and Double Standards."[4] Kirkpatrick claimed that Carter's human rights policy had led to the fall of traditional authoritarian allies of the United States, especially the Shah of Iran and Anastasio Somoza in Nicaragua. She argued that human rights pressures should focus on "totalitarian" regimes and that the United States should reestablish friendly relations with anticommunist authoritarian regimes, regardless of their human rights practices.

By the end of the second Reagan administration, the Kirkpatrick Doctrine had been discredited and deserted as a guideline for policy toward Latin America. The administration had abandoned its support for some authoritarian allies and had initiated a policy of support for democracy.[5] Even some critics of the Reagan administration's earlier policy referred to a virtual "sea change" in U.S. policy, especially toward Chile.[6] Where the Reagan administration switched gears to focus on democracy, it often used a range of "not-so-quiet" policy measures that looked more like the Carter policy than the Kirkpatrick Doctrine.[7] This chapter will explore the puzzling question of how one of the most ideologically conservative administrations in recent history had come to cautiously implement the very policies it had once so fervently challenged.

The Reagan policy toward Latin America can be divided into two phases: a first phase of active implementation of the Kirkpatrick Doctrine, and a second phase that included increasing emphasis on the promotion of democracy. These phases are most pronounced in Reagan policy toward South America. In Central America, and particularly with reference to the Sandinistas in Nicaragua, the administration maintained a single-minded and militant anticommunist focus throughout its two terms; it was committed to the military overthrow of the Sandinistas in Nicaragua and the military defeat of the guerrillas in El Salvador. Most of the administration's energy and funding was directed to the military defeat of leftist governments and insurgencies in Central America rather than to the promotion of democracy. All other areas of Latin America policy were subordinated to the militarized Central America policy. Reagan gave more speeches on Nicaragua in one year, 1986, than on all of the countries of South America during his entire presidency.[8]

During the second policy phase, the Reagan administration implemented a new policy of democracy promotion. Although efforts and funds were focused on fighting revolutions in Central America, the democracy-promotion policy became its major foreign policy legacy, sustained in future administrations. This policy toward South America and the Caribbean was implemented during the second term. In a few cases, such as Chile, Haiti, and Paraguay, such policies had positive effects. These successes eventually led the administrations of George H. W. Bush and William Clinton to a synthesis policy that increasingly institutionalized and normalized aspects of both Carter's human rights policy and Reagan's democracy-promotion policy as standard parts of U.S. foreign policy. This synthesis is embodied in the renamed Bureau of Human Rights in the State Department, now the Bureau of Human Rights, Democracy, and Labor. Some activists insist that we should examine democracy-promotion policies and human rights policies separately. Certainly, democracy promotion in and of itself does not automatically lead to improvements in other human rights, nor does the promotion of human rights automatically lead to transitions to democracy. In practice, however, democracy promotion and human rights policies are closely linked, so much so that it makes sense to discuss them together.

The Kirkpatrick Doctrine in Practice

From the moment of Reagan's election, allies and opponents alike scrutinized the campaign statements and the early acts of the administration for signals. Almost immediately after taking office, Reagan officials worked to reestablish cordial relations with the military regimes of the Southern Cone. They hosted visits of high-level military delegations to Washington from Chile, Brazil, Argentina, and Bolivia and abandoned the Carter administration policy of opposing loans in the multilateral development banks on human rights grounds. Congress was lobbied to renew military and economic assistance that had been cut or reduced for human rights violations. In an August 1981 trip to the region, Jeane Kirkpatrick praised the regimes of the Southern Cone and suggested they could offer valuable lessons to Central America on internal security.[9] Congress was not sympathetic to the new Kirkpatrick Doctrine and blocked most efforts to reestablish normal aid flows to these authoritarian regimes. Nevertheless, the symbolic dimension of the Reagan turnaround should not be underestimated. The new policy was even more important for its signals than for its changes to military and economic aid. The military regimes became convinced that they once again had an ally and a sympathetic ear in Washington, and these beliefs affected their actions.

Not surprisingly, the Reagan administration's authoritarian allies took its public disregard for human rights seriously. Alarmed by the upsurge in human rights violations in the period immediately after Reagan's election, a group of prominent church leaders sent an open letter to the president-elect, expressing concern that military governments were "viewing your election as a green light" to human rights abuses. Instead of taking rectifying measures, the administration reemphasized the new policy. In his first news conference, Secretary of State Haig announced that "international terrorism will take the place of human rights in our concern because it is the ultimate cause of abuses of human rights."[10] A few days later, Ernest Lefever was nominated assistant secretary of state for human rights. Lefever was a conservative activist who was on record stating that the United States should not be promoting human rights abroad and that the Bureau of Human Rights should be abolished. With a nominee committed to abolish both human rights policy and the very position for which he had been nominated, the administration clearly signaled its lack of commitment to human rights. To many senators, the ensuing debate was not merely about Lefever but about the very continuation of human rights policy.

Although it is impossible to link this "green light" directly to human rights practices on the ground, there was a notable upsurge in human rights violations in Latin America in the early period of the Reagan administration. Michele Montas, expelled from Haiti in December 1980, explained that Haitian authorities "thought the international climate was favorable to this sort of thing. They thought human rights was over."[11] The Salvadoran military may have had similar thoughts. On November 27, 1980, killers associated with the Salvadoran government abducted, tortured, and executed six top leaders of the main political opposition group in El Salvador. Less than a week later, Salvadoran National Guard officers abducted, raped, and murdered four U.S. churchwomen who worked in El Salvador. A month after that, a couple of Salvadoran National Guard agents killed two U.S. advisors and the Salvadoran head of the Institute for Agrarian Reform. No clear identification of the murderers was made at the time. Instead, the UN Truth Commission later established the responsibility of government agents.[12] Even at the time, however, there was strong reason to believe that the murders had been committed by individuals associated with the Salvadoran government. Security forces across Latin America apparently interpreted the signals from presidential candidate Reagan to mean that the United States would no longer criticize human rights violations in the region.

A week after Reagan's inauguration, Jeane Kirkpatrick asked her longtime friend Richard Shifter if he could serve as a member of the U.S. delegation to the UN Human Rights Commission in Geneva. Shifter, an avid anticommunist, had spent his boyhood in Vienna under the Nazis and lost his parents to the Holocaust.[13] Yet he admitted that he was a novice when it came to international human rights law and diplomacy. He had worked for thirty years in private law practice with substantial time devoted to representation of Indian tribes. "I had not been exposed to international human rights law and was only vaguely aware of the existence of the UN Human Rights Commission."[14]

As a novice to the meetings of the commission, Shifter was critical of its "ritual dances." "Predictable speech followed predictable speech," he recalled. To-

gether with Michael Novak, the head of the delegation, Shifter signaled publicly that the course of U.S. policy would be changing, stating that "all human
rights violations would have to be opposed and criticized, not merely those of
countries with few international friends."[15] The Kirkpatrick Doctrine entailed
a two-tiered system: human rights violations in communist "totalitarian countries" were opposed, but those of anticommunist authoritarian regimes were
not. Novak and Shifter's actions in the U.N. Commission meeting thus involved
the United States in a "full-blooded apology" for both the Chilean and the Argentine governments as the U.S. voted with these governments against mo-
tions that condemned Chile for torture and extended the mandate of the U.N.
working group on disappearances.[16]

As a signal of the new policy direction, the first Latin American head of
state invited to visit Washington was General Roberto Viola, the "president-
designate" of Argentina's military regime. Viola was a protégé of General Videla, who had held power during the peak of the repression during the "dirty
war." Though Videla and Viola were seen as soft-liners as compared to some
other members of the Argentine military, they were both deeply implicated in
the Argentine repression, something an Argentine court would recognize later
when it sentenced Videla to life imprisonment and Viola to seventeen years in
prison for human rights violations during their presidencies.

At the same time as the Reagan administration supported the Argentine government in Geneva and invited the future military dictator on a state visit, the
Argentine government arrested seven of the most effective and well-known
human rights activists in Buenos Aires. Emilio Mignone, Federico (Pippo) Westerkamp, and their associates had been active, virtually since the military regime's inception, in creating one of the most effective human rights organizations
in Argentina: the Center for Legal and Social Studies (CELS). The military not
only arrested these human rights workers but also ransacked their offices and
seized hundreds of documents. Mignone and his colleagues had traveled frequently to the United States and Europe and had established strong relations
with human rights organizations there. As soon as they were arrested, Westerkamp's wife Angela was on the phone to her contacts abroad, contacts which
in turn activated the entire human rights network on behalf of the detainees.
Congressional staff and the press subsequently peppered the State Department
with inquiries. The *New York Times* wrote an editorial accusing the Reagan administration policy of emboldening the junta to arrest the human rights workers.

Previously the Argentine military government had not dared to arrest these
high-profile CELS leaders, and it was only after the implementation of the
Kirkpatrick Doctrine that such arrests took place. The State Department, the
United Nations, and European governments all protested the arrests, and

Mignone and his colleagues were released a week later. The State Department claimed a victory for silent diplomacy, ignoring both the possibility that their open support of the Argentine government might have emboldened it to make the arrests in the first place, and that they mobilized private diplomacy only after strenuous lobbying from NGOs, the press, and Congress. Two weeks after the release of Mignone, an unrepentant General Viola arrived in Washington. "A victorious army is not to be investigated," he announced. "If the Reich's troops had won the last World War, the Tribunal would have been held not in Nuremberg but in Virginia." In some ways, Viola was only expressing a worldview held by many modern realists in international relations—that international law is a tool of the powerful who use it against their enemies. But the comments were not well received in Washington, since they equated U.S. behavior during World War II with Nazi war crimes. Viola's comments were even criticized in the censored press of Buenos Aires. "Viola is supposed to be a moderate, and if moderates think the only thing the Nazis did wrong is lose, the normal mind will find it hard to imagine what the view of the hardliners must be," editorialized the *Buenos Aires Tribune*.[17] Despite some embarrassment, the Reagan administration pressed ahead on its proposal to lift the 1978 embargo on military aid and arms sales to Argentina.

Yet, in the larger scheme, the Reagan administration's obsession with Central America led it to pay relatively little attention to South America. Administration officials mainly tried to recruit the South American military governments for their Central American anticommunist crusade.[18] They found the most willing partner in the Argentine military regime, which agreed to cooperate with their efforts to overthrow the Sandinista government in Nicaragua by supporting and training the Contras. The United States would provide the funds, while the Argentines would provide over two hundred advisors to train and oversee the operations on the ground.

This new relation with the Reagan administration was so cozy that Argentine military officials came to believe that the United States would remain neutral in a conflict between Argentina and Great Britain over the Malvinas, or Falkland Islands. By the time U.S. officials realized that the Argentines intended to invade the islands, they were unable to persuade the Argentine military leadership to call off their plan, even after President Reagan made a lengthy last-minute phone call to General Galtieri, president of Argentina.

Divisions within the Reagan administration may have contributed to this misperception. Jeane Kirkpatrick in particular was very friendly with the Argentine military, and she attended a dinner in her honor at the Argentine embassy in Washington on the day of the invasion.[19] The invasion of the Malvinas initially rallied wide support in Argentina. But the Argentine military, having mainly fought against unarmed civilians for the last decade, was unprepared for the war in the South Atlantic. Their resounding defeat and their abysmal execution of the war so undermined their legitimacy and credibility that they were forced from power shortly afterward. Thus the mistakes of the regime itself led to the final transition to democracy in Argentina. U.S. policy makers contributed only inadvertently to the transition by leading the Argentine military mistakenly to conclude that the United States would support their occupation of the Malvinas.

Once Argentina began the transition to democracy by holding elections in 1983, internal political forces took the initiative. The Reagan administration's lack of a human rights policy ultimately did not undermine progress toward democracy and human rights in Argentina, but neither was the Reagan administration viewed as a friend of democracy in Argentina. The newly elected president, Raúl Alfonsín, went out of his way to invite Patricia Derian to his inauguration to underscore his appreciation of her support for human rights and democracy during the Carter administration. Argentines applauded Derian as she participated in the inaugural parade.

Reagan officials did declare their support for the Alfonsín government when it faced military coup attempts in 1987 and 1988.[20] But even after the return to democracy in Argentina, after the publication of the definitive Argentine Truth Commission report, and after the trials and sentencing of junta members for murder and kidnapping, Reagan continued to refer to "rumors" of human rights violations there rather than recognize that such human rights violations were an established legal fact.[21]

Argentina was not the only country where Reagan policy emboldened authoritarian regimes to take measures they had not taken during the Carter administration. Jeane Kirkpatrick traveled to Chile in August 1981, where she firmly expressed the desire to fully normalize relations with Chile. During her visit, she refused to meet with Jaime Castillo, a senior Christian Democrat and president of the mainstream Chilean Commission for Human Rights. Two days later, Castillo and three other political leaders were expelled from Chile. The new ambassador to Chile, James Theberge, not only failed to protest the expulsion but said that there was nothing illegal about the decision to exile a Chilean citizen for his advocacy of human rights.

The increase in human rights violations in various countries directly after the election and during the first year of the Reagan administration suggests that repressive regimes are sensitive to messages they receive about the international environment of human rights. In virtually all cases, the Reagan administration had not yet had time to reestablish military or economic aid to these regimes—it had merely signaled its desire to reestablish cordial relations. The administration had urged Congress to reinstate military aid to Argentina, Chile, Guatemala, and Uruguay, and U.S. delegates to multilateral development banks had reversed the Carter administration opposition to loans to authoritarian regimes in Latin America. These policies promised or hinted of material benefits for authoritarian allies, but the benefits had not yet started to arrive. In some cases, like that of Guatemala, they would be sparse due to congressional opposition. But the authoritarian regimes responded to the rhetorical legitimation of the new policy. Their response suggests that the rhetoric of human rights, especially that of a superpower, cannot be ignored.

The first years of the Reagan administration are instructive. The decision to reorient policies away from an emphasis on human rights was a failure, both because it did not receive support from Congress or U.S. public opinion and because it contributed to an upsurge in human rights violations. It also did not enhance any version of U.S. national interests. The authoritarian allies that Kirkpatrick had praised turned out to be both unreliable (as in the case of the Argentine attack on the Malvinas) and brutal. These failures were perceived by policy makers within the administration, as well as by congressional and NGO critics, and eventually contributed to a reorientation of policy away from the Kirkpatrick Doctrine.

Policy Reorientation

One year into the Reagan administration, policy makers began to reorient policy toward democracy promotion. The sources of the policy change were multiple. Congress continued to have an active, if erratic, human rights policy during this period. The confrontation between the Reagan administration and Congress over human rights issues was one factor that led the Reagan administration to rethink its policy.

The Senate Foreign Relation Committee's defeat of Reagan's nominee for assistant secretary for human rights, Ernest Lefever, by a vote of 13 to 4 signaled that Congress and the U.S. public did not support the wholehearted dismantling of the Carter human rights policy. Individuals within the Reagan administration, seeing that Lefever ran into a "buzzsaw" in Congress, began to realize that "saying we don't care about human rights is a loser."[22] The confirmation hearings had made it clear that what was at stake was not just Lefever but the very decision of the administration to try to dismantle human rights policies. Jacobo Timerman, the Argentine journalist whom the Argentine military had disappeared, tortured, and eventually released only after pressure from Patricia Derian and many NGOs, was present in the room during the hearings for the Lefever nomination. His explosive memoir, *Prisoner without a Name, Cell without a Number,* had attracted broad attention in U.S. press and policy circles, and the charges of violent anti-Semitic repression directly called into question the Kirkpatrick Doctrine's distinction between totalitarian and authoritarian regimes. Two senators on the committee had dined with Timerman the night before the hearings. The following morning, Senator Percy noted Timerman's presence in the room and invited him to stand. He was greeted with lengthy applause. Aside from Timerman's dramatic presence, Lefever was his own worst enemy and his abrasiveness, impolitic statements, and revelations about improper financial relations sealed his fate. After the committee voted overwhelmingly against the nomination, Lefever withdrew his name rather than press forward to the full Senate. It was a clear defeat for the Reagan administration's approach to human rights.

Reagan's staff, worried that in foreign policy matters Reagan had become associated with a bellicose and negative image, tried to put a positive spin on the administration's foreign policy. The Argentine military's surprise attack on the Falkland Islands also called into question the administration's assumption that the military regimes of Latin America would be moderate and stable allies once cordial relations were reestablished.

After Lefever's defeat, William Clark, deputy secretary of state, began to look around for another nominee. Elliot Abrams, then assistant secretary of state for international organizations, recalled telling Clark jokingly: "I have a candidate for the position, who is not only brilliant, handsome, suave, and debonair, but I also have some good ideas for the human rights policy." Clark asked for a memo embodying those ideas. Abrams was a member of the neoconservative group once associated with Senator (Scoop) Jackson's Cold War liberal faction in the Democratic Party. When the party split over the Vietnam War, many of this group switched to the Republican Party and a number received appointments in the Reagan administration. The memo that Abrams produced was very much a product of the neoconservative, Scoop Jacksonian worldview of human rights. What distinguished this line from that of other Reaganites was that Jackson was committed to the idea of human rights but always saw it through a Cold War prism. In an eyes-only memo in late October 1981, Abrams proposed that "human rights should be at the core of our foreign policy."[23] What the memo did, in Abrams's words, was "elucidate a human rights policy that people could believe in as Reaganites."[24] In another analyst's view, it was the administration's attempt to "appropriate the banner of human rights for itself—to use it in battle not only against communist regimes but also, in a more defensive way, against domestic opponents of its human rights policy. It was a brilliant strategy, no more than half cynical, and it almost worked."[25]

Clark liked the memo, and Abrams was appointed to the post of assistant secretary of human rights. Because he had served on the staffs of both Senator Moynihan and Senator Jackson, Abrams had bipartisan support in the Senate, and the nomination was approved without problems. The memo, adopted for diverse political reasons in the State Department, foreshadowed the change in human rights policy that would eventually appear in the second Reagan administration.

The new policy of democracy promotion found another advocate in the new assistant secretary of state for inter-American affairs, Thomas Enders. Enders had first unveiled the policy in a speech to the World Affairs Council in Washington in July 1981, even before Abrams had written his memo. In his speech, Enders endorsed a "political solution" to the conflict in El Salvador, by which he meant not negotiations but elections. He argued that "El Salvador's leaders will not—and should not—grant the insurgents, through negotiations, the share of power they have not been able to win on the battlefield . . . but they should be—and are—willing to compete with the insurgents at the polls."[26] Enders used this policy stance successfully to defuse congressional opposition to military aid for El Salvador.

But the new policy would not appear in any consistent form in Latin America for four to five years. Why was there such a long delay between the articulation of an alternative "Reaganite" vision of democracy promotion and its actual implementation? Enders and other proponents of democracy promotion policies had to contend with Haig, Kirkpatrick, and other hard-liners in the administration who preferred cordial relations with authoritarian regimes in South America, and who sought a military, not a political, solution in Central America.

The policy was adopted after Secretary of State Haig was replaced by George Shultz. But the instinctive distrust that Reaganites had for the term "human rights" and for the Carter administration left them with no policy tools to implement their human rights policy. They refused to consider the public ones adopted by Carter, and they soon found that quiet diplomacy was notoriously inefficient. Tentative, trial-and-error policies implemented in El Salvador and Guatemala eventually led to more coherent democracy-promotion and human rights policies in the second administration.

Many individuals who in other circumstances would have been supporters of a democracy-promotion program were skeptical of the Reagan administration's motives and commitment to democracy. Often the administration claimed to be supporting democracy while it simultaneously ignored gross violations of human rights. Central America became one of the major arenas where the debate over democracy and human rights played out. Critics lambasted the apparent hypocrisy of an administration that claimed to be supporting democracy as it appealed for dramatic increases in aid to El Salvador, a regime that could be labeled democratic in the early 1980s only by an exercise of wishful thinking and apology.

The genesis of these new democracy-promotion efforts in foreign policy may explain the somewhat surprising division within the policy and NGO community, where democracy-promotion advocacy is often separated from, and sometimes even counterposed to, human rights policy. Human rights activists—having witnessed massive aid to the government of El Salvador at a time when its democratic credentials were shaky and when it was engaged in a campaign of massive human rights violations against its population—saw democracy promotion as a sham cover for counterinsurgency. And in Nicaragua, democracy-promotion policy, which had extensive military and political support for the Contras as its centerpiece, appeared to be an ideological cover for U.S. efforts to overthrow the Sandinistas. At the same time, Reagan administration officials viewed the "so-called human rights organizations" as ideologically motivated and dismissed their human rights reporting as unreliable. "At one point we said that we weren't going to get information from the creeps on the left who disguised themselves as human rights experts," said Elliot Abrams. "I was only half wrong. Many were passionately opposed to Reagan human rights policy and it clouded their vision. As it clouded our vision because we were passionate supporters of Reagan human rights policy."[27] Abrams suggests a scenario where the reporting of both sides is compromised by ideology. What this appraisal misses is that the Truth Commission reports, transcripts of trials, and records of exhumations found again and again that the reporting of the human rights organizations was far more accurate than that of the "highly skilled foreign service officers" upon which Elliot Abrams was basing his policy.

Guatemala

Perhaps the most troubling instance of the effects of the Reagan policy was Guatemala. The wave of state-sponsored violence that swept the country from 1978 until 1983 was on an order of magnitude that startled even hardened observers.[28] Responding to a perceived threat from the urban political opposition, the newly elected president, General Romeo Lucas García, unleashed national security forces and their associated death squads. The worst of this state-sponsored repressive activity was aimed at stemming the tide of union organizing in the countryside as well as suppressing new guerrilla activity there. Following a coup in 1982 by General Efrain Ríos Montt, the military

sought to stamp out the guerrillas through well-funded and -staffed rural counterinsurgency programs. A substantial portion of the highland peasant male
population was forced to serve in army-run civil defense patrols, and tens of
thousands of civilians and guerrillas were killed.[29]

Guatemala boasted the largest magnitude of human rights violations in the
hemisphere. In Guatemala, as throughout the hemisphere, political and economic elites had watched the U.S. elections carefully. "When Reagan won, we
celebrated in Guatemala just like New Year's Eve, with Mariachis, Marimbas,
and firecrackers," recalled Lionel Sisniega Oters, a leader of Guatemala's rightist National Liberation Movement.[30] Prior to Reagan's inauguration, a series of
advisors who claimed to speak on behalf of his transition team met with the
Guatemalan leaders. In December, two leading Guatemalan businessmen, Roberto Alejos and Manuel Ayau, met with President-elect Reagan to discuss the
administration's new policy toward Guatemala. These entrepreneurs had do-
nated $2 million to the Reagan campaign.[31] Alejos had been outspoken in his
criticisms of the Carter human rights policy. "Most of the elements in the State
Department are probably pro-communist," he complained. "Either Mr. Carter
is a totally incapable president or he is definitely a pro-communist element."[32]

Once elected, the Reagan administration pushed to reestablish military aid
to Guatemala and to increase levels of economic aid. Congress, however,
blocked the Reagan administration's efforts to reestablish military aid. Administration officials acquiesced, largely because their policies toward El Salvador
and Nicaragua were more important to them, and they didn't want to antagonize their congressional opponents by reestablishing military aid to Guatemala
over their objections. As a result, during most of the Reagan administration and
during the period of most intense repression in Guatemala, U.S. military aid
was cut off and economic aid was at fairly low levels. The Reagan administration did manage to provide more support than such numbers suggest—it re-
classified some military sales as nonmilitary. For example, the administration
arranged for the sale of twenty-five Bell helicopters to the Guatemala government, worth close to $25 million, by classifying them as civilian. Once they ar-
rived in Guatemala, however, the helicopters were outfitted with guns and used
for military purposes. The U.S. government encouraged Israel to expand dramatically its military aid, sales, and training program to Guatemala. Even taking all these alternative forms of assistance into account, however, the period
of most intense repression in Guatemala was one where U.S. direct and indirect aid levels were very low, in relation to previous aid levels and to other
countries in the region, especially El Salvador and Honduras, but also Costa
Rica, which was not an ally of the Reagan administration.

The Reagan administration encouraged increased lending to Guatemala from international financial institutions. In 1982, the height of human rights violations, the Reagan administration pressed for the approval of an Inter-American Bank loan to Guatemala, on the basis that "the basic human rights exception was no longer relevant since 'major human rights steps' taken by the Guatemalan government had placed it outside the purview of the human rights statutes."[33]

Nevertheless, the cutoff of military assistance to Guatemala gave it a "relative autonomy" vis-à-vis the United States that other regimes, such as that in El Salvador, did not have.[34] The Guatemalan government thus carried out its most intense repression at a time that it received very little U.S. military aid. This pattern calls into question arguments about a direct and immediate relation between military aid and human rights violations. Almost at the same time in neighboring El Salvador, the military was carrying out extreme repression and human rights violations, also in the context of civil war, with extensive and increasing military and economic support from the United States.

Comparing these two cases, direct military aid at the repressive moment cannot be seen as a necessary or sufficient condition for repression. Rather, military aid needs to be understood as part of a larger context of U.S. relations, including the history of military support and training and the symbolic and rhetorical messages communicated to the repressive governments. We therefore need to consider not only the level of military aid but the broader diplomatic context. The government of General Romeo Lucas García had been in power since July 1978. Repression had been high during the Lucas García regime, focused initially on the urban political opposition. Lucas García later instituted a program of indiscriminate repression in the countryside. But the level of repression, high during the first year and a half of the Lucas García government, increased dramatically in 1980 and 1981. There are various apparent reasons for this increase in repression. The July 1979 victory of the Sandinistas in Nicaragua reinforced the Lucas García government's determination to prevent any increase in social movement activity. The actions of the Salvadoran government to institute even limited land reform was also seen as an ominous precedent by the Guatemalan entrepreneurial class, and the Guatemalan right pointed to developments in El Salvador as examples of the error of making concessions to reform.[35]

When a group of Mayan Indians occupied the Spanish embassy in Guatemala City in January 1980 to denounce the murder and kidnapping of nine peasants in their villages, police threw incendiary devices into the embassy, killing thirty-nine people. Because the Guatemalan government had taken such a public act of repression against the urging of the ambassador, Spain broke off diplomatic relations with Guatemala.

The slaughter of the protesters in the embassy signaled that the Guatemalan government would no longer tolerate nonviolent protests by popular movements, and that it was prepared to disregard international public opinion and antagonize key states like Spain.[36] In this context of international isolation, the Lucas García government continued its program of repression against its urban political opponents and initiated a major counterinsurgency campaign in the countryside in 1981.

In 1981 the guerrilla movement in Guatemala reached a new peak. A church source estimated that by the end of that year the guerrillas had 6,000 people in arms, and a support base of another 276,000 people, acting in 16 of Guatemala's 22 departments.[37] During their counterinsurgency campaign, the Lucas García government and the Ríos Montt government that followed it carried out the episode in modern Latin American history that most clearly fits the definition of genocide. The total number of people killed was massive, and the great bulk of victims (over 85 percent) were indigenous people of Mayan descent.[38]

In this context of genocide, insurgency, and counterinsurgency, the Reagan administration decided to try to improve its relations with the Guatemalan government. As the Kirkpatrick Doctrine came to form the broader context for U.S.–Guatemalan relations in the early 1980s, the United States made clear to the Guatemalan government that human rights concerns would not be a central issue in bilateral policy. It had decided that the Carter policy had unnecessarily alienated the Guatemalan government and that to reestablish a dialogue, the United States would need to make some "condition-free demonstrations of our goodwill."[39] What this meant was clearly expressed in a meeting between Rafael Castillo, Guatemala's foreign minister, and Deputy Secretary Clark in May 1981. Castillo urged the United States to let the Guatemalans "do their own thing" in Guatemala. Clark "assured Castillo that the Reagan administration would not publicly castigate human rights offenders nor forget its friends." In their conversation, Clark signaled that he shared Castillo's views. Clark pointed out that human rights were a private matter and not something you wear on your lapel, and noted "that Guatemala had only one problem: [Fidel] Castro"; Castillo heartily agreed.[40] Given that this conversation took place in the context of mass killing, it is not surprising that the Guatemalan government interpreted this signal as a green light to continue repression.

Whenever the Reagan administration put any human rights pressures on the Guatemalan government, it always made clear that it was doing so not out of commitment but only to protect itself from congressional attacks. While these kinds of pressures were better than no pressures at all, they lacked conviction and were unpersuasive to the Guatemalan government. When the special en-

voy Vernon Walters met with President Lucas García in May 1981, for example, he was instructed to explain that the high level of violence in Guatemala
was causing "internal political and legal problems" for the Reagan administration that "impede our ability to maintain the level of military cooperation that
we would wish."[41] Walters avowed that the United States couldn't reestablish
military aid because "President Reagan would be subject to attack for any
change in U.S. policy." President Lucas essentially told Walters that the repression would continue because he believed that it was effective against the
leftist insurgency. The Guatemalans would prefer to have U.S. military assistance, but they were willing to "go it alone." In his report to the U.S. government on conditions in Guatemala, Walters downplayed the human rights
situation by claiming that "there is no evidence of a systematic campaign to
eliminate non-guerrilla opposition."[42] At the same time, the U.S. embassy reported an average of 356 deaths per month, the largest increase in deaths since
it had started reporting on such deaths, and said that "the [number of deaths
caused by the] right continues to outpace the left by almost a 4 to 1 ratio."[43]

In July 30, 1981, the deputy assistant secretary of inter-American affairs
testified before a hostile and skeptical congressional committee that the U.S.
policy of distancing itself from Guatemala "publicly and, at times confronta-
tionally," practiced over the previous three years, did not improve the status of
human rights in Guatemala. The administration recommended instead a "moderate" and "measured" program of establishing communication with the Guatemalan government, including increases in commercial sales of trucks, jeeps, and
spare parts, which would be aimed at lowering its "siege mentality."[44]

There is indeed some evidence that the international isolation of the Guatemalan government was giving some of the most reactionary groups a free
hand to engage in massive human rights violations. A policy of rapprochement
as a vehicle for improving human rights was thus not necessarily wrongheaded.
But the manner in which the administration proposed the policy once again
provided an apology (and a cover-up) for a murderous regime nearing the apex
of its violence. "There have been some positive developments in the past several weeks," the deputy assistant secretary stated. "The Guatemalan security
forces have made inroads in guerrilla operations. And they have done it while
taking care to protect innocent bystanders."[45] While expressing concern for
human rights violations in Guatemala, he characterized the violations as violence between rightist paramilitary groups and guerrillas. He made this claim
despite a recently released Amnesty International report documenting that
right-wing death squads operated directly out of the presidential palace. He
clearly was aware of the report, since he affirmed that the department had
taken note of it, but he refused further comment. He later announced that the

Guatemalan government "has formulated a very comprehensive plan to try to improve the lot of the Guatemalan Indians," referring to a counterinsurgency plan that would result in the murder of thousands of Indians. He went on to say that "there was some evidence, following Vernon Walter's visit, that there was a policy formulated or articulated within the Guatemalan government which sought to bring greater control over the activities of the Government's security forces."[46] The deputy assistant secretary of state thereby misrepresented the overall tenor of Walters's discussion with President Lucas, since Lucas had shown no inclination to end repression or bring security forces under greater control.

Unable to convince the Guatemalan government to limit repression in return for increased security assistance, and unable to convince a skeptical Congress of the wisdom of its "moderate, measured" program of improved relations with the Guatemalan government, the Reagan administration decided to wash its hands of the Guatemala repression. It would wait and see if Guatemalan repression could eliminate the insurgency. This position is outlined in a memo from the Human Rights Bureau in October 1981.

> Only in time will we and the Guatemalans know whether President Lucas is correct in his conviction that repression will work once again in Guatemala. If he is right and the policy of repression is succeeding and will result in the extermination of the guerrillas, their supporters, and their sympathizers, there is no need for the U.S. to implicate itself in the repression by supplying the GOG [Government of Guatemala] with Security Assistance. . . . If the repression does work and the guerrillas, their supporters and sympathizers are neutralized, we can in the aftermath of the repression work to restore normal relations with the successors to President Lucas. . . . If we are correct in our conviction that the repression will not succeed and will only exacerbate and compound the guerrilla threat, then we ought to distance ourselves form the GOG until such time as it arrives at this realization and is prepared to address our human rights concerns in return for renewed U.S. political and military support.[47]

This language is not foreign to the intent of U.S. human rights policy, because one of the initial concerns of Donald Fraser was indeed that the United States disassociate itself from repression abroad. During the Reagan administration, idealist expressions of support for the idea of human rights were frowned upon and ridiculed as remnants of the Carter policy, so it is not surprising that an officer in the Human Rights Bureau would express himself in such realpolitik terms, designed in part to persuade the Latin America Bureau not to press ahead with military support. Even so, this memo is chilling. It accepts as perhaps inevitable a government campaign of "extermination," not only of guerrillas but also of "their supporters and their sympathizers." It furthermore expresses a willingness to use Guatemala as a kind of human experiment to test whether repression will "work." Only then, when the dirty work is done, should the United States step in and reestablish cordial relations.

This sterile and indifferent language is characteristic of the cable traffic to and from the Guatemalan embassy during the 1980–82 period, the period of greatest repression in Guatemala. Messages are interspersed with grim reports of violence that express increasing mystification as to its origins. The tone is thrown into relief by the one exception, a "cry of conscience" from a political officer in the embassy, Raymond J. Gonzalez, in January 1982. Gonzalez was apparently expressing a personal view, to which Ambassador Chapin added his own comments in a cable to Washington. Gonzalez, responding specifically to the murder of priests, says,

> It is my belief that these recent acts by the GOG are only the tip of the iceberg. The U.S. government should avoid condoning these illegal acts by its silence. Eventually, the misdeeds and corruption of the GOG will come to light. I, for one, do not intend to serve as an apologist for GOG or my own government. It is the height of hypocrisy to participate in the civilities of diplomacy when we know the truth. We become silent partners in the barbarous and criminal deeds of this government if we do not speak out. I feel we are past the point of quote quiet diplomacy end quote in Guatemala.

Ambassador Chapin followed the message with a critique of some specific arguments but then goes on to say, in language most uncharacteristic of his cables during this period:

> I believe that Mr. Gonzalez's message is a profound cry of conscience from a deeply concerned and eminently honest officer. Nevertheless, I do not believe that we can, because of the national interests of the U.S. and the strategic importance of the struggle currently in process in Guatemala, allow ourselves the happy and the otherwise much-to-be-longed-for luxury of departing from the path of quiet diplomacy. Foreign policy cannot, unfortunately, be run on raw, gut emotion.[48]

The wording here is very unusual. Chapin associates a forthright condemnation of human rights violations with "raw, gut emotion," which he characterizes as a "luxury"—something "happy" and "much to be longed for," while reserving for himself the apparently more difficult task of diplomacy. Only within the confining limits of the Kirkpatrick Doctrine could criticisms of human rights violations in Guatemala be seen as a "luxury." It is frequently very difficult for an embassy to make a forthright criticism of human rights. Likewise, it was very difficult for Gonzalez, during the height of the Kirkpatrick Doctrine, to take a principled stand and request that the ambassador forward his message. He must have known that this memo would not lead to promotions in the Reagan administration State Department. So, what is so "happy" and "much to be longed for" about this? Chapin was shaken by his experience in Guatemala. Abrams described him as a "buttoned-down" WASPy ambassador, arriving in Guatemala for one of his last postings, who later appeared "tortured" and who "went off in a bad way."[49] Chapin's task was complicated by the expectation that embassies would shape their reporting to the overall policy the administration pursued in the country.[50] The Reagan administration policy was to improve relations with Guatemala, and it would have expected embassy communications to be consonant with that policy. But in the context of intense human rights violations, Chapin may have found it difficult to tailor his embassy's messages to fit the policy.

By early 1982, the embassy claimed that "as the number and ferocity of violent incidents increase, it is becoming difficult for the embassy to attribute responsibility for them to any particular source." But CIA reports from the embassy at the time betray no confusion about what is going on. A CIA cable reported that the Guatemalan army had

> launched a sweep operation into Ixil Province. The commanding officers of the units involved have been instructed to destroy all towns and villages which are cooperating with the EGP [Ejército Guerrillo de los Pobres—the main guerrilla organization in Guatemala at the time] and eliminate all sources of resistance. . . . When an army patrol meets resistance and takes fire from a town or village, it is assumed that the entire town is hostile and it is subsequently destroyed. . . . The army high command is highly pleased with the initial results of the sweep operation.

The report concluded that "the well documented belief by the army that the entire Ixil Indian population is pro-EGP has created a situation in which the army can be expected to give no quarter to combatants and non-combatants alike."[51]

Human rights organizations during the same period also had little trouble attributing responsibility for human rights violations. Amnesty International, Human Rights Watch, and other organizations clearly stated that a government-sponsored program of mass murder was under way. Yet the U.S. embassy and U.S. policy makers refused to state this publicly and tended to attack the messengers.

Despite the symbolic green light from the Reagan administration, the Guatemalan government was quite isolated internationally during the period of greatest repression. In August 1981, Washington issued a travel advisory saying it was dangerous for travelers to go to Guatemala. Yet the Guatemalan government seemed unperturbed by its isolation. President Lucas García summarized the general attitude: "Gringos are not going to teach us what democracy is."[52] International human rights activities were denounced as part of an international campaign in support of subversion and against the government and army of Guatemala. The Guatemala government maintained a distance even from the Reagan administration, refusing to cooperate directly in its regional military plan, for fear that some form of political conditionality would be involved.[53]

The most problematic aspects of this policy were its normative and discursive context and the way it justified decisions. Instead of saying, "We agree that there are grave violations of human rights and that there is clear evidence that the government is responsible; we condemn them, but we want to keep our lines of communication open with the government so we can continue to communicate our opposition to these abuses," the State Department chose to whitewash the practices of a murderous regime.

U.S. human rights legislation forbids military aid to countries engaged in a consistent pattern of gross violations of human rights. Guatemala, without doubt, fitted this definition. There was perhaps no way that the U.S. government could have recognized such levels of abuse while simultaneously justifying military sales or aid. To justify military aid and sales, it had to distort the picture of the human rights situation in Guatemala. The extreme corruption of the Lucas García government and the sense of increasing international isolation eventually led to the ousting of this government in March 1982 through a coup staged by junior officers. This brought General Efraín Ríos Montt, an evangelical Christian, to the presidency. U.S. military aid cutbacks were among the multiple factors that contributed to the coup against the Lucas García regime. As government reserves declined, junior officers had become increasingly concerned about the lack of adequate supplies, and some had even called for a reduced level of human rights violations to improve the military's image.[54]

Despite considerable uncertainty about the direction of the new government, the United States represented the Ríos Montt government as a more modern and less repressive alternative to Lucas García. After the coup, Enders stated that "in Guatemala, a coup has installed a new leader who has improved the human rights situation, and has opened the way for a more effective counterinsurgency."[55] Yet Ríos Montt oversaw a concerted program of genocide and mass murder in the Guatemalan highlands that yielded an average of eight hundred victims per month. Ríos Montt was part of the "modernized, technified sector of the Guatemalan army, trained in special warfare; during the mid-1970s, he had served as head of the Department of Studies at the Inter-American Defense College in Washington, developing close ties to the U.S. counter-insurgency establishment."[56]

Not only was the administration attempting to whitewash massive human rights abuses under way in Guatemala, but it also decided to attack the organizations responsible for trying to document and disseminate information about these violations. In September 1982, during this period of U.S.–Guatemala rapprochement and massive political killing, the Reagan State Department decided to pick a fight with Amnesty International, which had recently published a report finding the Ríos Montt government responsible for mass killings in rural areas. In a letter to an executive of Amnesty International, Enders stated that the organization's reporting "appears to contrast greatly" with embassy information and that the Ríos Montt government had "made significant progress" on human rights, implying that Amnesty data was flawed. The embassy later circulated the letter to the local press in Guatemala, apparently in an effort to bolster the administration's rapprochement with the Ríos Montt government. A few months later, the State Department again attacked the reporting on Guatemala by human rights organizations, accusing them of being part of "a concerted disinformation campaign . . . by groups supporting a left wing insurgency. . . ."[57]

Instead of working together with other countries to bring all pressure to bear on the Guatemalan government to stop the killings, the United States was negotiating a rapprochement with the government and attacking the very organizations that were trying to distribute reliable information on the human rights situation. This is the low point of U.S. policy in the region, not because of the level of military or economic aid, which were indeed quite modest, but because of the rhetorical stance taken by the U.S. government. The United States was in effect using its considerable resources to refute and discredit the reporting efforts of human rights NGOs rather than investigating those cases of human rights abuse, offering assistance to victims, or pressuring the Guatemalan government to change its practices.

The emblematic moment in this policy came in December 1982, when

Ronald Reagan traveled to Latin America and met with six presidents including Ríos Montt of Guatemala. We don't know what Reagan said in private, but
after the meeting he stated publicly that Ríos Montt was "a man of great personal integrity and commitment" whose country "is confronting a brutal challenge from guerrillas armed and supported by others outside Guatemala." That
same day, in a question-and-answer period, a reporter asked Reagan what he
thought about Ríos Montt's announcement about a new election law to prepare for elections in the future. Reagan replied that he thought Ríos Montt "is
totally dedicated to democracy in Guatemala. . . . They made quite a presen-
tation and brought a lot of information and material to us. And frankly, I'm inclined to think they've been getting a bum rap." A reporter asked if Reagan was
leaning toward resuming military aid. Reagan replied, "Well, this is going to
depend, of course, on all this information that's been provided to us. But I
would think so."[58]

We now know that in 1982, the year that Ronald Reagan called Ríos Montt
a "man of great personal integrity" who had gotten a "bum rap," the Guatemalan
government forces killed or disappeared at least 17,953 Guatemalan citizens,
most of them unarmed civilians and primarily rural indigenous peoples.[59] The
mass murder occurring in Guatemala in 1981–82 was no secret, even if the exact numbers were not known at the time. Human rights organizations had spent
much of 1982 denouncing the liquidation of whole villages in the highland areas of Guatemala. The most recent and careful research points to 1981 and 1982
as the years of greatest repression in Guatemala. The *Guatemala: Nunca Más* report shows that 80 percent of the 165 rural massacres they documented took
place in the years 1981 and 1982.[60] A detailed study by the forensic anthropol-
ogy team of Guatemala of the graves of massacre victims in the Rabinal region
also showed that all the victims were killed in the period 1980–83.[61]

Reagan's endorsement of Ríos Montt, at the very height of his planned program of mass murder, constitutes one of the most troubling moments of the
Reagan period. It was a gratuitous, thoughtless gesture made for a man guilty
of mass murder of his population. I use "thoughtless" here in the manner
suggested by Hannah Arendt, implying an incapacity to tell right from wrong.
We suspect that it was not only Reagan himself who was thoughtless at this
moment, but also the staff who briefed him for the meeting. Nor was the problem confined to the staff. The entire policy environment in the State Department made it difficult to raise human rights issues that would have contradicted
the Kirkpatrick Doctrine. Embassies were expected to bring their human
rights reporting in line with policy, not the other way around. Because
Guatemala is a small country, relatively unimportant for U.S. policy, the gesture has been largely forgotten. In my mind, it symbolizes the bankruptcy and

culpability of the Kirkpatrick Doctrine and its practitioners. To put it in comparable terms, it is equivalent to an American president saying that Milosevic was a man of great personal integrity, who was totally dedicated to democracy but who had gotten a bum rap from the international community, at the height of repression in Bosnia or Kosovo. We would have seen this as a morally and politically bankrupt gesture.

But the embrace of Ríos Montt was more than a gesture; it was a message to the Guatemalan government and military. It was a cue to the Guatemalan military that the United States was not going to criticize them, much less sanction them, for their human rights practices. The Guatemalan military would have interpreted this cue in the context of their national security ideology and in the context of what they thought the U.S. government knew about the nature of repression. Like the earlier cues from Clark, Walters, and Enders discussed above, this signal gave a green light to repression.

Efforts of other international actors to call attention to human rights violations in Guatemala were unsatisfactory. When a special UN human rights investigator was appointed in 1983, he was largely ineffectual in contributing to improving the human rights situation and became what one author referred to as the most "politicized human rights investigator ever appointed in the U.N."[62] Later, in 1985, Guatemala did make a transition to the civilian regime of Cerezo, but not to full democracy. Since the military retained extraordinary power, human rights abuses continued at very high levels. U.S. policy makers encouraged Guatemalan elites to move toward civilian-led governments. Although mass murder had subsided in Guatemala, these tenuous civilian regimes during the period 1985–93 coincided with unacceptably high levels of extrajudicial executions and other human rights violations. Nevertheless, these governments did establish institutions, such as a Constitutional Court and a human rights ombudsman's office, that became important actors in the struggle for human rights and democracy in Guatemala during the 1990s.[63]

El Salvador

Initially, the Reagan administration did not have its own human rights policy toward El Salvador. As in the case of Guatemala, the Reagan administration was initially determined to reverse what they saw as the wrongheaded policies of the Carter administration. As they downplayed human rights and emphasized counterinsurgency, the administration occasionally felt obliged to deliver congressional messages on human rights. This was preferable to no discussion of human rights whatsoever, but just as in the case of Guatemala, the messages lacked conviction and thus were ineffectual. Enders was advocating more democracy and a "political solution" to the military conflict, but he faced opposition from hard-liners in the administration.

During the first two years of the Reagan administration—years that the UN Truth Commission called the period of the "institutionalization of violence" in El Salvador—repression was especially intense: 3,836 deaths in 1981; 2,477 in 1982.[64] Indeed, "over 75% of the serious acts of violence reported to the Commission on the Truth took place during the first four years of the decade" and continued at high yearly levels throughout the entire Reagan period.[65]

As a result of the escalation of human rights violations, personnel in the U.S. embassy in El Salvador began to push for a more forceful policy. At one point, the U.S. embassy in San Salvador developed an almost textbook case of using a "two-level game" in human rights negotiations with El Salvador. The centerpiece of congressional human rights policy toward El Salvador during the Reagan administration was "certification," which required that the executive certify the improvement of human rights and efforts made to investigate past violations by the Salvadoran government, especially those against U.S. citizens.

The certification policy has been deeply criticized as an escape valve for a divided Congress that was unwilling to take a strong stand on human rights but wanted to protect its image. At a certain point, "an odd symbiosis developed between the Reagan administration and its Congressional opponents. The administration hated the certification requirements and bitterly opposed the aid cuts that its opponents were always threatening."[66] One of the main tools that the ambassador and the State Department used in negotiations with right-wing allies in San Salvador, however, was the threat of an aid cutoff. At one point, Reagan's ambassador to El Salvador, Deane Hinton, began handing out copies in El Salvador of the certification legislation—a law he had once called stupid—"to show the right that an aid cut-off would be required" if the human rights situation worsened.[67]

Basically, Reagan had been so rhetorically supportive of the worldview of the right in Central America that right-wing leaders didn't believe that the Reagan administration would cut aid. By rhetorically embracing the right without asking for any concessions in return, in other words, the Reagan administration gave away bargaining leverage it might have used. When the embassies in Guatemala City or San Salvador began expressing concern over human rights, the military and the right in these countries thought that the problem was with the embassies. They never doubted that they had the support of Reagan. The embassies then needed the threats of the U.S. Congress to give them any leverage with the right wing. So, in April 1982, General Vernon Walters traveled to San Salvador with an aide of Jesse Helms, with the explicit task of convincing the Salvadorans that the threat of a congressional cutoff of aid was "real—not a chimera invented by the State Department." "In [Ambassador] Hinton's battle with the Salvadoran right, it was precisely the onerous certification and the threat of reduced aid that, time after time, gave him the crucial leverage he needed."[68] Eventually, that game began to wear thin—especially as Reagan himself insisted on making statements that appeared to contradict and undermine the State Department's position. But it remained a crucial tool through the early period of U.S.–Salvadoran relations.

El Salvador was also a crucible where the administration experimented with the democracy-promotion policies that would later be used in a less politicized fashion. In the 1982 Constituent Assembly elections, the State Department, with funding from the Agency for International Development (AID), arranged for a group of prominent Americans to observe balloting and report to Washington. "This superficial and highly politicized" election observer mission nevertheless set the stage for the minor growth industry in election observation missions in the 1980s and 1990s, which would later achieve more objectivity.[69] Likewise, for the presidential election of 1984, AID paid for computers and the voter registration system to ensure more credible elections, experimenting with types of funding that would later be used in Chile to help the opposition defeat Pinochet. The Administration of Justice Program for judicial training also saw its origins in El Salvador, after the State Department was "struck by the incompetence of the Salvadoran judicial and police system" while working with the Salvadoran government to resolve the murders of the churchwomen and the U.S. AID workers.[70]

The Reagan State Department had to work with the Salvadoran government on these murder cases because congressional certification legislation required evidence of progress. The main problem, as the truth commission later documented, was not the incompetence of the judiciary and the police. It was that the Salvadoran military murdered its opponents with impunity, even when those opponents were citizens of the government that provided massive aid. It wasn't just that the Salvadoran government lacked political will to *investigate*. A focus on investigative resolve would miss the point. The Salvadoran government was engaged in a program of mass murder against its political opponents. To focus on the subsequent administration of justice in such a situation seemed politically disingenuous to congressional critics, and this tarnished the whole notion of a judicial training program. Until the military stopped killing its opponents as a matter of policy, and until the government developed the political will to investigate such murders, it hardly seemed important that the Salvadoran state also lacked the judicial and police capacity to carry out such investigations. Nevertheless, administration of justice programs in such politically controversial settings as El Salvador paradoxically laid the groundwork for later judicial programs where such training was more productive.

Conflicts over policy toward El Salvador reflected divisions within the executive as well as those between the executive and Congress. The Reagan administration was divided between hard-liners, including Clark, Kirkpatrick, William Casey, head of the CIA, and Casper Weinberger, and "moderates," led by Secretary of State Shultz. This was a true two-level game: intense fights within the executive as well as between the executive and Congress interacted with divisions within the Salvadoran government to produce particular policy outcomes. This fight came to the forefront in U.S. policy toward El Salvador after Ambassador Hinton made a forthright speech to the American Chamber of Commerce in El Salvador in October 1982, during a traditional gathering of the Salvadoran economic elite. Hinton announced that as many as thirty thousand people had been "murdered, not killed in battle, murdered," and added that the "mafia" responsible for these killings must be stopped. Despite a decrease in killings since 1981, Hinton said, "by no stretch of the imagination can current levels be considered acceptable by any civilized person." Unless El Salvador made progress in the human rights area, "U.S. aid would end."[71]

The White House had not approved the speech, and Ronald Reagan didn't like it. It clearly was not "private diplomacy." Hinton was muzzled, and eventually both Hinton and Assistant Secretary Enders were forced to resign due to being too forthright about their support for a negotiated end to the war in El Salvador. The hard-liners had won the day, and the exit of Hinton and Enders silenced any other critics within the administration. But Shultz was not to be beaten so easily. He named a top-notch career foreign service officer, Thomas Pickering, as the new ambassador and told him privately to "raise hell" about Salvadoran human rights abuses.[72]

Pickering was outraged by the continuation of death squad killings, particularly of Christian Democrats and others allied with the U.S. embassy. He too gave an equally forceful speech at the next annual Chamber of Commerce meeting, condemning the death squads and chiding the elite for failing to speak out against human rights abuses. Even as Pickering condemned the death squads, the hard-liners in the administration contradicted his efforts. Reagan pocket-vetoed the legislation extending certification requirements and suggested publicly that right-wing violence in El Salvador was the product of guerrillas masquerading as rightists.

To contain the damage of this statement, Vice President Bush was sent to El Salvador to deliver a personal message from President Reagan. He first endorsed Pickering's earlier comments and then condemned the death squads. "Tom Pickering's remarks, which I greatly admire and which the president and I fully endorse—were right on the mark," Bush said. "Every murder they [the death squads] commit poisons the well of friendship between our two countries. . . . If these death squad murders continue, you will lose the support of the American people, and that will be a tragedy."[73] In his private meetings with the military, Bush was apparently consistent. Once again, the Reagan administration had demonstrated that private diplomacy alone was not going to be sufficient for effective human rights policy. Clear public language backed up by the possibility of material sanctions was necessary.

Material sanctions were not forthcoming, however. In the months following Bush's visit, and despite CIA reports that deaths attributed to political violence had not declined significantly, U.S. aid to El Salvador expanded dramatically. The May 1984 election of Christian Democrat José Napoleón Duarte had led Congress to change its attitude about aid to El Salvador, permitting an increase in military and economic aid.[74] Despite the increase in aid, truth commission data indicate that the levels of deaths declined between 1983 and 1984, reaching their lowest level since 1978.

Whatever the equivocation and double messages involved in Reagan policy toward El Salvador, it differs from the almost complete silence and apologies in Guatemala during a period of genocide. The United States had far greater responsibility in El Salvador, for it was sending millions of dollars annually in economic and military aid. By 1984 the Reagan administration had adopted a human rights policy toward El Salvador, but it was permeated with profound contradictions. It gave major military and economic aid as well as training to support the counterinsurgency, but meanwhile it pressured the government to end the death squad killings. At the same time, in order to sustain high levels of military and economic aid, it repeatedly had to certify to Congress that the human rights conditions were far better than the embassy in fact knew them to be. The counterinsurgency war and the death squad killings were intrinsically linked in the Salvador system, and U.S. policy was at an impasse.

The United States and El Salvador remained in this impasse until the late 1980s and early 1990s, when the convergence of three factors made it possible to end the civil war and reduce repression. First, both sides in the war became convinced that neither side could win. The stalemate created the internal will for a peace settlement. Second, elections had brought the right-wing ARENA Party to power, and the Salvadoran right had learned that it could win power democratically and did not have to rely on the military to serve as its proxy.[75] Finally, the 1989 murder of six Jesuit priests, their housekeeper, and the housekeeper's daughter by members of a U.S.-trained crack battalion undermined U.S. confidence that its training efforts could lead to a fundamental reorientation of the Salvadoran military. The Salvadoran case suggests that human rights abuses would have ended sooner had the civil war not lasted so long. The Reagan administration, however, never tried to promote peace and instead actively blocked peace efforts by both internal and international actors, including efforts by its own staff.

Chile

The Reagan administration initially made consistent efforts to improve relations with the Pinochet government. The Letelier case was downplayed, and cordial diplomatic relations were established, especially between Ambassador James Theberge and the Pinochet government. Theberge reversed the policies of the Carter administration, refused to meet with Chilean human rights leaders, and declared that he intended to "devote all my energies to the deepening and strengthening" of his relationship with Pinochet.[76] When the administration lobbied to reestablish military aid, however, Congress refused.

U.S. policy makers eventually became discouraged with the slow pace of progress toward democracy in Chile. As other Southern Cone countries such as Argentina, Uruguay, and Brazil made successful transitions in the mid-1980s, Chile remained an aberration. Policy makers in the Reagan administration became convinced that Pinochet's intransigence about democratic transition was going to provoke increasing violence as a result of the emergence of a guerrilla organization, which unsuccessfully attempted to assassinate Pinochet in 1986. Public opinion and congressional pressure were also a factor. By 1985, U.S. policy shifted to favoring a faster transition to democracy through the development of a centrist political consensus within Chile.[77]

This policy shift was the result of the growing influence of the moderates over the hard-liners within the administration. After William Clark stepped down as national security advisor in October 1983, his hard-liner replacement, Robert McFarlane, did not have his same ability to impose the National Security Council decisions over those of the State Department.

State department policy makers began to craft policies toward Chile similar to those developed by the Carter administration. They publicly condemned the lack of progress toward democracy and human rights, grew increasingly critical of Chilean human rights practices in the State Department human rights reports, postponed visits of high-level officials, and even considered vetoing loans in the multilateral development banks. In October 1984, Assistant Secretary Abrams called for vetoing loans to Chile in the Inter-American Development Bank, but he was overruled by the Latin America Bureau and Ambassador Theberge. By December 1984, the administration finally began to use its stronger weapon—public statements by President Reagan. In a Human Rights Day speech, Reagan cited as "an affront to human consciences the lack of progress toward Democracy in Chile and Paraguay."[78]

By 1986 three crucial personnel changes had an important impact on U.S. policy toward Chile. A senior career foreign service officer, Harry Barnes, replaced James Theberge as ambassador to Chile, part of George Shultz's efforts to replace political appointees with career diplomats during the second term; Jeane Kirkpatrick was not offered a sufficiently senior position in the second Reagan administration and had returned to academia; and Elliot Abrams was named as deputy assistant secretary for Latin America. With both Theberge and Kirkpatrick gone, Pinochet lost two of his most important advocates in the Reagan administration. Abrams, a hard-liner on Central America and the main point man on Contra aid to Nicaragua, was an advocate for a prodemocracy policy in Chile. His congressional and NGO opponents had attacked him strenuously for inconsistency: he opposed the Sandinistas for their lack of democracy and yet failed to criticize authoritarian anticommunist regimes. Of course, this was the essence of the Kirkpatrick Doctrine. However, Abrams had first proposed a more even-handed policy in 1981 and still didn't have a single clear example of that policy in practice in Latin America four years later. Chile was an obvious choice, because its strong opposition movement offered a clear centrist alternative to Pinochet. Abrams's tenure as assistant secretary of state for human rights had brought him into frequent contact with the political opposition in Chile. He was aware of the ongoing repression and concerned that Pinochet's intransigent opposition to an accelerated transition to democracy could lead to increased violence. Chile was still not an "easy" case for the Reagan administration, given the strong support among its contacts on Wall Street for Pinochet and his economic policies. Shultz, who had once been dean of the Business School at the University of Chicago, also had sympathy for the economic policies of the "Chicago Boys," implemented under Pinochet.[79] Increasingly, however, as the U.S. government sought guarantees from the emerging opposition alliance that it would continue to pursue a similar neoliberal economic model, the opposition to transition declined within the U.S. government.

A crucial turning point in U.S.–Chilean relations came in early 1985 over the renewal of the state of siege. The United States made it clear that it would not vote in favor of much-needed World Bank loans unless the Chilean government met certain conditions. Privately, it was clear that lifting the state of siege was one of these crucial conditions. On June 16, Chile lifted the state of siege and on the following day, the U.S. voted in favor of a package of loans. Again, the Reagan administration officials effectively used the same human rights policy tools that Carter had used: economic pressures in exchange for specific human rights changes that could open key space for the domestic opposition.

By 1986 a bipartisan consensus was in place for a new policy, a shift that was signaled most clearly by the arrival of the new ambassador, Harry Barnes. Barnes, whose appointment had been vehemently opposed by Senator Jesse Helms, moved immediately to expand the embassy's contacts with the Chilean political opposition, inviting members of the Socialist Party to the embassy for the first time since the coup and maintaining close contact with human rights groups such as the Vicaría de Solidaridad.[80]

By 1987, increasing attention was directed toward the October 1988 plebiscite, in which the public would vote Yes or No to Pinochet's being allowed to serve as president until 1997. The United States was clearly supportive of the many sectors working within Chile in favor of a No vote, which had coalesced into an alliance of parties called the "Coalition for the NO."

In 1987, Congress agreed to appropriate $1 million for the promotion of democracy in Chile, via the National Endowment for Democracy. It also added new economic sanctions against Chile by excluding it from trade benefits under the General System of Preferences and by terminating its eligibility for OPIC insurance. But the Reagan administration also continued to offer some mixed signals, abstaining on United Nations votes against Chile for its human rights violations and abstaining on a crucial World Bank loan that allowed Pinochet financial support at a crucial time.[81]

By 1988 U.S. assistance began to benefit the opposition Coalition for the NO, engaged in a full-fledged electoral campaign against the Pinochet constitution. The United States supported the democratic opposition and helped to improve campaign conditions by providing extensive funds for voter registration, civic education, the opposition media, polling (prior and during the elections), and a crucial "quick-count" on the day of the elections. Some of the policy tools that had been used experimentally in El Salvador now came into play in Chile. Here, however, the United States was using them to support the opposition. Pinochet denounced U.S. assistance as "aggression" and foreign intervention in the domestic affairs of Chile, but U.S. policy makers argued that they were "leveling the playing field" so skewed by Pinochet's repressive regime.

The euphoria surrounding the victory of the NO vote in the plebiscite led many observers to see the Chilean case as a model for future democracy-promotion efforts. Many others attributed the victory to the "unity, political skills, and determination of the Chilean opposition." Ambassador Barnes perhaps came closest when he described U.S. aid as marginal, but significant on the margins.[82] The main lesson to take away from the Chilean campaign is one found in all success stories discussed in this book: a clear and forceful United States human rights and democracy policy makes a difference only when it interacts with strong and relatively united internal groups in favor of democracy and human rights.

By the end of the Reagan administration, the human rights policy that Reaganites had tried so hard to overturn in their first years in office had not only survived the onslaught but had added a new dimension—that of democracy promotion. This was due to several factors: firm opposition from Congress and public opinion, the desire of Reagan staff to promote a more positive image of the president, and the departure of the most intransigent supporters of the Kirkpatrick Doctrine.

In the end, human rights policy during the Reagan administration was not abandoned but transmuted into a program for the promotion of democracy. A major analyst of the Reagan administration democracy efforts concludes,

> Although the Reagan administration embraced the promoting democracy theme for its rhetorical value, there is no question that over the course of the Reagan years the theme gathered some real substance and that an administration initially unsympathetic to what it saw as moralistic crusades abroad became sincerely interested in being a force for democracy in Latin America. This shift was the result of a number of factors: three major ones stand out. The first was the consistent pressure on the Reagan administration from many Democrats in Congress to pay attention to democracy and human rights in Latin America. . . . A second cause of the rise of promoting democracy in the Reagan administration's Latin American policy was the changing balance between the moderates and hard-liners in the policy-making process. . . . The rise of promoting democracy in the Reagan administration's Latin American policy was also the result of a third cause, the tendency in U.S. foreign policy making for rhetoric to influence reality. Government officials sometimes set out lofty rhetoric on a foreign policy issue and then find that, almost without their intending it, the actual policy begins to gravitate toward that rhetorical line.[83]

When the Senate defeated the Reagan nominee for assistant secretary for human rights, who was on record expressing his disapproval of the human rights policy, it sent a message to the new administration that it would not tolerate the overt dismantling of the human rights policy. The Reagan administration next attempted what amounted to a covert dismantling of the human rights policy. It endorsed human rights in principle, but in practice it often subverted policies to goals not consistent with human rights. Over time, and especially with regard to South America, however, some members of the Reagan team changed their minds about human rights policy, in part because they became increasingly aware of broad support for human rights policies among members of Congress, the American public, and Western allies. Once adopted, the new policy in support of democracy demanded a minimal inner consistency. Reagan administration officials who used the human rights and democracy banner in their crusade against Nicaragua felt obliged occasionally to protect the administration from charges of bias by also criticizing human rights abuses in some right-wing regimes such as Chile and Uruguay.

In the United States, the institutionalization of human rights policy within laws and the policy apparatus made it more difficult for an administration much less supportive of human rights to completely abandon the policy. The institutional modifications of the 1970s, with the creation of the Bureau for Human Rights and Humanitarian Affairs in the State Department, and the delegation of human rights issues to specific congressional subcommittees, provided a strong institutional basis for human rights policies.

Although human rights policies survived the Reagan administration, and some important progress was made in thinking about more coherent policies for the promotion of democracy, there were also grave defects in the manner in which the Reagan administration implemented its policy toward Latin America. By dismissing human rights in the early years and embracing some of the more repressive dictators of the region, Reagan sent a gratuitous signal to the region, one that emboldened leaders to believe they could arrest, imprison, kill, or exile their opponents without facing any serious international repercussions. It is very difficult, of course, to provide convincing evidence for the counterfactual argument that a different Reagan administration policy would have led to different outcomes. Nevertheless, there is strong reason to believe that a clearer and more forceful initial human rights policy during the early Reagan administration could have led to significantly fewer human rights violations in both El Salvador and Guatemala during this period at little if any cost to the United States. In the context of counterinsurgency wars against guerrillas in El Salvador and Guatemala, more explicit insistence by the United States on respect for the laws of war and protection of noncombatants could have limited the civilian victims of human rights abuse.

The Reagan administration's intense distrust of the human rights organizations in both the United States and in Latin America clouded its vision and limited its ability to interpret the human rights situation on the ground. A highly politicized atmosphere where human rights concerns were discredited led the administration to underestimate the seriousness of most human rights violations in embassy reports. The U.S. government showed more ability to attack the bearers of bad news (the NGOs or the media) than to use its investigative capacity to identify human rights problems. Elliot Abrams attacked the "so-called human rights organizations" as excessively ideological. His judgment should be evaluated in light of the fact that these organizations' reporting and rendering of events have been confirmed by the work of definitive truth commissions and trials in the region time and again.

No human rights policy in U.S. history was more hotly contested in its time, or is more controversial today, than the practices and legacy of the Reagan administration. In the midst of the acrimony, it is necessary to sort out some basic conclusions. The Reagan administration's attempts to dismantle human rights policy failed. The claims that Reagan officials substituted private diplomacy for public diplomacy cannot be taken seriously. The administration's nonuse of a key tool of human rights policy—the symbolic power of public comments by the president and his closest advisors—was interpreted as a reversal, a desertion of that policy, and the very notion of a "quiet diplomacy" of human rights was puzzling to allies and critics alike. Imagine policy makers claiming that they had a "quiet" policy in favor of liberalism and free trade, although they wouldn't mention it publicly and wouldn't back it with decisions on economic or military aid.

Surprisingly, the Reagan administration succeeded in one area of human rights policy where Carter had failed. It took the first halting steps toward the adoption of multilateral human rights policy. During the presidential campaign, Ronald Reagan was approached by members of an ad hoc citizen committee working for ratification of the Genocide Treaty, composed primarily of members from Jewish organizations. According to William Korey, a key committee member and the research director for B'nai B'rith, Reagan was much more responsive to efforts to ratify the Genocide Treaty than were either Carter or Mondale. In response to a campaign promise made before the B'nai B'rith in 1984, Reagan delivered the Genocide Treaty to the Senate for ratification and signed the implementing legislation in 1988. The ratification of the Genocide Treaty finally "pried open the door" that had been closed to the ratification of human rights treaties since the Bricker debate in the 1950s.[84]

Reagan administration attempts to change human rights policy to a pro-democracy policy were more successful, but in the process a policy was created that was different from what either the Reagan policy makers or their critics intended. That policy is the true outcome of the debate and struggle of the Reagan years. In many ways it resurrected the policy tools of the Carter period, but it also invented new tools and institutions, the National Endowment for Democracy and the Administration of Justice Program being two of the more visible examples. In some cases, this hybrid policy worked to promote human rights in Latin America, but the cases where it worked were not instances of the much-vaunted private diplomacy—they were cases where high-level policy makers used the range of tools at their disposal to send a clear and unequivocal signal of their concern for human rights and their willingness to back up their signal with sanctions.

The Reagan administration made some contributions to democracy, especially in places like Chile and Paraguay. But its most significant contributions to democracy and human rights came where it abandoned the policy of "silent diplomacy" and engaged in active, consistent, and relatively high profile policies of support for democracy and for human rights. In other words, where Reagan's policy worked was where it most resembled Carter's policy, a combination of public rhetorical support backed by military and economic assistance.

The forgotten tragedy of the Reagan administration policy toward Latin America was its green light for repression in Guatemala. At the height of the only genocide in recent Latin American history, the Reagan administration gave rhetorical and moral support to a murderous regime through both its public and private diplomacy. It even attempted to provide economic and military support but was blocked in its attempts by the U.S. Congress. The Guatemalan case suggests that the rhetorical dimension of foreign policy is even more important than is usually admitted. Despite the congressional cutoff of military and economic aid, the Reagan administration sent a wide range of cues and messages that signaled its acceptance of the Guatemalan government's brutal counterinsurgency campaign. This acceptance, and the corresponding commitment not to criticize and intervene, was just what the Guatemalan government needed at that point to continue its repression.

Chapter Eight

*Institutionalizing Human Rights Policy
toward Latin America during the
George H. W. Bush and Clinton Years*

In 1999 the UN-sponsored truth commission in Guatemala, the Historical Clarification Commission, issued a report confirming that the Guatemalan state had carried out genocide resulting in as many as 200,000 deaths. The report also said that U.S. military assistance "was directed toward reinforcing the national intelligence apparatus and for training the officer corps in counterinsurgency techniques, key factors which had significant bearing on human rights violations during the armed confrontation."[1] During a visit to Guatemala after the release of the report, President Clinton offered a near apology for U.S. complicity in the violations and a statement of future policy: "I think it imperative, as we begin, for me just to say a few words about the report of the Historical Clarification Commission. . . . For the United States, it is important that I state clearly that support for military forces or intelligence units which engage in violent and widespread repression of the kind described in the report was wrong, and the United States must not repeat that mistake."[2]

And yet, only a year later, the Clinton administration embarked upon an ambitious plan to provide over a billion dollars of emergency aid for the Colombian government, 80 percent of which would go to the Colombian military to support counternarcotics operations. In the context of a bitter armed conflict with guerrilla organizations, the Colombian military had been accused both of directly engaging in human rights violations and of cooperating with paramilitary organizations that carried them out. This aid was the largest such aid package to Latin America since the end of the Cold War.

The Colombia aid package raises the question of whether U.S. human rights policy has advanced or simply circled back. Human rights policies were, I believe, strengthened and institutionalized during the administrations of George H. W. Bush and Bill Clinton, although advocates of human rights within the U.S. government continued to struggle against those with opposing visions of U.S. identity and national interests. An institutionalized human rights policy meant that human rights concerns were now a regularized part of the policy process. It did not mean that human rights concerns would dominate any particular policy decision.

By the 1990s, as the end of the Cold War diminished the importance of anticommunism in U.S. policy, the global context had changed. Multilateral and regional actors now made diverse responses to human rights violations, as evidenced by the Guatemalan Historical Clarification Commission. And within the United States, human rights policy had become institutionalized. State Department human rights reporting had improved, and the foreign service had accepted human rights policy as part of its mandate. These changes started during the last years of the Reagan administration and continued during the administrations of George H. W. Bush and Clinton. The similarities between the policies of the first Bush administration and those of the Clinton administration in relation to human rights in Latin America allow us to treat them together in the same chapter. (When I refer below to "the Bush administration," I have in mind of course the first Bush administration, that of George H. W. Bush.)

The major human rights challenges faced by both the Bush and the Clinton administrations were outside Latin America, in the former Yugoslavia, China, the Middle East, and Africa. As was the case during both Carter and Reagan, Latin American human rights issues rarely reached the top of these administrations' foreign policy agendas. Nor did they garner active and sustained attention from Congress.

Neither George H. W. Bush nor Bill Clinton had a pronounced interest in human rights, in contrast with Jimmy Carter. Nor did they exhibit a deep preoccupation with political developments in a particular Latin American country on a par with Ronald Reagan's almost obsessive focus on Nicaragua and Central America. George H. W. Bush entered office determined to refocus U.S. foreign policy on traditional allies and issues in Europe, but his attention turned early to the Gulf War and later to its aftermath. President Clinton's early commitments were to domestic policy issues, especially the economy and health policy. Indeed, Clinton asked Secretary of State Warren Christopher to keep foreign policy off his desk so he could focus on the economy in his first year in office.[3] Investigations of financial and sexual misconduct plagued the administration throughout both terms in office, limiting its ability to launch new foreign policy initiatives. Human rights issues in Latin America in the late 1980s and 1990s thus tended to be handled by officials in the State Department. The department's new "standard operating procedures" of human rights policy are therefore very important if we wish to understand the policies adopted during these administrations. Standard operating procedures had changed significantly since the Carter administration to incorporate human rights concerns as an accepted part of the foreign policy calculus.

As an exception to this general lack of attention to Latin America, the Bush and Clinton administrations both carried out military operations in the Caribbean Basin: Bush in Panama and Clinton in Haiti. The differences between these two military operations in the region tell us how the world had changed, and U.S. policy with it. Although the Bush administration used some prodemocracy language in justifying the invasion of Panama in December 1989, this invasion was similar to old-style U.S. military invasions in Latin America, designed to protect U.S. citizens, U.S. property, and U.S. security interests. But it was an old-style military invasion with a new twist—the administration also justified it as a means to bring General Manuel Noriega to trial on drug charges. Rather than the harbinger of a new style of military intervention to promote democracy and human rights that we would later see in the case of Haiti, the Panama invasion was similar to earlier invasions like that of Grenada in 1983 during the Reagan administration. The UN General Assembly and the OAS General Assembly both deplored the Panama intervention, viewing it as a violation of international law. Only the Thatcher government of the United Kingdom voiced active support.

Although not justified as part of human rights policy, the Panama invasion had human rights effects, both positive and negative. Human rights organizations documented genuine improvements in the human rights situation in Panama with the return to civilian rule after the invasion. A report by Human Rights Watch, issued a year and a half after the invasion, reported that the Panamanian State "is not systematically engaged in acts of physical violence against its citizens; criminal law no longer is employed routinely to suppress political dissent; freedom of expression, while not absolute, is exercised and respected; and courts and prosecutors, though still subject to political direction and influence, operate far more independently than they did under the Noriega regime."[4] Human Rights Watch also documented ongoing human rights problems in Panama, especially the prolonged pretrial detentions and overcrowded and violent prisons. By defeating and weakening the Panamanian defense forces, which had been responsible for most of the violations of human rights in Panama, the invasion may have contributed to improving the situation of human rights and democracy in Panama. But it left an estimated three hundred civilians dead. Humanitarian law requires militaries to minimize harm to civilians, yet civilian casualties were far higher than military casualties among Panamanian or U.S. troops.[5] Prior to the invasion, the Panamanian defense forces had used excessive force against demonstrators, resulting in some executions and many injuries. They arbitrarily arrested hundreds of individuals for political reasons and held them without trial in harsh conditions, frequently torturing and abusing them. Noriega had annulled elections apparently won by Guillermo Endara and had himself sworn in as Panama's new president. The serious human rights violations of the Noriega regime, however, were minor compared to the much more significant violations in Guatemala and El Salvador in the 1980s. Over the five years preceding the U.S. invasion of Panama, Amnesty International's *Annual Reports* list a combined death toll of twenty-one or twenty-two people from summary execution by Panamanian security forces.[6] About fourteen times more Panamanian civilians were killed during the invasion than those killed by Panamanian security forces in the five preceding years. Military intervention can be justified only when the situation is so grave that immediate intervention is necessary to stem massive violations of human rights. The human cost of the invasion should not be far greater than the lives lost during the repressive regime. Panama thereby doesn't even begin to meet the definition of humanitarian intervention.

The threatened military invasion of Haiti in 1994 was quite different than that of Panama. In the case of Haiti, the United States used economic sanctions, threatened military invasion, and eventually put a military peacekeeping force on the ground in Haiti for over five years. The main U.S. security interest at stake was the flow of Haitian refugees to U.S. shores. NGOs and some members of Congress criticized the Clinton administration for sending Haitians intercepted at sea back to a situation of grave human rights abuses under the authoritarian Cedras regime in Haiti. The political effect of the intervention was eventually to allow Jean-Bertrand Aristide, a leftist priest, to regain the presidency stolen from him in a right-wing military coup. U.S. policy in Haiti was carried out in tight cooperation with the United Nations and the OAS. In the early 1990s, both the OAS and the UN Security Council had imposed embargoes and comprehensive economic sanctions, not to be lifted until President Aristide was restored. When the sanctions began to seriously undermine the well-being of the poor in Haiti without loosening the control of the military leaders, the UN Security Council authorized a multinational peacekeeping force to use "all necessary means" to facilitate the departure of the military leadership from Haiti. President Clinton held back the U.S.-led multinational invasion of Haiti to allow a delegation headed by former president Jimmy Carter and including General Colin Powell to carry out final negotiations with the Haitian military. The Carter delegation secured a last-minute agreement from General Cedras to step down, and U.S. troops arrived peacefully on September 11, 1994, to oversee the return of President Aristide.[7]

The resolution of this first major post–Cold War crisis in Latin America was unprecedented. For the first time, the U.S. government, backed by the United Nations, was willing to use the threat of military intervention to reverse a military coup, even though the situation raised no serious national security interests for the United States; nor did it present a threat to international peace and security, previously a requirement for UN Security Council endorsement of military action. Contrary to the case of Panama, the United States operated within the context of multilateral diplomacy, and it achieved its ends without open combat and the loss of large numbers of civilian casualties.[8] This last-minute agreement with the Haitian regime, however, prevented U.S. forces from disarming either the Haitian military or the right-wing paramilitary groups responsible for the violations of human rights. Eventually, the Haitian government reached an accord to abolish the army, and the United States acquiesced to the demilitarization process. The Clinton administration also failed to follow up on the occupation with ample financial support for the institution building and economic development needed to support democratization.[9]

The Institutionalization of Human Rights Policy

By January 1989, when President George H. W. Bush took office, U.S. human rights policy had become an institutionalized part of the U.S. foreign policy apparatus. It is indeed noteworthy that Bush administration personnel did *not* make efforts similar to those of the Reagan administration to dismantle human rights policy. A survey of the presidential papers during the administration of George H. W. Bush reveals that he did not even pay lip service to human rights. On those occasions when the president did mention human rights, he tended to refer to repression in Iraq or China. The president, particularly in the early years of his administration (1989–90), stressed the same themes of democracy and freedom that the Reagan administration had introduced and sustained since 1983, especially in his speeches lauding the end of the Cold War.[10] And yet, because human rights policy had been institutionalized, policy makers continued to implement it despite the lack of strong interest shown by the president and his top appointees.

Richard Shifter, appointed assistant secretary for human rights in 1985 during the Reagan administration, continued during the Bush administration. Shifter, an Austrian Jew who lost his parents in the Holocaust, was a member of the "neocons" who had been active during the Reagan administration. He shared with Jeane Kirkpatrick and Elliot Abrams an intense anticommunism and a tendency to see human rights through that lens. Shifter gave hundreds of speeches on human rights topics during his tenure, almost all of which he wrote himself, and raised the rhetorical profile of human rights discourse. Shifter was most interested and involved in human rights policy toward the USSR and other communist countries. But during his tenure, the end of the Cold War opened more space for human rights concerns, and Shifter took advantage of that space to raise human rights issues with other governments, including Israel, Chile, and Taiwan.

According to Shifter and other actors familiar with human rights policy during the Bush administration, the foreign service increasingly accepted human rights as part of its job description at this time. Initially, the foreign service had resisted the idea of incorporating human rights into foreign policy. Generations of foreign service officers had received no training in human rights. Human rights, furthermore, ran against the grain of their training, which taught them to maintain cordial relations with their counterparts in foreign governments. Ambassadors tended to see other governments as clients, even if the government was authoritarian. Human rights policy required the embassy to reconceive its mission, especially when human rights issues put ambassadors in conflict with governments. The long-term relations with the people of the country, not necessarily the government in power, had become the ambassador's priority. Even foreign service officers who were open to this new concept didn't initially have the skills to do the new work, since they were familiar neither with human rights organizations nor with the process of documenting human rights violations.

The Bureau of Human Rights and Humanitarian Affairs, which Congress required the State Department to establish, embodied human rights concerns in the foreign policy apparatus and created bureaucratic interests based on the perpetuation of these concerns. The creation of the Human Rights Bureau was a crucial turning point in U.S. policy, but it took years for the bureau to gain status and capability. At the same time as it created the bureau, Congress also required the State Department to issue annual human rights reports on each country receiving U.S. aid. This requirement altered the job requirements of at least one foreign service officer in every embassy around the globe, who for the first time had to gather systematic information on human rights abuses. Shifter pointed out that having to prepare human rights reports helped "enlist the foreign service" in human rights policy. Human rights officers were responsible each year for drafting the cables used to write the human rights reports. In order to do the job right, these foreign service officials had to be in contact with the opposition, read opposition newspapers, and attend meetings. In this process, some foreign service officials "became friendly with persecuted people" and were sensitized to human rights concerns. "Younger people began to grow up in a foreign service with human rights on the agenda, and they began to accept it."[11] The Human Rights Bureau was often seen as a "backwater assignment," not in the mainstream of U.S. foreign policy in the same way as the regional bureaus. But over time, as human rights became increasingly important in the formulation of policy, it lost some of its marginal status. By 1992 human rights thinking had been inculcated into the decision-making process. The end of the Cold War gave impetus to human rights policy. In the words of one foreign service officer, "we can pursue these concerns more freely without worrying that the other side is going to take advantage."[12]

One clear indicator of the institutionalization of human rights policy was the changing nature of the annual country reports. As the staff of the Human Rights Bureau grew and gained experience, their published reports acquired greater detail and accuracy. Mutually reinforcing links were established—not always congenial ones—between human rights NGOs and the bureaucratic and institutional interests. NGO lobbying contributed to the adoption of human rights legislation. NGOs contributed to human rights legislation by providing information about human rights abuses, by graphically bringing human rights to the attention of members of Congress and staff through personal testimony, and by encouraging the public to write to their representatives in support of human rights. As Shifter pointed out in a speech, "During my years in government service, I have been struck by the attention paid by the State Department to letters received from members of Congress, particularly those who hold key positions on committees of concern to the department. And I have noted how often small groups of constituents can persuade a member to weigh in on behalf of their cause."[13]

Relations between the State Department and human rights NGOs were often conflictive. A former official in the Human Rights Bureau, for example, said: "There is such disdain for the community of nongovernmental organizations at the State Department. At State, you can't talk to these organizations with ease, so you are left talking to each other."[14] Yet the Human Rights Bureau considered the human rights NGOs as one of its core constituencies and valued its fluid relations with these groups.

Country human rights reports provide a clear example of this interaction. Because State Department officials didn't want to offend officials in a country, or undermine other policy goals, their human rights reports were often weak. But these reports then served as a focal point for human rights groups, who created an annual event by issuing responses to the State Department reports.[15] The reports and counterreports attracted press coverage on human rights, and the critiques of its reports held the State Department up to higher standards. Shifter pointed out that he asked his staff to peruse these critiques for factual allegations and omissions.

During the Bush administration, the Senate ratified several basic human rights treaties. This was both a key advance and further evidence of the institutionalization of human rights policy. In 1991 the United States ratified the Convention on the Abolition of Forced Labor and the Convention against Torture and Other Cruel, Inhuman or Degrading Treatment or Punishment, and in 1992 it ratified the Covenant on Civil and Political Rights. The Carter administration had signed this covenant and submitted it to the Senate in 1978. When the Senate held hearings in 1979, witnesses and senators revealed many of the same attitudes that had led to the Bricker amendment in 1953.[16] Yet by 1992 the legacy of the Bricker coalition appeared to be dying in the Senate, as even Senator Jesse Helms eventually voted in favor of recommending ratification of the Covenant on Civil and Political Rights.[17]

A number of important changes had occurred. An important lobby against UN human rights treaties in the 1950s, the American Bar Association, reversed its position in the late 1970s.[18] Most important, however, were changes in international conditions. With the transformation of the former Soviet Union and Eastern Europe, U.S. officials expressed increased confidence in multilateral institutions, including the United Nations. Administration testimony on the Covenant on Civil and Political Rights stated that a "radically altered world picture" led them to change their position on ratifying the Covenant. "Ratification of the Covenant would have been an empty gesture 10 years ago, but now it has new meaning and effect."[19] Specifically, without ratification of the covenant, the United States could not be a member of the UN Human Rights Committee. The administration believed that the Human Rights Committee would become a central forum for shaping future international human rights law, and without ratification the United States would be marginalized from that process.

Richard Shifter pushed particularly hard for ratification of the Covenant on Civil and Political Rights. Before the fall of the Soviet Union, he explained, he thought that "with the Soviet Union and all the members of the Soviet bloc having ratified it, the covenant was damaged goods. It was just signing on to a fraud. When the Soviet Union and the whole Soviet Bloc changed and then began to take this stuff seriously, I thought that under the circumstances we were dealing with a totally different situation, and we should ratify it and I started pushing for it."[20]

Concerns with human rights and democracy were also becoming institutionalized within the inter-American system at this time. Between 1990 and 1993, strong normative developments occurred in the region around the "right to democracy." At the 1991 OAS General Assembly meeting in Santiago, all thirty-five member states declared "their firm political commitment to the promotion and protection of human rights and representative democracy." The General Assembly unanimously approved Resolution 1080, which instructs the secretary-general to convene an emergency meeting of OAS foreign ministers to decide on a collective reaction "in the case of any event giving rise to the sudden or irregular interruption of a democratic government." The resolution proved to be an effective means of coordinating and legitimating political sanctions by member states.

In 1992 the members of the OAS took this commitment to democracy further and amended the OAS charter to include Article 9, which gives the General Assembly the power to suspend from membership by a two-thirds vote any government that overthrows a democratic regime. This important reform was originally proposed by Argentina and was supported by all OAS members except Mexico. Although the amendment didn't enter into force until 1997, it enhanced the perception of support for democracy norms in the Americas.[21]

The Santiago Declaration and Resolution 1080 provided the procedural means for the rapid regional response to the military coups in Peru, Guatemala, and Haiti and put the OAS in the forefront of international organizations acting to promote democracy. U.S. policy thus took place within a regional framework that was very different from the context of a decade earlier.

The First Bush Administration and Human Rights Policy in Latin America

The major initiatives of the Bush administration toward Latin America focused on measures to combat drug trafficking and to promote investment, free trade, privatization, and debt reduction (including the Enterprise for the Americas Initiative and the Brady Plan). The end of the Cold War led to a change in foreign policy priorities during the Bush administration. Anticommunism became a less compelling justification for human rights violations, and the Bush administration began to distance itself from dictators in some parts of the world, such as Mobutu in Zaire and Moi in Kenya.[22] But in Latin America at this time, with the exception of Cuba, the issue was not dictatorship but the continuing high level of human rights violations in the formally democratic regimes of El Salvador, Guatemala, Colombia, and Peru.

The crucial Latin American human rights issues during the first period of the Bush administration were the still unresolved conflicts in El Salvador and Nicaragua. The main in-depth academic studies of U.S. policy toward El Salvador and Nicaragua concur that the Bush administration departed from the Reagan policy of military victory in El Salvador and military destabilization of Nicaragua.[23] Bush administration officials negotiated with Congress to find an "exit strategy" for the Contra war against Nicaragua. They focused instead on the bipartisan goal of free elections in Nicaragua, a goal the Sandinistas had committed themselves to as part of the Central American peace process.[24] The Sandinistas' defeat in elections in Nicaragua in 1990 both effectively took Nicaragua off the U.S. policy agenda and, by signaling the willingness of former revolutionary actors to play by democratic rules, opened up new possibilities in El Salvador.

El Salvador

Change in El Salvador took longer. Although the end of the Cold War altered the general context for policy in Central America, it took a dramatic event and shock to rearrange policy makers' basic assumptions underpinning U.S. policy toward this country. The FMLN guerrilla offensive against the city of San Salvador in November 1989 demonstrated that the Salvadoran government's claims to be winning the war were exaggerated. At the same time, the failure of the FMLN offensive to ignite a widespread popular revolt suggested that neither side could win the war.

In the midst of the FMLN offensive, on the evening of November 15, 1989, several dozen soldiers from the special commando unit of the U.S.-trained Atlactl Battalion went to the Jesuit-run Central American University, pulled five Jesuit priests from their beds (among them the rector, Ignacio Ellacuria), forced them to lie face down, and executed them. They also killed the Jesuits' housekeeper and her daughter, who had witnessed the executions. The soldiers wrote graffiti to implicate the FMLN in the killings. Most observers rejected the suggestion that the FMLN had killed the priests, since they lacked both a motive and the capability of operating in the zone where the university was located. The guerrillas did not see the Jesuits as enemies, and Ellacuria had been actively seeking a negotiated resolution to the conflict. The military, under the leadership of Colonel Guillermo Benavides, was in charge of a special security zone including the university, the Defense Ministry, and the armed forces joint command headquarters. U.S. Ambassador Walker and many embassy staff nonetheless accepted the story of the massacre as the work of guerrillas for weeks. Eventually the State Department condemned the murders and demanded a full investigation.[25]

The murders shocked the public and policy makers in the United States who had been told that human rights abuses were on the decrease. As it became clearer over the following months that the murders were carried out by the U.S.-trained elite battalion, at the orders of the highest levels of the Salvadoran military, claims that U.S. training was transforming the Salvadoran military sounded hollow.

This realization galvanized congressional critics of aid to El Salvador, who made it clear that aid would dry up unless the government of El Salvador made progress toward a negotiated settlement of the conflict. Under pressure from Congress, the Bush administration reversed the Reagan policy of intransigent support only for a military solution and finally became supportive of political negotiations. The new ARENA president, Alfredo Cristiani, initiated negotiations with greater commitment than in the past. Although the U.S. government came to support the peace negotiations very late, the clear warning by Congress that aid would be cut off may have provided a final impetus to the Salvadoran government to reach an agreement.[26]

Guatemala

U.S. relations with Guatemala had improved after 1985, when the elected government of Vinicio Cerezo took office. Under the new constitution of 1985, the Cerezo government recognized the legitimacy of international human rights norms. The 1985 constitution mandated the preeminence of international law over domestic law in human rights matters and created an independent human rights ombudsman office to investigate human rights abuses, recommend policy changes, and censure or promote legal action against human rights violators.[27] Initially, however, the ombudsman was not able to systematically address abuses, nor could the office help protect nongovernmental human rights monitors. Violations continued at high levels, and the military operated with autonomy from the civilian government.[28]

During the Bush administration, two well-documented Guatemalan cases revealed how the CIA often worked at cross-purposes with the emerging human rights policy. Congressional hearings, press reports, and executive branch documents released through the Freedom of Information Act have since allowed us to piece together parts of the story.

On June 9, 1990, armed men kidnapped and killed Michael Devine, an American innkeeper living in Guatemala. His wife, Carole Devine, immediately hired a private investigator and a lawyer and contacted the U.S. embassy for help. U.S. government sources later confirmed that after a few weeks, they became convinced of the involvement of the Guatemalan military in the murder. U.S. Ambassador Thomas Stroock took intense personal interest in the case and made it a test for U.S.–Guatemalan relations. Stroock demanded that the Guatemalan government bring to trial the soldiers responsible for the murder. Unsatisfied with the progress of the investigation, he requested and secured a cutoff of U.S. military aid to Guatemala in 1990. In December 1990, just three weeks before President Cerezo was to hand over power to the newly elected government of Jorge Serrano, the United States cut off $2.8 million in military aid because of Guatemala's failure to criticize or exhaustively investigate those responsible for human rights abuses.

When President Serrano took office, he said that his government would refuse a renewal of U.S. military aid. "They offered us $100,000 and a human rights checklist, . . . but as president I'm not going to accept their orders. Our dignity must be respected. My government has decided not to accept their military aid."[29] Nevertheless, the Serrano government did pursue the Devine case more seriously and in 1992 secured the conviction of five soldiers for the murder. A sixth soldier, an officer, was convicted but apparently immediately allowed to escape from prison. He has never been located.[30]

In 1991 an American human rights lawyer, Jennifer Harbury, married the Guatemalan guerrilla leader Efraín Bamaca. He disappeared after a skirmish with the military in March 1992, and the army announced that they had buried a body after the combat. Harbury assumed he was dead until an escaped URNG combatant told her that he had seen Bamaca detained and tortured in two army bases in 1992. Harbury began a vigorous campaign to locate Bamaca. She argued that it was illegal to detain and torture prisoners in clandestine prisons, and that the government should have him reappear in prison and then put him on trial for any crimes of which they accused him. Harbury carried out three hunger strikes in Guatemala and in Washington with the goal of securing information about the whereabouts of her husband. Two years later, during the filming of a *60 Minutes* story on the Bamaca case and the Harbury hunger strike, the journalist Mike Wallace told her that the CIA had long ago sent a cable to the U.S. embassy and State Department revealing that Bamaca had been captured alive by the Guatemalan army. The U.S. ambassador in turn stated her belief that Bamaca was dead, but she wouldn't provide Harbury with the basis for this belief. It would take a whole year until Representative Torricelli of the House Intelligence Committee informed Harbury about an anonymous communication stating that a Guatemalan army colonel and CIA-paid "asset" named Alpirez had given the order to kill Bamaca sometime in 1992. Torricelli also revealed that the same Alpirez had given the order to kill Michael Devine several years earlier.[31] Torricelli's accusation generated extensive press coverage, hearings in the Senate Select Committee on Intelligence, a review by the House Permanent Select Committee on Intelligence, and an investigation by the President's Intelligence Oversight Board. They concluded that the CIA failed to notify congressional committees of the case and that the CIA headquarters and station did not keep ambassadors appropriately informed. The reports also implicate Alpirez in the torture of Bamaca.[32] It is noteworthy that Alpirez received substantial payment as a CIA asset *after* he was implicated in both the Devine and Bamaca cases.

These cases raise the issue of how to evaluate human rights policy whenever a distinct foreign policy is carried out by the CIA. In principle, the CIA is mandated to collect and analyze information but not make foreign policy. In this case, the agency overstepped these bounds and apparently advocated a foreign policy different from that of the embassy. Any foreign policy is more forceful when the executive branch speaks with one voice. In the case of human rights policy toward Guatemala, the United States once again sent mixed signals. On the one hand, the embassy was stressing its support for democracy and human rights. On the other, the CIA was paying members of the Guatemalan military for information, apparently aware that these individuals were implicated in crimes against U.S. and Guatemalan citizens and that some of the information they were purchasing was almost certainly extracted under torture. Investigations suggest that the CIA sometimes failed to keep ambassadors informed about their activities, which compromised the ambassadors' efforts to carry out coherent policy. The Guatemalan government may have interpreted this as tacit U.S. government support.

Some U.S. government spokespersons claimed that the information gathered by the CIA formed an essential part of the human rights demarches that the United States made to foreign governments. But a close look at human rights reporting reveals that the great bulk of human rights information comes from public sources, especially domestic human rights organizations, rather than from CIA assets. The taboo against revealing publicly any criticism of the CIA, for fear of endangering U.S. intelligence-gathering capabilities, makes it very difficult to end this two-track diplomacy. In the case of Devine and Bamaca, only the exceptionally forceful campaigns of their wives, with the support of the news media, brought the episodes to light.

The Clinton Administration and Human Rights Policy in Latin America

By the time the Clinton administration came into office in January 1993, most of the countries discussed in this book had made the transition to democracy and had experienced a significant decrease in human rights violations. As in the Bush administration, therefore, Latin America was not at the center of debate over human rights and U.S. policy during the two Clinton terms in office.[33]

Bill Clinton focused on domestic policy rather than foreign policy in the 1992 campaign. Indeed, he attacked Bush for being so engaged with foreign policy that he ignored the economic problems of ordinary Americans. But when Clinton discussed foreign policy, he argued that "our nation has a higher purpose than to coddle dictators and stand aside from the global movement toward democracies," and he criticized Bush for preferring a foreign policy that "embraces stability at the expense of freedom."[34]

Clinton invoked American identity when he discussed democracy promotion. "A pro-democracy foreign policy is neither liberal nor conservative; neither Democrat nor Republican; it is a deep American tradition. And this is for good reason. For no foreign policy can long succeed if it does not reflect the enduring values of the American people."[35] Clinton carried through on his commitment in some critical foreign policy appointments. He named John Shattuck as his assistant secretary of state for human rights. Few nominees for this post have longer experience with civil and human rights concerns than Shattuck, who had worked for thirteen years with the American Civil Liberties Union, been the vice-chairman of Amnesty International USA, and taught human rights courses at Harvard University. Other appointments likewise signaled a commitment to a liberal internationalist foreign policy of promoting democracy and human rights.

Guatemala

Despite the return to electoral politics in 1985, by the beginning of the Clinton administration Guatemala was still far from democratic. Power was not effectively exercised by elected officials; the military evaded executive control, and continuing human rights abuses made it impossible for citizens to meaningfully and safely exercise democratic freedoms. Nevertheless, electoral politics and a somewhat improved human rights climate opened space for the growth of a more vibrant political and civil society. Although civilian presidents didn't control the military, the legislature and the judiciary had gained some independent life, and NGOs, political parties, and grassroots social movements developed throughout the country.

A significant "critical juncture" for democracy in Guatemala came in May 1993, when the elected president Jorge Serrano carried out a "self-coup" by closing the legislature and judiciary and censoring the press. International and domestic pressures combined to force the military to step in and remove Serrano from power. Many human rights organizations, both domestic and international, were now addressing rights violations in Guatemala. Domestically at least five nongovernmental human rights organizations had been set up by the early 1990s, as well as the human rights ombudsman's office. Internationally a large number of human rights organizations were publishing reports on Guatemala.

These organizations, in turn, had been able to work together with more effective leverage from governments and international organizations. Immediately after the self-coup, networks of European NGOs disseminated information on developments in Guatemala that they received from their Guatemalan counterparts. These networks then coordinated a lobbying effort to pressure governments and the European Political Cooperation to take a strong position in opposition to the Guatemalan coup.[36] Later Germany announced it would suspend $78 million of aid to Guatemala, and the Dutch also conditioned their aid on the restoration of parliamentary democracy. The United States immediately suspended all military and police aid and most economic aid to Guatemala, stating that it would press for sanctions against Guatemala at an emergency meeting of the OAS. President Clinton's spokesperson issued a short but strongly worded statement that read: "This illegitimate course of action threatens to place Guatemala outside the democratic community of nations. We strongly condemn efforts to resolve Guatemala's problems through nondemocratic means. We hope the Guatemalan leadership will reverse its course, and immediately restore full constitutional democracy."[37] One of the most powerful sanctions was the U.S. threat to withdraw Guatemala's trade benefits under the General System of Preferences (GSP).

Two large groups in Guatemalan civil society formed (the Multisectoral Forum, led by the business association CACIF, and the Social Multisectoral Forum, led by unions and social movements) and took leadership to oppose the coup and press for a return to democracy.[38] Once Serrano was out, politicians, under pressure from organized citizens in the streets, unexpectedly elected the former human rights ombudsman Ramiro de Leon Carpio as the new president of Guatemala.

To most observers of Latin American politics, this scenario was surprising.

For decades, Guatemalan regimes had been among the most severe violators of human rights and the most impervious to international human rights pressures. What had changed? The Guatemalan case illustrates the way a society can move from less democracy to more, and the role that international forces play in that process. It shows that in the last instance, internal forces must be the promoters and protectors of democracy. External groups can nonetheless offer crucial support and assistance and thus foster the growth of political and civil society.

U.S. policy was only one factor among many influencing the direction of human rights and democracy in Guatemala.[39] Prompt and forceful international action combined with internal pressures brought about the change. Human rights organizations established in the mid-1980s linked up with newly formed state-level offices, especially the Office of the Human Rights Ombudsman and the newly formed Constitutional Court, to work together toward human rights change.

Bilateral policies toward Guatemala were made more effective because they were coordinated with and channeled through the OAS. Just four days after the coup, an OAS fact-finding mission headed by the secretary-general of the OAS, João Baena Soares, arrived in Guatemala. The mission's discussions with diverse groups in civil society helped them send a clear message to Serrano and members of the military high command: the self-coup had violated the constitution, and unless a legal resolution was found to the crisis, the OAS would probably adopt economic sanctions against the country.[40]

The action against Serrano in 1993 marks a critical moment in Guatemala's movement toward democracy. Had the self-coup been allowed to go forward, it is unlikely that the progress in securing peace and human rights would have developed. By the late 1990s, however, the government had signed a peace agreement with the guerrillas, and the United Nations in-country human rights verification mission, known as MINUGUA, documented significant reductions in the level of human rights violations.[41] Two major truth commissions issued devastating reports about past human rights violations. Guatemalan human rights victims, as well as their families and NGOs, directly began to use the domestic judicial system to file cases against state officials.[42]

Vienna 1993

The high point of a human rights foreign policy during Clinton's first term came in June 1993 at the World Conference on Human Rights in Vienna. Secretary of State Warren Christopher made a forceful speech on human rights, reaffirming the importance of national values and identity in U.S. human rights policy: "Over the course of the last two centuries, Americans have found that advancing democratic values and human rights serve our deepest values as well as our practical interest. . . . That is why President Clinton has made reinforcing democracy and protecting human rights a pillar of our foreign policy. . . . Our agenda for freedom must embrace every prisoner of conscience, every victim of torture, every individual denied basic human rights." Human rights NGOs gave the administration high marks for its rhetoric and performance at the conference. The United States was particularly active in helping secure two key advances in the human rights agenda: the explicit incorporation of women's rights into human rights discourse and institutions, and the creation of the position of a UN high commissioner for human rights.

The high hopes of Vienna were dissipated in the foreign and domestic policy crises the Clinton administration soon confronted. The debacle of U.S. troops killed in Somalia and the inability to resolve the crisis in Bosnia contributed to U.S. unwillingness to intervene to block genocide in Rwanda. After the catastrophic Democratic defeat in the midterm elections of 1994, when Republicans gained control of the Senate and won a majority in the House for the first time since 1954, the possibility of a joint foreign policy agenda involving Congress disappeared.

As a result of these crises, which were largely out of the control of the Clinton administration, human rights issues were sidelined during most of the first term and into the second. By 1997 John Shattuck found himself forced into a "human rights ghetto" in the State Department after he lost bureaucratic struggles to advocates of trade, jobs, and national security.

China policy was perceived as a crucial test case for human rights policy during the Clinton administration. During the campaign, Clinton criticized the Bush administration for being soft on China and committed himself to a more forceful stand against human rights violations there. Specifically, Clinton called for ending China's trade status as a most favored nation (MFN). This policy was advocated by human rights organizations and was strongly supported by Shattuck. But it had the disadvantage of applying human rights policy conditionality to an issue where it had rarely been used successfully: trade policy and MFN status.

The retraction or not granting of MFN status had never been used in Latin America. The closest example was Cuba, which was subject to an even more far-reaching trade embargo. But in the case of Cuba, there was little evidence that these trade embargoes had any positive effect on human rights. Clinton signed an executive order saying that the MFN status could only be renewed if China could demonstrate progress on seven major areas. But China resisted, and Clinton discovered he had inadequate support for such conditionality within his own administration and in Congress. The strong business lobby, anxious for better access to the huge Chinese market, also opposed it. Eventually, the Clinton administration backed down. On the advice of the Commerce and Treasury departments, the administration decided to "de-link" trade and human rights. This didn't necessarily entail defeat for the human rights movement, but since Shattuck and the human rights community had invested considerable effort and prestige in the campaign over China policy, it was nonetheless perceived as a loss.

Ultimately, Clinton would be remembered primarily as a president who put "economic diplomacy at the core of his diplomacy," often arguing that capitalism and free trade would lead to political change and democracy.[43] But a policy of "constructive engagement" could often be an excuse for abandoning a strong human rights agenda and substituting the hope that economic engagement would indirectly contribute to progress in human rights.

Clinton's Second Term

During Clinton's second term, human rights policy gained somewhat more prominence than during the first. Like Bush, Clinton was not strongly committed to human rights in foreign policy. A review of his presidential papers and his annual speeches to the UN found no more attention to human rights issues than that of the Bush administration, and less rhetorical attention to the issues of democracy and freedom.[44] He did appoint staff with high levels of commitment, however. For the most part, he also supported their work. This was particularly apparent in his second term.

For his secretary of state Clinton chose Madeleine Albright, a woman who argued that democracy and human rights had been "the lodestars of my entire life," while adding that she was very pragmatic.[45] Albright, born in Czechoslovakia, had moved with her family to the United States when she was eleven. Her father had been a Czech diplomat and cared passionately about international events, a passion Albright inherited.[46] Albright did not have a background and interests in Latin American political issues, though she had worked effectively for a more forceful policy toward Haiti and Cuba while U.S. ambassador to the United Nations during Clinton's first term. "You can depart voluntarily and soon," she told Haitian dictators in July 1994, "or you can depart involuntarily and soon."[47] In February 1996, when she denounced Cuba for shooting down two civilian planes, she became a heroine of the Cuban-American community in Florida. Borrowing the vulgarity of the Cuban fighter pilots' boasting of the attack, Albright stated that "This is not *cojones* [balls], this is cowardice." This support may have helped her secure the appointment as secretary of state from Clinton, who had trouble gaining the support of Cuban voters.[48]

The assistant secretary of state for democracy, human rights, and labor during 1998–2001, Harold Hongju Koh, resembled Albright in a number of respects. He was also the child of a diplomat who had taken refuge from repression in the United States. Koh's family became political exiles after the Korean coup d'état in 1960. While a law professor at Yale University, Koh and his law students had spearheaded a series of high-profile human rights lawsuits, in some cases against the U.S. government. When the Clinton administration took office, Koh was suing it for human rights violations as counsel for Haitian refugees. These refugees had been intercepted on the high seas while trying to escape Haiti and come to the United States; they were either returned to Haiti or held in a camp in Guantanamo, Cuba, by the American authorities. Koh said that for him, "the Haitian litigation was a career-transforming experience. During the three thousand hours that I worked on the case, I was driven by the memory of my own parents and how they had found refuge in the country. It was because of America's willingness to take them in that I became a lawyer. When the Haitians did precisely the same thing, however, they were summarily returned to those from whom they were fleeing."[49]

When Albright asked Koh to be the assistant secretary of state for human rights, his first thought was that he had "far more to lose than to gain by joining the U.S. government." Koh sought the advice of his old professor at Harvard, the late Abram Chayes, a former legal adviser at the State Department who later successfully sued the United States at the World Court for mining Nicaraguan harbors as part of its support for the Contra war. Chayes argued that whether inside or outside of government, "there's nothing wrong with an American lawyer holding the United States to its own best standards."[50] Koh had also worked on cases of Cuban boat people seeking to keep from being returned to Cuba. The Cuban community wrote letters on his behalf to senators, including Jesse Helms, which may help explain why Koh was confirmed so easily.[51]

When he first arrived at the State Department, a colleague took him aside and said, "You know, in the State Department, we hate four things—political appointees, functional bureaus, lawyers, and professors."[52] Koh fit all four categories. But Koh soon surprised his detractors and turned out to be a far more effective assistant secretary for human rights than predicted. Central to his effectiveness was the support he received from Albright. "Albright was key," he said. "Here is a person living the human rights story. We are never going to have a secretary of state who cares more about human rights in the fiber of her being."[53] The bulk of Koh's work was not focused on Latin America, but crucial Latin American issues were on the agenda. One of these was Colombia.

Colombia

Colombia was the most controversial human rights issue in Latin America that faced the Clinton administration. The Bush administration's preoccupation with drug trafficking in Colombia had overshadowed its concern for human rights. Despite strong evidence of violations in its own human rights country reports, the Bush administration formally determined that Colombia was meeting the human rights conditions that U.S. law requires for antinarcotics security assistance. Under Bush, substantial military and economic assistance was provided to Colombia.[54]

The Clinton administration initially continued the policies of the Bush administration. By the mid-1990s, however, the Clinton administration moved to a strategy that combined support for counternarcotics and counterinsurgency with support for the peace process, while at the same time trying to stress human rights. Administration officials were frustrated both by the Colombian armed forces' reluctance to engage in counternarcotics operations and by the human rights violations of the military. During the Ernesto Samper presidency, bilateral relations reached a low point. On a number of occasions, the State Department announced that it could not certify that Colombia was cooperating with U.S. antinarcotics objectives and initiated sanctions mandated by law. During this period aid levels remained relatively modest, and assistance was provided primarily to Colombia's police force.

This policy was supported by Congress. In 1996 Congress passed the Leahy provision, legislation aimed at preventing international antinarcotics funds from going to members of foreign security forces who violate human rights. Specifically, the provision prohibits funding to any unit of a foreign security force if there is credible evidence that the unit engages in gross human rights abuses and if no effective measures are being taken to bring those responsible to justice. The Leahy provision applies to any country, but it has been most significant in Colombia.[55] In attempting to apply the provision, however, the United States discovered that is was very difficult to find units with no history of human rights violations in Colombia.

In December 1998 a cooperation agreement with the Colombian military laid the groundwork for a shift in policy. This agreement established a bilateral working group of U.S. and Colombian defense officials and created a counternarcotics battalion staffed by the Colombian army and equipped and trained by the United States.[56]

In 1999 Congress introduced country-specific legislation with human rights conditions that required Colombia's military to break long-standing ties to paramilitary groups, pursue these groups in the field, and prosecute those responsible for repression. Both the White House and the Colombian government lobbied heavily against the conditions. Unable to defeat the legislation, supporters of military aid were able to insert an amendment that allowed the president to waive the conditions if he determined that aid was in the national security interests of the United States.

President Clinton exercised this waiver in August 2000, thus permitting lethal weapons, intelligence support, and counterinsurgency training to flow to the Colombian military, even while many of its units were working with paramilitary forces responsible for human rights violations. "Behind closed doors, administration officials said strict enforcement of human rights law was impractical given the need to fight drug trafficking."[57]

Colombia's situation in the 1990s was broadly similar to that of El Salvador or Guatemala in the 1980s. In all cases, repressive governments and their paramilitary allies faced major guerrilla insurgencies, leading to massive violations of human rights. But there were important differences. The Colombian guerrillas carried out more human rights violations than their counterparts in Central America. Because of the drug trade, there were more actors with vested interests in the continuation of violent politics.[58] Clinton policy makers were nonetheless more committed to promoting peace in Colombia than the Reagan administration was to conflict resolution in Guatemala and El Salvador. Nevertheless, the Clinton administration appeared to be forgetting a key lesson of the Central American crisis. By providing extensive military and financial support for the Colombia military and simultaneously waiving or relaxing human rights conditions, the United States strengthened the military's grip and lost crucial leverage over its human rights practices.

Harold Koh saw the policy differently. Human rights change only occurs, he felt, when you have internal political actors committed to political change. President Pastrana was exactly such an actor, and thus the U.S. intention was to support Pastrana as the "best hope for a comprehensive solution to the triple problems of drugs, war, and human rights violations." Koh said that the waiver didn't imply that the human rights situation was good; it meant only that they recognized that Pastrana was making an effort and that there was progress.[59]

Contrary to Clinton administration policy in Haiti and Guatemala in 1993, the United States did not have the cooperation of other regional and international actors in Colombia. These other actors expressed support for Pastrana's efforts to negotiate an end to the civil war but voiced concern about his use of the military to end drug trafficking and fight guerrillas.

It is too early to judge the final outcome of the complex political situation in Colombia, which remains the country with the most serious human rights situation in the hemisphere. By deciding to use the waiver, the Clinton administration gave up what has been perhaps the most useful tool in U.S. human rights policy—the tension between the Congress and the executive over human rights policy. This tension has been a productive one, allowing the executive to focus on dialogue while Congress plays the role of "bad cop," threatening sanctions in the background. A total aid cutoff, as in Guatemala in 1980s, leads to isolation and disengagement that can exacerbate human rights violations, as they did in the case of the Guatemalan genocide. On the other hand, a lack of human rights conditionality in the context of extensive military aid is easily interpreted as a green light for continuing human rights violations. The tension between the offer of aid and the conditionality of that offer on the recipient's performance in human rights throws the weight of the donor country behind advocates of improved human rights.

Debate over the School of the Americas and Training Manuals

During the Bush and Clinton administrations, a debate intensified over the role of the U.S. government in training Latin American armed forces. The debate focused on the School of the Americas (SOA), the main training center for Latin American militaries since it was established in 1946 in the Panama Canal Zone. The SOA trained more than sixty thousand members of the military between 1946 and 2000. After the Cuban revolution, the SOA focused increasingly on counterinsurgency training. Critics of the SOA began to call attention to coups and human rights violations carried out by its Latin American military graduates. In 1984 the school was moved to Fort Benning, Georgia. In 1990 a Maryknoll priest, Father Roy Bourgeois, founded a group called SOA Watch with the explicit goal of closing down the school. Criticism intensified after SOA Watch published an analysis of military officers in El Salvador whom a UN Truth Commission report had cited for involvement in major massacres: more than 75 percent of them had been trained at the SOA.[60]

In 1993 a group of members of Congress under the leadership of Representative Joseph Kennedy proposed legislation to close the school or cut funds from its budget. Kennedy opposed the school because "it ends up giving the imprimatur to these types of human rights abusers. It gives the impression that America has somehow blessed this kind of activity."[61] Like Donald Fraser two decades earlier, Kennedy was concerned about the appearance of U.S. support for repression.

Kennedy asked the administration to declassify army manuals used for training at the SOA. The *Baltimore Sun* also secured release of two CIA training manuals through the Freedom of Information Act. In 1996 the Pentagon released seven manuals used in intelligence training courses at the SOA from 1987 to 1991. At the same time, the Pentagon disclosed the following conclusion, reached by an investigation during the Bush presidency:

> Five of the seven manuals contained language and statements in violation of legal, regulatory or policy prohibitions. . . . The manual *Handling of Sources* . . . refers to motivation by fear, payment of bounties for enemy dead, beatings, false imprisonment, executions, and the use of truth serum. . . . [The manuals] evolved from lesson plans used in an intelligence course at USA SOA. They were based, in part, on old material dating back to the 1960s from the Army's Foreign Intelligence Assistance Program. . . . We found that neither the Army element at USSOUTH-COM [U.S. Army Southern Command] nor the faculty at USA SOA followed the Army policy for the doctrinal approval of the manuals. . . . To compound the problem, no English language versions of the manuals were ever prepared. . . . [C]opies of the four manuals were issued as supplemental reading material to military students from 10 Latin American countries at USA SOA until 1991.[62]

The manuals provide a rare opportunity to see the types of messages and cues given by U.S. Army sources to the Latin American military over time. They also reveal that the faculty at the SOA had significant autonomy even from U.S. army policy, not to mention from the human rights policies of the executive and Congress. Significant numbers of SOA students used these manuals (and the lesson plans that were their precursors) until the early 1990s.

The Pentagon review and decision to discontinue use of the manuals was a positive move that illustrates how civil society and congressional human rights pressures can contribute to the implementation of human rights policy even in the more resistant and autonomous spheres of the U.S. government. The Department of Defense advised governments in Latin America that the manuals contained passages that did not represent U.S. policy and destroyed copies of the manuals. But the army did not discipline the individuals responsible for writing or teaching the lesson plans, nor were they retrained.

Much of the debate over the SOA has been concerned with whether or not U.S. military trainers actually taught members of the Latin American military to torture or assassinate their opponents. For example, the manuals mention "information obtained involuntarily from insurgents who have been captured," and say that agents "must offer presents and compensation leading to the arrest, capture or death of guerrillas." Various passages in the manuals refer to the "neutralization" of targets.[63] Neutralization is defined in one manual as "detaining or discrediting" but was "commonly used at the time as a euphemism for execution or destruction," according to a Pentagon official.[64]

The focus on a small handful of the most egregious passages fails to appreciate that these manuals offered not only cues about specific tactics but an entire framework of national security ideology. Whether U.S. trainers intended neutralization to mean "execute" or just "detain" is less important than how the Latin American military made sense of their U.S. military training. There is ample evidence that Latin American militaries interpreted the (sometimes ambiguous) cues they received at the SOA in the context of a national security doctrine that they assumed they shared with their U.S. trainers. Researchers associated with the SOA have argued that U.S. counterinsurgency doctrine "was distorted by Argentine and Chilean military leaders in the 1970s into the French Algerian concept of national security, meaning military praetorianism and intentional repression and abuse of selected citizens."[65] It is indeed the case that French military advisors, using lessons they drew from their experience in Algeria, initially introduced national security doctrine in many countries in Latin America.[66] But the U.S. counterinsurgency training became predominant after the Cuban revolution, and Latin American military sources rarely distinguish between the lessons they learned from the French and those from the United States. The crucial issue is that large parts of national security doctrine are homegrown in Latin America, but for the Latin American military they were consistent with equivalent doctrines in the United States and France.

Lisa Haugaard made a fascinating analysis of army and CIA manuals that is consistent with the theoretical argument presented in this second part of the book. She points out that the manuals offer "an entire framework that should be deemed inconsistent with U.S. policy and democratic standards." Specifically, Haugaard argues that the framework contains the following key elements: (1) a lack of distinction between civilian movements and armed rebellion; (2) a willful ignoring of the rule of law; and (3) a purely military response.[67] These elements are consistent with national security ideology, as we saw in chapter 3. Thus, the training manuals are yet another example of why Latin American militaries continued to interpret U.S. policy cues in the context of a shared national security framework. Like other cues we have examined, what the manuals *don't* say is just as important as what they do. "What they leave out is any understanding of democracy and the rule of law."[68] While it is important for the Pentagon to condemn specific passages of the manuals, it is more important for the United States to provide an alternative policy framework within

which future cues will be interpreted. Human rights offer such a policy framework.

Kennedy and his successors attempted to cut funds from the SOA budget
every year from 1994 to 1999, finally succeeding in 1999. Top civilian and military leaders in the Clinton Defense Department lobbied on behalf of the SOA.
Although the cut to funds didn't survive a conference committee on the bill,
the Clinton administration officially closed the SOA in 2000 and reopened it
under a new name, the Western Hemispheric Institute for Security Cooperation, in January 2001. While the new school does not satisfy the critics, a report by Amnesty International found that the training at the SOA today had
greater human rights content and much greater transparency than other U.S.
programs training military students from around the world.[69] This is a direct
result of the pressures placed upon the school by human rights advocates inside and outside the U.S. government. In addition to the SOA, the United
States has approximately 275 military schools and installations, offering over
4,100 courses and training tens of thousands of students. Although some U.S.
military training now includes human rights content, "there is no systematic
requirement for such content in the majority of U.S. training and education
provided to foreign forces."[70]

This illustrates once again that the "institutionalization" of human rights policy does not mean that human rights will necessarily be taken into account in
U.S. policy. Institutionalization means that human rights issues now figure in
U.S. policy debates. Whether they will have an impact on outcomes depends
on whether individuals committed to human rights continue to make concerted efforts to ensure that human rights policy is implemented in the broad-
est range of policy arenas.

Institutionalization, then, doesn't mean that the battle of human rights and
foreign policy has been resolved. As Harold Koh points out, simply having a
place in the bureaucratic structure "gives no guarantee that you will be part of
the decision-making process, and it takes great energy, perseverance and sheer
hard work simply to insert oneself and one's bureau into that process."[71]

During the Bush and Clinton administrations, human rights became an institutionalized part of the U.S. foreign policy. By the end of the Bush administration, the Human Rights Bureau had a staff of approximately 40–45
professional and administrative staff.[72] At the beginning of the Clinton presidency, Secretary of State Christopher, at the urging of John Shattuck, mandated
that one political officer in each embassy serve as the human rights officer, either full-time or as part of his or her job description. In 1993 the Human Rights
Bureau was transformed into the Bureau of Democracy, Human Rights, and

Labor, gaining staff and turf as a result. By the end of the Clinton administration, the bureau had more than a hundred staff. Even so, it was still understaffed and underfunded compared to the regional bureaus in the State Department. The bureau's budget accounted for less than 1 percent of the State Department budget, while the European Bureau accounted for 46 percent. In the late 1990s, only three computers in the bureau had access to the Internet, and one of those was an unauthorized telephone hookup.[73]

Having an institutionalized human rights policy did not mean that human rights usually took precedence in foreign policy decisions. It simply meant that diplomatic staff accepted that human rights issues were now part of the policy calculus, that the Human Rights Bureau was seen as having a place in the bureaucratic structure, that staff routinely acquired training in human rights as part of foreign service training, and that the human rights practices and procedures of the State Department were now part of its standard operating procedures. During the second term of Clinton's presidency, the human rights reports became so extensive and carefully researched that the main human rights organization charged with writing an annual critique, the Lawyers Committee for International Human Rights, decided to no longer issue a counterreport. The Lawyers Committee staff person met with the State Department staff person in charge of the report and told him that "they no longer needed a sledgehammer to swat a fly."[74]

Human rights concerns frequently lost out to compelling arguments about the importance of trade and commerce and to competing perceptions of national security interests, including the drug trafficking issue and the preservation of smooth bilateral relations. The purpose of the Human Rights Bureau, a Clinton administration policy maker pointed out, "is to advance human rights within the framework of U.S. policy. . . . It is not the Amnesty International office in the State Department." How much influence the bureau can exercise "gets fought out issue by issue, day by day."[75] At the end of the Clinton administration, Harold Koh concluded that the global human rights community was "like the famous dog that walks on two legs: given the practical difficulties, it is amazing that any human rights response happens at all."[76]

In crucial cases discussed in this chapter—Haiti in 1993, El Salvador in 1992, Guatemala in 1993—U.S. government actions contributed to the promotion of democracy and human rights. U.S. policy was most effective when it worked in tandem with other regional and international actors. It did so in Haiti, El Salvador, and Guatemala, where UN or OAS actions and those of countries supplemented and complemented U.S. policy. In other cases, U.S. policy was ineffective in promoting human rights and democracy, as it is currently in Colombia.

The executive branch frequently spoke with a divided voice on human rights issues. In Guatemala in the early 1990s, some U.S. policy makers were promoting human rights while others, particularly those associated with the CIA, were providing payments to agents deeply implicated in human rights violations. Policy was least effective where mixed messages pitted one part of executive policy against another.

In the Americas in the early twenty-first century, progress on human rights and democracy has been hard and slow but ultimately has created a virtuous and self-reinforcing circle. As more regional actors strengthen their democracies, and as human rights and democratic principles are institutionalized not only in U.S. policy but in the inter-American system, we can expect that these democracies will continue to work together to sustain democracy and enhance human rights practices in the hemisphere.

CHAPTER NINE

Conclusion: The Lessons of Human Rights Policies

Human rights advocates both in government and outside, in the United States and abroad, succeeded in securing a major shift in U.S. policy and international institutions in the last quarter of the twentieth century. Human rights issues, long seen as moral concerns inappropriate for foreign policy, have become an integral part of U.S. policy and of international and regional institutions. Advocates of human rights succeeded in this endeavor against considerable odds, taking on not only long-standing foreign policy doctrine but also powerful individuals and governments who adamantly opposed the policy change. Visionary leaders like Eleanor Roosevelt, Hernán Santa Cruz, Donald Fraser, Emilio Mignone, Wilson Ferreira Aldunate, Jimmy Carter, Patricia Derian, Richard Shifter, F. Allen "Tex" Harris, and Harold Koh helped to bring about this change.

Human rights issues, as we have seen, have become a routine and institutionalized part of the policy process. Outcomes still depend on political struggles, "fought out issue by issue, day by day," where human rights advocates require skill, energy, and fortuitous circumstances to prevail. A major accomplishment of the human rights movement has been to discipline and change U.S. foreign policy and subject its impact on human rights to scrutiny. U.S. policy was not subject to such scrutiny before the 1970s. Earlier foreign policy episodes with significant implications for human rights and democracy, like the coup in Guatemala in 1954 and the invasion of the Dominican Republic in

1965, provoked little of the debate and inquiry that has become routine since the advent of human rights policy. Some critics of human rights policies miss this point. Human rights policy is not only a policy through which the United States monitors and criticizes other countries. It is also a framework and set of laws that make it possible for the U.S. public and government officials to monitor U.S. policy itself. Human rights policy is both about outcomes and about a policy process in the United States. Policy makers must take human rights and democracy issues into account and scrutinize U.S. policy to consider its complicity with authoritarianism and human rights violations.

This policy change within the United States operates within a broad regional and international context. Human rights and democracy promotion have been institutionalized within international and regional institutions and in the foreign policies of other governments. These international and regional changes are incomplete, and we cannot predict how human rights concerns will affect particular situations. But we can say that human rights policy no longer depends on the whims or commitment of particular leaders or countries. Member states of the OAS, for example, have developed clear norms and procedures for democracy promotion that operate even without U.S. support.

An example occurred in 2002, when the U.S. government encouraged a military coup in Venezuela against the elected populist president, Hugo Chávez. Departing from over a decade of successful cooperation with other regional actors to prevent coups in the region, officials in the administration of George W. Bush appeared to offer a green light to the leaders of the coalition that ousted Chávez. In the months prior to the coup, Bush administration officials met several times with Venezuelan opposition leaders and agreed with them that Chávez should be removed from office. A Defense Department official involved in policy toward Venezuela said, "We were not discouraging people. . . . We were sending informal, subtle signals that we don't like this guy."[1] The assistant secretary of state for inter-American affairs, Otto Reich, had a phone conversation with the business leader who sought to replace Chávez on the very day he took over. Reich claimed that he pleaded with him not to dissolve the National Assembly. Others saw it as evidence that Mr. Reich was "stage managing" the takeover.[2] After the coup, the White House spokesman did not condemn the coup and suggested that the administration was pleased that Chávez was gone. Reich called ambassadors from Latin America to his office after the coup and stressed that "the ouster of Mr. Chávez was not a rupture of democratic rule because he had resigned." Reich urged the diplomats to support the new government, but most refused.

On the one hand, U.S. backing for the coup highlights the continuing fragility of U.S. policies for the promotion of democracy and human rights.

The administration of George W. Bush had apparently forgotten or decided to disregard the key Reagan administration contribution to U.S. policy. The administration of George H. W. Bush in 1991 had firmly supported the regional efforts to incorporate democracy promotion into regional norms and institutions through the Santiago Declaration. But on the other hand, the final outcome in Venezuela underscores that human rights policy no longer depends on the whims of individuals. Regional leaders firmly implemented OAS policy and condemned the coup, the coup makers stepped down, and Chávez returned to power. The regional regime in support of democracy was now sufficiently strong that it operated successfully even against the wishes of the U.S. government. The Venezuelan case is not a simple victory of the democratic leader against the forces of authoritarianism. On the contrary, Chávez has distinct authoritarian tendencies, and his government has a troubled history of human rights practices. Rather, the countries of the region said that they would not support a coup, no matter how reasonable the opposition appeared to be, to resolve a political conflict. The opposition would need to find a constitutional means to unseat the Chávez government. One of the fundamental changes that have occurred in the hemisphere in the last two decades is that certain commonly accepted practices, in this case the military coup, have been taken off the menu of options for policy makers in the region.

Congressional, NGO, and media critics immediately demanded that the Bush administration explain its actions, and the administration was put on the defensive. Senator Christopher Dodd requested a report by the State Department's inspector general after the outcry about the administration's apparent embrace of Chávez's ouster. The inquiry concluded that department officials did not act inappropriately and that it "sent a consistent message of support for democracy in Venezuela."[3] As with many of the episodes recounted in this book, we will probably not know the full story until relevant documents are released to the public. Yet the response of congressional leaders and NGOs revealed once again that they were not going to let administration policy makers easily dismantle long-standing policy.

Policy Implications

The central question in the second part of this book is what difference human rights policy made. It is difficult to isolate a single factor, like U.S. policy, and evaluate its impact on human rights practices in a diverse region like Latin America. Human rights policy toward Latin America was successful in some cases because of Latin America's unique history and tradition, including its long embrace of human rights norms and law as part of national identity. We saw in the first part of this book the role that Latin American diplomats, lawyers, and activists played in the origins of international and regional human rights norms. Even as repression intensified in the 1970s and 1980s, human rights values resonated with the political history and national identity of most Latin American states. Latin American exiles condemned the human rights abuses of the military regimes and sought international solidarity. Activists and dissidents who stayed behind organized new domestic human rights organizations, often at great personal risk, to document and denounce repression and provide legal and social services to the victims of repression and their families. Human rights policies were successful, in part, because of a strong network of human rights organizations throughout the region. And it was often successful in spite of U.S. policy toward the region, as in the case of Venezuela.

U.S. policies have sometimes contributed to repression in Latin America and sometimes to greater respect for human rights, depending on how the policies were implemented and what kinds of messages they conveyed. This sounds deceptively simple, and yet it flies in the face of the claims that U.S. policy has consistently exacerbated repression or has consistently promoted human rights. U.S. policy toward the region has brought both harm and benefits. In some cases, like that of Guatemala, an earlier harm outweighs any later benefits. No amount of funding for human rights and democracy in the 1990s can outbalance the hugely harmful U.S. policy of the 1950s and 1960s, which set Guatemala on its course of increasingly intense repression. It is impossible to know what would have happened in Guatemala without U.S. intervention in the 1950s, but in retrospect it appears that the 1954 coup set Guatemala on a path of increasingly authoritarian regimes that resulted in the genocide of the early 1980s.

In other cases U.S. policy contributed to improvements. Carter policy helped get people out of jail in Uruguay and Argentina. The Carter administration pressured the Argentine military regime to invite the Inter-American Commission on Human Rights to Argentina. The visit marked a crucial turning point in human rights and led the regime to end its practice of disappearing and murdering its citizens. But Carter policy had to counteract the go-ahead that Kissinger and other top-level policy makers gave the Argentine military government at the height of disappearances in 1976. In Uruguay in 1978, Chile in 1988, Mexico in 1992, Haiti in 1993, Guatemala in 1993, Paraguay in 1996–2000, and Peru in 2000, diverse U.S. administrations, both Democratic and Republican, got it right and were able to help promote human rights and democracy in the region. When I say the administrations "got it right" I mean they delivered a policy that spoke clearly and consistently, in public and in private, of a firm commitment to human rights and democracy. They backed up verbal diplomacy with a judicious use of cutoffs of military and economic aid. They worked with democratic elements within the country and coordinated with regional and international actors. Again this sounds deceptively simple. Yet how many times did the United States get it wrong by breaking these simple guidelines?

The single most damaging manner in which the United States got it wrong were the gratuitous green lights it gave publicly and privately to the officials of repressive regimes, which signaled that the U.S. government was not concerned about human rights and would not grant them priority in bilateral relations. Green lights sometimes took the form of blanket and vague statements that U.S. officials "understood" the problems of fighting "terrorism" and would not criticize regimes that were detaining, torturing, executing, and disappearing their citizens. These statements sometimes implied that the United States didn't want to know all the details of how the regime intended to handle its opponents, but would support the regime nonetheless.

Sometimes green lights took the symbolic form of inviting dictators to Washington on state visits, or refusing to meet with the leaders of opposition political parties or human rights organizations. The green light for the coup in Venezuela consisted of "informal, subtle signals" that the United States wanted to get rid of Chávez. Green lights sometimes took the much more specific form of the CIA paying informants who were deeply associated with repression. Routinely U.S. policy makers justified such actions as being in national security interests. In retrospect, it is difficult to see what U.S. being national security interests were served by promoting a coup in Chile in 1973, encouraging repression in Argentina in 1976, or standing by while the Guatemalan government carried out genocide.

Even in the case of the notorious army manuals used at the School of the Americas, the problem was less with the exact language and more with the overall message that the manuals communicated. The manuals recommended techniques for infiltrating social movements, interrogating suspects, spying, and controlling the population. Few believe that Latin American militaries could not have come up with these techniques on their own. The manuals are important for the overall signal or message they convey. One analyst points out that "in the name of defending democracy, the manuals advocate profoundly undemocratic methods." They fail to distinguish between legitimate civilian movements or organizations and armed rebellions; they ignore the rule of law, advocate routine spying on the civilian population, and encourage solely military responses to political problems.[4]

Human rights policy is most effective when high-level private diplomacy underscores the human rights message of public diplomacy, and when it is re-inforced by various forms of sanctions and cutoffs of assistance. Decisions about aid are more important as signals of broader policy directions than as tools for affecting specific human rights practices. Military and economic aid cutoffs can be used as one part of an overall communicative signal from the U.S. government to Latin American governments about the importance of human rights practices in determining the tenor of relations between the countries. What is most important, however, is not the amount of aid that is cut but the clarity and consistency of the overall signal. To be effective, private diplomacy must convey real resolve, and thus the more forceful public aspects of human rights policy may provide a backdrop against which private diplomacy takes on new meaning.

It is unlikely that the U.S. government will ever speak with one voice on human rights issues. Disagreements will continue within the executive, between the executive and Congress, and among the members of Congress about the correct tools to implement this policy. These disagreements can even be used to reinforce a human rights message, as ambassadors to El Salvador learned during the Reagan years. Human rights policy can survive and even thrive in the midst of such disagreements. What undermines the policy are the subtle and not-so-subtle signals from U.S. officials that gross violations of human rights are acceptable.

The minimum standards for a human rights policy should be of attempting to "do no harm" and working to communicate a clear, firm, and consistent commitment to human rights. Once these standards have been met, there will still be many differences over what policy mix will best promote human rights and democracy in a particular circumstance. In general, an effective policy has tended to use a range of policy tools. So, for example, in the case of Guatemala in 1993, U.S. policy makers sent public and private messages that the coup was unacceptable. They worked within the OAS to develop a joint regional strategy with other countries. They immediately stopped certain forms of aid and threatened to stop others. The threat of aid cutoffs is an essential part of the tool kit of human rights policy. It is also a negotiating tool, and the selective approval of previously blocked aid has also been a useful part of human rights policy, for example, in the case of the Export-Import Bank loan to Argentina. Because these signals and messages are so important, human rights policy should avoid absolute isolation of a rights-violating government. The case of Guatemala suggests that isolation of rights violators combined with verbal green lights and a washing of hands increased the autonomy of the Guatemalan military and made genocide more possible.

The most important parts of U.S. policy toward Latin America are the worldviews and doctrines that policy communicates. From the 1950s into the 1980s the worldview that much of U.S. policy communicated was that of national security doctrine. While national security doctrine is motivated by anticommunism, it also goes well beyond it. An anticommunist policy could have been perfectly consistent with a policy promoting human rights and democracy. It was not anticommunism per se that was the problem—it was the specific kind of anticommunist policy adopted in Latin America. National security doctrine identified unarmed domestic communists and leftists as enemies and thus legitimate military targets, and it justified or even advocated the use of unlimited means against them. National security doctrine allowed national militaries and police essentially to carry out war against their citizens, even the unarmed. Governments are justified in using force to confront armed insurgents, but they must do so within the bounds of law. National security doctrine implied that in this internal war the security apparatus was not bound by domestic law or even the laws of war. It appeared to justify security forces using methods against their own population that they could not legitimately use in a declared war, such as the torture and murder of prisoners.

Human rights policy was such a dramatic about-face because it represented a very different worldview. Human rights treaties and laws recognize that under circumstances of national emergency, governments may take exceptional measures. Terrorism and armed insurrection can be fought using all the legitimate tools at the disposal of the state, including force. But under no circumstances can a government use torture, murder, disappearance, or indefinite imprisonment without charge. Civilians are never legitimate military targets, and in confrontations with armed insurgencies the laws of war do apply.

These lessons of the 1970s and 1980s are so important today because there is a danger that the new doctrine of antiterrorism will resemble aspects of national security ideology. An antiterrorist policy can be fully consistent with human rights policy. But the form that some antiterrorism discourses and policies are taking in the early twenty-first century put it into conflict with basic aspects of human rights policy.

National security doctrine defined the war against "subversion" as a permanent and global war, in which there was "no distinction between periods of peace and periods of war, no formal declaration of the start or end of hostilities," and "no distinction between the civil front and the military front." It saw the war against guerrillas as a total, moral, and nonconventional war "involving two antithetical visions of the world," the objective of which was the annihilation of the adversary. The enemy employed "dirty tactics, techniques, and methods," which in turn justified and indeed required the use of similar unconventional tactics by the forces of order.[5]

The "war against terrorism" as formulated and practiced by the administration of George W. Bush and allies after September 11, 2001, has virtually all of these characteristics. It too is seen as a permanent and global war in which there is no distinction between periods of peace and periods of war, no formal declaration of the start or the end of hostilities, and no distinction between the civil front and the military front. It is a war in which the tactics of the enemy justify unconventional tactics by the forces of order. Just like national security doctrine, this new type of antiterrorist doctrine runs the risk of undermining the subordination of military to civilian power. If the doctrine used in the war against terrorism continues to mirror national security doctrine, the foreign policy of the United States could once again become complicit with repression. Our domestic institutions and civil society may be strong enough to protect civil liberties in this country. But projected into countries with weaker institutions, such a doctrine could become exactly the legitimation that powerful groups need to carry out repression against their population.

Theoretical Conclusions

This discussion of cues and worldviews moves ideational or constructivist accounts of foreign policy toward specific propositions about how language and identity interact to produce foreign policy outcomes. I offer a modification of the spiral model of human rights change that I developed with Thomas Risse and Stephen Ropp. The spiral model shows how increasing domestic and international human rights pressures can overcome the denial and backlash of an authoritarian regime to contribute to lasting human rights change. But the spiral model does not adequately address how ambiguous and contradictory messages from a powerful actor like the United States can affect the spiral of human rights change.

Risse has proposed important ways to think about argumentation, deliberation, and persuasion in international relations.[6] While many of the foreign policy interactions I study in this book could be seen as argumentation, deliberation, and persuasion, often something far more indirect is going on. When President Reagan, in the midst of genocide in Guatemala, says that Ríos Montt is a "man of great integrity" who has gotten a "bum rap," he is not arguing, deliberating, or persuading. He is, however, sending a powerful cue to the Guatemalan military. In addition to argumentation and persuasion, constructivists need to pay more attention to indirect processes of sensemaking. Diplomacy in particular seems to be permeated by such indirect cues. A sensemaking approach sees that communication often takes the form of fragmentary cues in uncertain situations. "Meaning is created when these cues are linked to well-learned and / or developing cognitive structures."[7] Individuals then act on these interpretations. Top-level leaders don't just argue, they are "sense-givers."[8] As we have seen, U.S. policy makers gave cues that were linked to broader policy frameworks, which allowed Latin American policy makers to make sense of the cues and act upon their interpretations.

I conclude that in regions like Latin America where the United States has a powerful influence, ambiguous or contradictory messages from the United States can block the spiral of human rights change. When U.S. policy makers give a green light for repression, they may at least temporarily trump other human rights messages and short-circuit the spiral. If they send ambiguous messages, other states, NGOs, and international organizations must intervene more forcefully than they otherwise would have.

Why and how do ambiguous or contradictory cues from the United States short-circuit a spiral of positive human rights change? We start with the understanding that neither U.S. policy makers nor the authoritarian regimes of Latin America were unified in their policy making. Advocates of human rights policy in the United States struggled against those who believed that more traditional national security concerns should prevail. In Latin America, military leaders had to negotiate between hard-liners and soft-liners on human rights issues. This led to a very complicated two-level negotiation game over human rights, as a divided U.S. government interacted with different factions of the authoritarian regimes. Ambiguous or contradictory messages on human rights will tend to empower the hard-liners in repressive regimes.

Human rights messages are intrinsically hard to deliver and hard to hear. A government engaged in repression does not want to hear messages about human rights. Government forces involved in repression are breaking both domestic and international law. Because they know that what they are doing is illegal, they usually work to hide the information about what is occurring. They hide this information not only from international observers but also from their own public, and sometimes even from parts of the government itself. The practice of disappearances, for example, was a complex repressive tool that was designed to terrorize the population while at the same time hiding the fact that state repression was occurring. This hiding of information makes human rights policy more difficult, because it must work with uncertain information provided by unofficial sources. Human rights reports were important for the genesis and development of human rights policy because they provided a public source of information about human rights practices. But the problems of gathering reliable information on human rights practices means that even in the best of circumstances there will be a lag between the time a government initiates repression and the moment when domestic and international observers can identify the nature of the problem and who is responsible for it.

In order to convince their security forces to violate human rights, governments develop complex justifications about why such law breaking is permitted or even necessary. National security doctrine provides one such justification— repressive measures normally forbidden are needed to protect the nation against subversion. Such justifications are used to sustain individual and national identity and esteem. The human rights message, however, undermines this justification; and doing so, it attacks the state identity and the individual identities of leaders. In these circumstances, leaders will try not to hear these messages, and they will vilify and attack the messenger. A government engaged in repression will often mishear or misinterpret what it hears if it can. Ambiguous or contradictory messages on human rights thus play into the tendency for human rights abusers to mishear messages that attack their identity and undermine self-esteem.

Other scholars have suggested that on the contrary, human rights messages are easy to deliver because they buttress the identity of the deliverers and support their sense of moral superiority. I believe that the evidence from Latin American–U.S. relations suggests that human rights messages ran contrary to the ethos of the foreign service because they exacerbated relations with foreign governments. It was an article of faith among Latin American experts in the State Department in the 1970s and 1980s that U.S. national interests depended upon cordial relations with militaries in the region. They believed that human rights messages undermined positive bilateral relations.

Thus, when U.S. policy makers gave a cue like "get terrorism over quickly," and failed to mention that this should be done within the rule of law and while respecting human rights, military regimes in the region were all too ready to hear the cue and see a green light. It was taken as a reaffirmation that the illegal choices they had made had the blessing of the powerful and influential United States. It affirmed their common identity as defenders of freedom against the evil of communism.

Human rights and democracy promotion constitute an alternative, potentially overarching foreign policy framework. If this framework were firmly entrenched, a policy maker could say "Get terrorism over with quickly" and take it for granted that the message would be interpreted within the human rights and democracy framework. But although human rights and democracy policy is institutionalized, it is not yet deeply entrenched or overarching. Any cue about fighting terrorism today must continue to specify the relevant framework—for example, "Use all the tools at your disposal to fight terrorism within the rule of law"—and then go on to specify what exactly is meant by the rule of law.

The overall lesson I take from my study of U.S. foreign policy is one of both hope and humility. By expanding the human rights agenda, we restrict U.S. complicity with repression, and we sometimes save lives, stop torture, and release people from prison. Human rights policies bring about positive outcomes that provide long-term benefits. U.S. human rights policy helped create the conditions for a democratic and relatively stable hemisphere, with substantial long-term benefits for the people and countries of the region, including the United States.

But we also need to understand that the United States can contribute to human rights abuses as well as end them. Such policy failures can come back to haunt us and undermine our long-term interests. Some of the failures of human rights policy are the result of insufficient application, mixed signals, and equivocation. Others are the result of hubris, of believing that the United States can unilaterally impose a solution through extensive and excessive involvement. In this book I argue for a strong continuation of human rights policy, but one that steers a middle ground between equivocation and hubris. I stress the need for both greater consistency and firmness, together with the realization of the necessary limits of U.S. power.

These messages are particularly important after September 11, 2001. Because authoritarianism and human rights violations are linked, it is ultimately counterproductive to fight terrorism by supporting and arming authoritarian regimes. But we also shouldn't be too optimistic that we can improve the situation quickly simply by encouraging countries to democratize. Although democracies have better human rights records than authoritarian regimes, during a transition to democracy ethnic conflict and related human rights violations often increase. Perhaps the strongest finding of the quantitative literature on repression is that there is a strong connection between war and human rights violations. Decades of civil war in Afghanistan created conditions where terrorism and human rights violations flourished prior to the attacks of September 11. Countries marked by war, authoritarianism, and poverty will find it a long and difficult process to protect human rights and establish the rule of law.

During the administration of George W. Bush, the Human Rights Bureau continues to operate. Its day-to-day work has not changed dramatically. The danger is that once again the very highest levels of government are sending signals that the goal of fighting terrorism justifies the violation of human rights.

The United States offers cues not only through specific public and private remarks to foreign governments. We also offer cues through the nature and volume of our economic and military assistance program, and our military and nonmilitary training.

But the most important cues we send about human rights policy come through our own human rights behavior. When the U.S. government holds people incommunicado without access to lawyers, it flaunts the rule of law and invites similar illegal detentions elsewhere. When members of the U.S. military torture and humiliate prisoners, as they did in the Abu Ghraib prison in Iraq, they signal that such behavior is acceptable, and they destroy U.S. credibility to protest torture anywhere in the world. When the U.S. government refuses to ratify human rights treaties or "unsigns" them, it sends a message that it doesn't believe in international human rights law.

The full explanation for U.S. use of torture in Iraq will take years to uncover. But, consistent with the main argument of this book, high level U.S. officials gave signals and cues that made repression more likely. In January 2002, Secretary of Defense Donald H. Rumsfeld publicly declared that hundreds of people detained by U.S. forces in Afghanistan "do not have any rights," under the Geneva Conventions. The Bush administration refused to submit the people it held in Guantánamo Bay to formal hearings, as required by the Geneva Conventions, to determine if they were prisoners of war. Instead, it created a category—illegal combatant—and acted as if the people it classified arbitrarily in this category could be permanently deprived of all rights. These acts sent signals, not only to foreign governments but also to members of the U.S. military, that detainees could be considered outside the realm of both international and domestic law. That U.S. soldiers could read these signals is clear from some of their comments and testimony. "One member of the 377th Company said the fact that prisoners in Afghanistan had been labeled as 'enemy combatants' not subject to the Geneva Conventions had contributed to an unhealthy attitude in the detention center." "We were pretty much told that they were nobodies, that they were just enemy combatants," he said. "I think that giving them the distinction of soldier would have changed our attitudes toward them."[9]

At the same time, the Bush administration continued its campaign against the International Criminal Court (ICC). It unsigned the treaty and pressured the Security Council to grant permanent immunity for U.S. peacekeeping forces from legal action by the ICC. Congress passed a bill that would cut off military aid to countries that had ratified the ICC treaty unless they promised not to transfer U.S. citizens to the Court. The U.S. government may have believed these acts were a statement of its distrust of international law and international institutions. But it was possible to interpret these signals, in the context of the war against terrorism, as a promise that the U.S. government would protect its soldiers from prosecution if they violated the laws of war.

Past evidence suggests that high-level public signals are likely to be echoed in private conversations that may be construed as green lights for repression. The green lights of the past have had tragic effects on people's lives. They have sometimes come back to haunt the policy makers who issued them, as they have haunted Henry Kissinger. Increasingly, as the many truth commissions and human rights trials attest, the victims of repression will not be forgotten. The search for justice and attribution of responsibility will continue. In the name of fighting the grave human rights abuses of terrorism, we must not again risk contributing to repression. Our commitment to civil liberties and the rule of law is an essential part of our identity and should not be squandered by the shortsighted policies of any administration.

Jacobo Timerman, the Argentine journalist who was disappeared and imprisoned in Argentina, and later released into exile after Patricia Derian pressured the Argentine government, told a story that was emblematic of the change that U.S. human rights policy wrought in the image of the United States in Latin America. He described seeing a prison wall in Argentina where "Yankee, Go Home" had been scrawled. But the "Go Home" had been crossed out, and in its place someone had written "Yankee, Take Me Home."[10] For Timerman, this symbolized that as a result of human rights policy, instead of being identified with repression, the United States was identified "with our hopes." The tragedy of Abu Ghraib prison in Iraq is not only the suffering of the victims of torture, but also that this prison has become a powerful symbol that identifies the United States with our worst nightmares, not our hopes.

NOTES

Preface

1. U.S. Department of State, "Foreign Minister Guzzetti Euphoric over Visit to U.S.," embassy cable, October 19, 1976.

2. U.S. Embassy (Buenos Aires), "Demarche to Foreign Minister on Human Rights," document no. 1976Buenos03462, May 28, 1976.

3. This is from a verbatim transcript of a memorandum of the conversation between Guzzetti and Kissinger, one of a set of newly declassified State Department documents obtained by the National Security Archive. "Secretary's Meeting with Argentine Foreign Minister Guzzetti," memorandum of conversation, October 7, 1976, New York.

4. U.S. Embassy (Buenos Aires), "Other Aspects of September 17 Conversation with Foreign Minister," document no. 1976Buenos06130, September 20, 1976.

5. Philip Agee, *Inside the Company: CIA Diary* (New York: Stonehill , 1975), p. 455.

6. Lawrence Pezzullo, interview by author, Baltimore, Md., August 29, 1991.

7. Agee, *Inside the Company,* pp. 455, 458.

8. F. Allan "Tex" Harris, interview by author, Washington, D.C., March 5, 2003.

9. Ibid.

10. Alejandro Vegh Villegas, interview by author, Washington, D.C., August 29, 1991.

11. Jason Donovan, interview by author, Guatemala City, March 28, 2001.

12. Jennifer K. Harbury, *Searching for Everardo* (New York: Warner Books, 1997),

p. 323; Senate Select Committee on Intelligence, *Hearing on Guatemala,* 104th Cong., 1st sess., April 5, 1995 (Washington, D.C.: GPO, 1995).

13. *Washington Post,* May 22, 1981.

1. Introduction to the Origins of Human Rights Policies

1. Michael Ignatieff, "Is the Human Rights Era Ending?" *New York Times,* February 5, 2002, p. A29; David P. Forsythe, "Human Rights Fifty Years after the Universal Declaration: Reconciling American Political Science and the Study of Human Rights," *PS: Political Science and Politics* 31, 3 (1998).

2. Ignatieff, "Is the Human Rights Era Ending?"

3. Senate Subcommittee on Western Hemisphere Affairs, *United States Policies and Programs in Brazil: Hearings,* 92d Cong., 1st sess., May 4, 1971 (Washington, D.C.: GPO, 1971), p. 290.

4. Ibid., p. 1.

5. U.S. Embassy (Stockholm), "A National Security Strategy of Enlargement and Engagement, III: Integrated Regional Approaches," February 1996, http://www.usis .usemb.se/usis/1996strategy/integrat.html.

6. See also Paul Gordon Lauren, *The Evolution of International Human Rights: Visions Seen* (Philadelphia: University of Pennsylvania Press, 1998), p. 17. See Louis Henkin, "The First Two Hundred Years of an Idea," in *The Rights of Man Today* (Boulder, Colo.: Westview, 1978), pp. 5−13; David P. Forsythe, *The Internationalization of Human Rights* (Lexington, Mass.: Lexington Books, 1991).

7. Stephen Krasner, *Sovereignty: Organized Hypocrisy* (Princeton: Princeton University Press, 1999). In particular, issues of religious toleration in the sixteenth and seventeenth centuries, and of minority rights in the nineteenth and early twentieth centuries, led states to concern themselves routinely with the relation between ruler and ruled in other states.

8. This paragraph draws on material from Krasner, *Sovereignty,* pp. 14−25.

9. Organization of American States, *Annual Report of the Inter-American Commission on Human Rights, 1989−1990* (Washington, D.C.: OAS General Secretariat, 1990), pp. 103−105.

10. Peter Katzenstein, ed., *The Culture of National Security: Norms and Identity in World Politics* (New York: Columbia University Press, 1996); Martha Finnemore, *National Interests in International Society* (Ithaca, N.Y.: Cornell University Press, 1996).

11. David Campbell, *Writing Security: U.S. Foreign Policy and the Politics of Identity,* rev. ed. (Minneapolis: University of Minnesota Press, 1998), p. 170.

12. James D. Fearon and David D. Laitin, "Violence and the Social Construction of Ethnic Identity," *International Organization* 54, 4 (autumn 2000), p. 848.

13. See, for example, Campbell, *Writing Security.*

14. John G. Ruggie, "The Past as Prologue: Interests, Identity, and American Foreign Policy," *International Security* 21 (1997): 110; see also Campbell, *Writing Security.*

15. See, for example, Robert A. Pastor, ed., *A Century's Journey: How the Great Powers Shape the World* (New York: Basic Books, 1999).

16. See, for example, Walter Russell Mead, *Special Providence: American Foreign Policy and How It Changes the World* (New York: Routledge, 2001); John Hartz, *The Liberal Tradition in America: An Interpretation of American Political Thought since the Revolution* (New York: Harcourt, 1955); Walter McDougall, *Promised Land, Crusader State: The American Encounter with the World since 1776* (New York: Houghton Mifflin, 1997).

17. For example, Mead, *Special Providence*.

18. See Ruggie, "Past as Prologue"; Robert Pastor, "The United States: Divided by a Revolutionary Vision," in *A Century's Journey: How the Great Powers Shape the World*, ed. Robert Pastor (New York: Basic Books: 1999), pp. 191–238.

19. Judith Goldstein and Robert Keohane, eds., *Ideas and Foreign Policy: Beliefs, Institutions and Political Change* (Ithaca, N.Y.: Cornell University Press, 1993).

20. On norm entrepreneurs, see Ethan Nadelmann, "Global Prohibition Regimes: The Evolution of Norms in International Society," *International Organization* 44, 4 (autumn 1990), p. 482.

21. See, for example, Bruce Russett, *Controlling the Sword: The Democratic Governance of National Security* (Cambridge: Harvard University Press, 1990), chap. 5.

22. Although the United States has ratified the Covenant on Civil and Political Rights, it is unlikely that the United States will adopt a multilateral policy in the near future. This policy would involve ratifying the Optional Protocol of the covenant, the statute of the International Criminal Court, or the American Convention on Human Rights and accepting the compulsory jurisdiction of the Inter-American Court of Human Rights.

23. A number of small Caribbean countries also do not yet have a multilateral human rights policy. See table 3 in chapter 1.

24. Stephen D. Krasner, "Sovereignty, Regimes, and Human Rights," in *Regime Theory and International Relations*, ed. Volker Rittberger (Oxford: Clarendon, 1993), p. 166.

25. Ibid., p. 141.

26. These theorists are also sometimes called critical constructivists, or poststructuralists.

27. Jutta Weldes et al., *Cultures of Insecurity: States, Communities, and the Production of Danger* (Minneapolis: University of Minnesota Press, 1999), p. 13.

28. Roxanne Lynn Doty, "Introduction," in *Imperial Encounters: The Politics of North-South Relations* (Minneapolis: University of Minnesota Press, 1996), p. 137.

29. Ibid.

30. Andrew Moravcsik, "Taking Preferences Seriously: A Liberal Theory of International Politics," *International Organization* 51, 4 (1997): 513–533.

31. Anne-Marie Slaughter, "International Law in a World of Liberal States," *European Journal of International Law* 6, 4 (1995).

32. These paragraphs draw on Andrew Moravcsik, "The Origins of Human Rights

Regimes: Democratic Delegation in Postwar Europe" *International Organization* 54, 4 (2000).

33. This point of view is called sociological institutionalism or the world polity school. For an overview of this approach, see Martha Finnemore, "Norms, Culture, and World Politics: Insights from Sociology's Institutionalism," *International Organization* 50 (1996): 325—347.

34. John Boli and George M. Thomas, eds., *Constructing World Culture: International Nongovernmental Organizations since 1875* (Stanford: Stanford University Press, 2000).

35. Lauren, *Evolution of International Human Rights,* pp. 2, 139.

36. John G. Ruggie, "International Regimes, Transactions, and Change: Embedded Liberalism in the Postwar Economic Order," in *International Regimes,* ed. Stephen Krasner (Ithaca, N.Y.: Cornell University Press, 1983), pp. 195—231.

37. Kathryn Sikkink, "Human Rights, Principled Issue Networks, and Sovereignty in Latin America," *International Organization* 47, 3 (summer 1993): 411—441; Margaret Keck and Kathryn Sikkink, *Activists beyond Borders: Advocacy Networks in International Politics* (Ithaca, N.Y.: Cornell University Press, 1998); Thomas Risse, Stephen C. Ropp, and Kathryn Sikkink, eds., *The Power of Human Rights: International Norms and Domestic Change* (Cambridge: Cambridge University Press, 1999).

38. Graham Allison, *Essence of Decision: Explaining the Cuban Missile Crisis* (Boston: Little, Brown, 1971); Graham Allison and Morton Halperin, "Bureaucratic Politics: A Paradigm and Some Policy Implications," *World Politics* 24 (1972): 40—79.

39. This may help explain Oona Hathaway's conclusions about the lack of connection between treaty ratification and human rights practices in "Do Treaties Make a Difference? Human Rights Treaties and the Problem of Compliance," *Yale Law Journal* 111, 8 (2002): 1935—2042.

40. Ruggie, "Past as Prologue."

41. Ignatieff, "Is the Human Rights Era Ending?"; Thomas Friedman, "The War on What?" *New York Times,* May 8, 2002.

2. The Idea of Internationally Recognized Human Rights

1. Mary Ann Glendon, *A World Made New: Eleanor Roosevelt and the Universal Declaration of Human Rights* (New York: Random House, 2001), p. 21.

2. Hernán Santa Cruz, *Cooperar o perecer: El dilema de la comunidad mundial* (Buenos Aires: Grupo Editor Latinoamericano, 1984), p. 37 (translations my own unless otherwise indicated).

3. Glendon, *World Made New,* p. 22.

4. In particular, see ibid.

5. Santa Cruz, *Cooperar o perecer,* pp. 38—40.

6. Ibid., pp. 41, 42.

7. See Robert William Fogel, *Without Consent or Contract: The Rise and Fall of American Slavery* (New York: Norton, 1989), p. 205; Ethan A. Nadelmann, "Global Prohibition Regimes: The Evolution of Norms in International Society," *International*

Organization 44, 4 (autumn 1990): 491–498; J. D. Armstrong, "The International Committee of the Red Cross and Political Prisoners," *International Organization* 39 (autumn 1985); Ann Towns, "Norms and Inequality in International Society: Global Politics of Women and the State" (Ph.D. diss., University of Minnesota, 2004); Arnold Whittack, *Woman into Citizen* (London: Athenaeum, 1979).

8. Jan Herman Burgers, "The Road to San Francisco: The Revival of the Human Rights Idea in the Twentieth Century," *Human Rights Quarterly* 14 (1992): 449.

9. This entire section draws heavily on Burgers, "Road to San Francisco," pp. 450–459, as well as on an interview with Jan Herman Burgers, The Hague, Netherlands, November 13, 1993.

10. William Korey, "Raphael Lemkin: The Unofficial Man," *Midstream,* June–July 1989, pp. 45–46; Samantha Power, *A Problem from Hell: America and the Age of Genocide* (New York: Basic Books, 2002).

11. Burgers, "Road to San Francisco," p. 455.

12. Ibid., pp. 459–464.

13. Larry Rohter, "Panama's Plan to Pardon Human Rights Abusers Draws Fire," *New York Times,* May 14, 1996, p. A4.

14. Santa Cruz, *Cooperar o perecer,* p. 58.

15. G. Pope Atkins, *Latin America in the International Political System,* 2d ed. (Boulder, Colo.: Westview, 1989), p. 228.

16. Ibid., pp. 203, 215–216.

17. Alejandro Alvarez, "Declaración sobre las bases fundamentales y los grandes principios del derecho internacional moderno," *La Reconstrucción del Derecho de Gentes* (Santiago de Chile: Editorial Nascimento, 1943), pp. 89–91.

18. Alberto Rodriguez Larreta, "Inter-American Solidarity: Safeguarding the Democratic Ideal: Note from Uruguayan Foreign Minister to Secretary of State," U.S. Department of State, *Bulletin,* November 25, 1945, pp. 865–866.

19. Johannes Morsink, *The Universal Declaration of Human Rights: Origins, Drafting, and Intent* (Philadelphia: University of Pennsylvania Press, 1999), pp. 130–131.

20. David C. Smith, *H. G. Wells: Desperately Mortal: A Biography* (New Haven: Yale University Press, 1986), p. 428.

21. Samuel I. Rosenman, *Working with Roosevelt* (New York: Harper and Brothers, 1952), pp. 262–264.

22. M. Glen Johnson, "The Contributions of Eleanor and Franklin Roosevelt to the Development of International Protection for Human Rights," *Human Rights Quarterly* 9 (1987): 21–23.

23. Ibid., p. 21.

24. Burgers, interview.

25. Dorothy B. Robins, *Experiment in Democracy: The Story of U.S. Citizen Organizations in Forging the Charter of the United Nations* (New York: Parkside, 1971), pp. 27–28.

26. Santa Cruz, *Cooperar o perecer,* p. 59.

27. Cited in Paul Gordon Lauren, *The Evolution of International Human Rights* (Philadelphia: University of Pennsylvania Press, 1998), p. 165.

28. Lauren, *Evolution,* pp. 162, 164–165, 167.

29. Jacob Robinson, *Human Rights and Fundamental Freedoms in the Charter of the United Nations* (New York: Institute of Jewish Affairs, 1946), p. 17.

30. Lauren, *Evolution,* pp. 174–179; and Sumner Wells, *Where Are We Heading?* (New York: Harper and Brothers, 1946), p. 34.

31. Lauren, *Evolution,* p. 178.

32. Ibid., p. 130.

33. Robins, *Experiment in Democracy,* p. 41.

34. Barbara Blaustein Hirschhorn, "The United Nations and Human Rights, 1945–1995" (speech at the We the Peoples Conference panel on Citizen Action in International Affairs, San Francisco, June 22, 1995), p. 2.

35. Robins, *Experiment in Democracy,* p. 104.

36. Ibid., p. 103.

37. John P. Humphrey, *Human Rights and the United Nations: A Great Adventure* (Dobbs Ferry, N.Y.: Transnational, 1984), p. 13; U.S. Department of State, *The United Nations Conference on International Organization, San Francisco, California April 25 to June 26, 1945: Selected Documents* (Washington, D.C.: GPO, 1946).

38. Copy of letter submitted to Secretary Stittinius by consultants regarding human rights, May 2, 1945, in Robins, *Experiment in Democracy,* pp. 218–219.

39. Blaustein Hirschhorn, "United Nations," p. 3.

40. Blaustein Hirschhorn, "United Nations" p. 4; Robins, *Experiment in Democracy,* pp. 131–132.

41. Lauren, *Evolution,* p. 337 n. 86.

42. Ibid., p. 193.

43. Morsink, *Universal Declaration,* p. 130.

44. Santa Cruz, *Cooperar o perecer,* p. 69.

45. Quoted in Robins, *Experiment in Democracy,* p. 132.

46. Johnson, "Contributions," p. 24.

47. "Statement of Uruguayan Delegation of Its Position with Reference to Chapters I and II of the Charter as Considered by Committee I/1," June 15, 1945, in *Documents of the United Nations Conference on International Organization,* vol. 6 (New York: United Nations Information Organization, 1945), 628–633.

48. "Report of Rapporteur," Subcommittee I/1/A (Farid Zeineddine, Syria), to Committee I/1, June 1, 1945, in *Documents of the United Nations Conference on International Organization,* vol. 6 (New York: United Nations Information Organization, 1945), 705.

49. In particular, see Lauren, *Evolution,* chaps. 6–7; Morsink, *Universal Declaration;* Glendon, *World Made New.*

50. Cited in Glendon, *World Made New,* p. 134.

51. Morsink, *Universal Declaration,* p. 131.

52. Santa Cruz, *Cooperar o perecer,* pp. 179–180.

53. Glendon, *World Made New,* p. 43.

54. John Humphrey, cited in Glendon, *World Made New,* p. 44.

55. Glendon, *World Made New,* p. 70.

56. Humphrey, *Human Rights,* pp. 31–32.

57. Morsink, *Universal Declaration,* p. 131.

58. Ibid.

59. Ibid., p. 157.

60. Korey, "Raphael Lemkin," pp. 45, 47.

61. Johnson, "Contributions," pp. 31, 42.

62. This section draws on Azza Salama Layton, *International Politics and Civil Rights Policies in the United States, 1941–1960* (New York: Cambridge University Press, 2000); Mary Dudziak, *Cold War Civil Rights: Race and the Image of American Democracy* (Princeton: Princeton University Press, 2000); Doug McAdam, "On the International Origins of Domestic Political Opportunity Structures," in *Social Movements and American Political Institutions,* ed. Anne Costain and Andrew McFarland (Lanham, Md.: Rowman and Littlefield, 1998), pp. 251–267.

63. Layton, *International Politics,* p. 18.

64. Ibid., p. 16.

65. Ralph Beddard, *Human Rights and Europe* (London: Sweet and Maxwell, 1980), p. 17.

66. Economic and social issues are discussed in the European Social Charter.

67. Gaddis Smith, *Morality, Reason, and Power: American Diplomacy in the Carter Years* (New York: Hill and Wang, 1986), p. 21.

68. U.S. Department of State, *Foreign Relations of the United States,* 1950, vol. 1 (Washington, D.C.: Government Printing Office), 244.

69. Ibid., 2:607.

70. Ibid., 2:615, 616.

71. Piero Gleijeses, *Shattered Hope: The Guatemalan Revolution and the United States, 1944–1954* (Princeton: Princeton University Press, 1991), p. 366.

72. Natalie Hevener Kaufman and David Whiteman, "Opposition to Human Rights Treaties in the United States Senate: The Legacy of the Bricker Amendment," *Human Rights Quarterly* 10 (1988): 309–337.

73. Glendon, *World Made New,* p. 193.

74. Duane Tananbaum, *The Bricker Amendment Controversy* (Ithaca, N.Y.: Cornell University Press, 1988), p. 25.

75. This characterization differs from that of some other experts on U.S. human rights policy. See, for example, Richard A. Falk, "Ideological Pattern in the United States Human Rights Debate: 1945–1978," in *The Dynamics of Human Rights in U.S. Foreign Policy,* ed. Natalie Hevener Kaufman (New Brunswick, N.J.: Transaction Books, 1981), p. 32.

76. Cited in Bruno V. Bitker, "The United States and International Codification of Human Rights: A Case of Split Personality," in Hevener, *Dynamics of Human Rights,* p. 90.

77. Falk, "Ideological Pattern," pp. 32–33.

78. Jerome Levinson and Juan de Onis, *The Alliance That Lost Its Way: A Critical Report on the Alliance for Progress* (Chicago: Quadrangle Books, 1970), pp. 86–88, 338.

79. Beth Simmons, "Why Commit? Explaining State Acceptance of International Human Rights Obligations" (Dept. of Government, Harvard University, manuscript, 2003).

80. Ibid.

3. The Reemergence of Human Rights in U.S. Foreign Policy in the 1970s

1. Jo Marie Griesgraber, "Implementation by the Carter Administration of Human Rights Legislation Affecting Latin America" (Ph.D. diss., Georgetown University, 1983).

2. Donald Fraser, interview by author, Minneapolis, March 18, 1991.

3. Donald Fraser, interview by author, telephone, May 2, 1996.

4. House Subcommittee on International Organizations and Movements, *Human Rights in the World Community: A Call for U.S. Leadership: Report,* 93d Cong., 2d sess., March 27, 1974 (Washington, D.C.: GPO, 1974), pp. 3-8.

5. House Subcommittee on International Organizations, *Human Rights in Uruguay and Paraguay: Hearings,* 94th Cong., 2d sess., June 17, July 27, and August 4, 1976 (Washington, D.C.: GPO, 1976), p. 8.

6. See Lars Schoultz, *Human Rights and United States Policy toward Latin America* (Princeton: Princeton University Press, 1981), pp. 146-148. This situation changed in 1981, when Rep. Michael Barnes took over the chairmanship of the Subcommittee on Inter-American Affairs.

7. David P. Forsythe, *Human Rights and U.S. Foreign Policy: Congress Reconsidered* (Gainesville: University of Florida Press, 1988), pp. 49-50.

8. Piero Gleijeses, *Shattered Hope: The Guatemalan Revolution and the United States, 1944-1954* (Princeton: Princeton University Press, 1991), pp. 362-365.

9. Ibid., p. 369.

10. Tad Szulc, *Latin America* (New York: Athenaeum, 1966), p. 162.

11. Piero Gleijeses, *The Dominican Crisis: The 1965 Constitutionalist Revolution and American Intervention* (Baltimore: Johns Hopkins University Press, 1978), pp. 296-297.

12. William L. Wipfler, interview by author, telephone, April 29, 1996.

13. Abraham Lowenthal, *The Dominican Intervention,* 2d ed. (Baltimore: Johns Hopkins University Press, 1995), pp. xi, ix.

14. Ibid., pp. 161-162.

15. Fraser, interview, May 2, 1996.

16. Philip Agee, *Inside the Company: CIA Diary* (New York: Stonehill, 1975), p. 419.

17. Social movement theory has explored the concept of *issue framing,* the process by which meaning is assigned to events. See, for example, David A. Snow et al., "Frame Alignment Processes, Micromobilization, and Movement Participation," *American Sociological Review* 51 (1986): 464-481.

18. Emilio F. Mignone has also stressed this point as regards the human rights movement in Argentina. *Derechos humanos y sociedad: El caso Argentino* (Buenos Aires:

Centro de Estudios Legales y Sociales, Ediciones del Pensamiento Nacional, 1991), p. 127.

19. Margaret Keck and Kathryn Sikkink, *Activists beyond Borders: Advocacy Networks in International Politics* (Ithaca, N.Y.: Cornell University Press, 1998).

20. Mark Schneider, interview by author, Washington, D.C., March 16, 1992.

21. Rep. Donald Riegle, comments in House Committee of Appropriations, *Foreign Assistance and Related Agencies Appropriations for 1971: Hearings before a Subcommittee of the Committee of Appropriations,* 91st Cong., 2d sess., pt. 2 (Washington, D.C.: GPO, 1971), pp. 887—888.

22. *Congressional Record,* 92d Cong., 1st sess., 1971, 117:29111.

23. *Congressional Record,* September 16, 1971, p. 32157.

24. Edward Kennedy, "The Alianza in Trouble: Beginning Anew in Latin America," *Saturday Review,* October 17, 1970, p. 19.

25. Ibid., p. 20.

26. Lincoln Gordon, letter to the editor, *Commonweal,* August 1970.

27. Archdiocese of Sao Paulo, *Torture in Brazil* (New York: Vintage Books, 1986), p. 79.

28. Brady Tyson, interview by author, telephone, April 22, 1996.

29. William L. Wipfler, "The Price of 'Progress' in Brazil," *Christianity and Crisis,* March 16, 1970; Brady Tyson, "Brazil Twists Thumbscrews," *Washington Post,* April 5, 1970; Ralph de la Cava, "Torture in Brazil," *Commonweal,* April 24, 1970; Philip C. Schmitter, "The Persecution of Political and Social Scientists in Brazil," *PS: Political Science and Politics* (spring 1970); and Tyson, interview.

30. Gordon, letter to the editor.

31. Wipfler, interview.

32. Ibid.

33. On Cardinal Arns see Lawrence Weschler, *A Miracle, a Universe: Settling Accounts with Torturers* (New York: Pantheon Books, 1990), pp. 10, 12—15, 21—30.

34. Senate Subcommittee on Western Hemisphere Affairs, *U.S. Politics and Programs in Brazil: Hearings,* 92d Cong., 1st sess., May 4, 1971 (Washington, D.C.: GPO, 1971), p. 290.

35. Ibid., pp. 290—291, 295.

36. House, *The Status of Human Rights in Selected Countries and the United States Response: Report Prepared for the Subcommittee on International Organization of the Committee on International Relations of the United States House of Representatives by the Library of Congress,* 95th Cong., 1st sess., July 25, 1977 (Washington, D.C.: GPO, 1977), p. 2.

37. A. J. Langguth, *Hidden Terrors* (New York: Pantheon Books, 1978), pp. 241—243.

38. Ibid., p. 244.

39. Agee, *Inside the Company,* p. 337.

40. Ibid., p. 456.

41. Langguth, *Hidden Terrors,* pp. 286—287.

42. William Korey, *The Promises We Keep: Human Rights, the Helsinki Process, and American Foreign Policy* (New York: St. Martin's, 1993), pp. 53—54.

43. Forsythe, *Human Rights,* pp. 74–77.

44. Fraser, interview, May 2, 1996.

45. John Salzberg, interview by author, Washington, D.C., April 5, 1991.

46. Fraser, interview.

47. Salzberg, interview.

48. House Subcommittee on International Organizations and Movements, *International Protection of Human Rights: The Work of International Organizations and the Role of U.S. Foreign Policy: Hearings,* 93d Cong., 1st sess. (Washington, D.C.: GPO, 1974).

49. Ibid., pp. 9–12.

50. Ibid., pp. 27–29.

51. Salzberg, interview.

52. House Subcommittees on Inter-American Affairs and International Organizations and Movements, *Human Rights in Chile: Hearings,* 93d Cong., 2d sess., December 7, 1973; May 7, 23; June 11, 12, 18, 1974, pp. 122–135.

53. Joseph Eldridge, interview by author, Washington, D.C., March 18, 1992.

54. House Subcommittees, *Human Rights in Chile,* pp. 19, 23, 27.

55. House Subcommittee, *International Protection,* p. 217. For a sense of the conversation with witnesses, see the discussion of October 3, 1973, pp. 202–217.

56. House Subcommittee, *Human Rights in the World Community.*

57. Ibid., p. 1.

58. Fraser, interview.

59. Foreign Assistance Act of 1961, sec. 502B, 22 U.S.C. 2304 1988, in International Human Rights Law Group, *U.S. Legislation Relating Human Rights to U.S. Foreign Policy,* 4th ed. (Buffalo: W. S. Hein, 1991), p. 20.

60. House Subcommittee on International Organizations and Movements, "Recommendations," in *Human Rights in the World Community: A Call for U.S. Leadership: Report,* pp. 3–8.

61. Korey, *Promises,* p. xvii.

62. Forsythe, *Human Rights,* pp. 49–50.

63. See William P. Avery and David P. Forsythe, "Human Rights, National Security, and the U.S. Senate: Who Votes for What, and Why," *International Studies Quarterly* 23, 2 (June 1979): 312; Forsythe, *Human Rights,* p. 37.

64. Forsythe, *Human Rights,* pp. 49–50.

65. Salzberg, interview.

66. Ibid., pp. 196–197.

67. House Subcommittee on International Organizations, *Human Rights in Uruguay and Paraguay: Hearings,* 94th Cong., 2d sess., July 27, 1976 (Washington, D.C.: GPO, 1976). The evidence was submitted by Edy Kaufman, Latin American Research Department, Amnesty International, London.

68. Ibid., August 4, 1976.

69. Lawrence Pezzullo, interview by author, Baltimore, August 29, 1991.

70. Ibid.

71. "Consejeros de estado reaccionan contra Congresales de los EE.UU.," *El Dia,* September 29, 1976, p. 1.

72. *Latin America* 10, 41 (October 22, 1976); and *Latin American Political Report* 11, 18 (March 13, 1977).

73. Joshua Muravchik, *The Uncertain Crusade: Jimmy Carter and the Dilemmas of Human Rights Policy* (Lanham, Md.: Hamilton, 1986), p. 1; and Zbigniew Brzezinski, *Power and Principle: Memoirs of the National Security Adviser, 1977–1981* (New York: Farrar, Straus, and Giroux, 1983), p. 49.

74. This is the argument made by Muravchik, *Uncertain Crusade,* pp. 2–5. It is supported by a careful reading of the Carter campaign speeches in House Committee on House Administration, *Jimmy Carter,* vol. 1 of *The Presidential Campaign 1976* (Washington, D.C.: GPO, 1978–79).

75. Daniel P. Moynihan, "The Politics of Human Rights," *Commentary* 64, 2 (August 1977): 22, cited in Muravchik, *Uncertain Crusade,* p. 4.

76. Brzezinski, *Power and Principle,* p. 49.

77. Elizabeth Drew, "Reporter at Large: Human Rights," *New Yorker* July 18, 1977, p. 37, cited in Muravchik, *Uncertain Crusade,* p. 9.

78. Muravchik, *Uncertain Crusade,* p. 7.

79. Fraser, interview, May 2, 1996.

80. One to B'nai B'rith on September 9, 1976, and one at Notre Dame University, October 10, 1976. House Committee on House Administration, *Jimmy Carter,* pp. 710–714, 993–998.

81. Ibid., p. 713.

82. Senate Committee of Foreign Relations, *Vance Nomination: Hearings,* 95th Cong., 1st sess., January 11, 1977 (Washington, D.C.: GPO, 1977), p. 48.

83. House Committee on House Administration, *Jimmy Carter,* pp. 77, 111, 221, 245, 831, 911, 917, 919, 975, 994, 1001.

84. Ibid., pp. 710, 712, 955.

85. Jimmy Carter, *Keeping Faith: Memoirs of a President* (New York: Bantam Books, 1982), p. 144.

86. Ibid., p. 145.

87. Weschler, *A Miracle,* p. 153.

88. Ibid., p. 159.

89. Ibid., pp. 170–171, 174.

4. Introduction to the Effectiveness of Human Rights Policies

1. Excellent studies of the implementation of human rights policies during specific administrations or toward specific regions or countries already exist. For the Carter administration, see Lars Schoultz, *Human Rights and United States Policy toward Latin America* (Princeton: Princeton University Press, 1981); Jo Marie Griesgraber, "Implementation by the Carter Administration of Human Rights Legislation Affecting Latin

America" (Ph.D. diss., Georgetown University, 1983); for the Reagan administration, see Thomas Carothers, *In the Name of Democracy: U.S. Policy toward Latin America* (Berkeley: University of California Press, 1991). With regard to Central America, see Cynthia Arnson, *Cross-roads: Congress, the Reagan Administration, and Central America* (New York: Pantheon Books, 1989); William Leogrande, *Our Own Backyard: The United States in Central America, 1977–1992* (Chapel Hill: University of North Carolina Press, 1998). On the role of Congress from 1973 to 1984, see David P. Forsythe, *Human Rights and U.S. Foreign Policy: Congress Reconsidered* (Gainesville: University of Florida Press, 1988).

2. Ruth Berins Collier and David Collier, *Shaping the Political Arena: Critical Junctures, the Labor Movement, and Regime Dynamics in Latin America* (Princeton: Princeton University Press, 1991), p. 29–30.

3. Hannah Arendt, *Eichmann in Jerusalem: A Report on the Banality of Evil* (New York: Penguin, 1964), p. 297.

4. Conway Henderson, "Conditions Affecting the Use of Political Repression," *Journal of Conflict Resolution* 35, 1 (1991): 120–143; Christian Davenport, ed., *Paths to State Repression: Human Rights Violations and Contentious Politics* (Lanham, Md.: Rowman and Littlefield, 1996); Steven Poe and C. Neal Tate, "Human Rights and Repression to Personal Integrity in the Late 1980s: A Global Analysis," *American Political Science Review* 88 (1994): 853–872; Steven Poe, C. Neal Tate, and Linda Camp Keith, "Repression of the Human Right to Personal Integrity Revisited: A Global Cross-national Study Covering the Years 1976–1993," *International Studies Quarterly* 43 (1999): 291–315.

5. Helen Fein, *Genocide: A Sociological Perspective* (London: Sage, 1993); Jack L. Snyder, *From Voting to Violence: Democratization and Nationalist Conflict* (New York: W. W. Norton, 2000).

6. Poe and Tate, "Human Rights and Repression"; Poe, Tate, and Keith "Repression."

7. Neil J. Mitchell and James M. McCormick, "Economic and Political Explanations of Human Rights Violations," *World Politics* 40, 4 (1988): 476–499; Poe and Tate, "Human Rights and Repression"; Poe, Tate, and Keith, "Repression."

8. Heinisch, "Basic Human Rights."

9. Poe and Tate, "Human Rights and Repression."

10. Adam Przeworski and Fernando Limongi, "Modernization: Theories and Facts," *World Politics* 49, 2 (1997): 155–184.

11. William H. Meyer, "Confirming, Infirming, and 'Falsifying' Theories of Human Rights: Reflections on Smith, Bolyard, and Ippolito through the Lens of Lakatos," *Human Rights Quarterly* 21, 1 (1999): 220–228; Meyer, "Human Rights and MNCs: Theory versus Quantitative Analysis," *Human Rights Quarterly* 18, 2 (1996): 368–397.

12. Noam Chomsky and Edward Herman, *The Political Economy of Human Rights: The Washington Connection and Third World Fascism* (Boston: South End, 1979).

13. Jackie Smith, Melissa Bolyard, and Anna Ippolito, "Human Rights and the Global Economy: A Response to Meyer" *Human Rights Quarterly* 21, 1 (1999): 207–220.

14. However, antiglobalization activists are often referring to a very broad range of economic and social and cultural rights that are not considered in the quantitative literature on repression.

15. Leo Kuper, *Genocide: Its Political Use in the Twentieth Century* (New Haven: Yale University Press, 1982); Fein, *Genocide.*

16. David Pion-Berlin and George A. Lopez, "Of Victims and Executioners: Argentine State Terror, 1975–1979," *International Studies Quarterly* 35, 1 (1991): 63–87; Carina Perelli, "The Military's Perception of Threat in the Southern Cone of South America," in *The Military and Democracy: The Future of Civil-Military Relations in South America,* ed. Louis W. Goodman, Johanna S. R. Mendelson, and Juan Rial (Lexington, Mass.: Lexington Press, 1990), pp. 93–105.

17. Stanley Millgram, "Some Conditions of Obedience and Disobedience to Authority," *Human Relations* 18, 1 (1965); Ervin Staub, *The Roots of Evil* (Cambridge: Cambridge University Press, 1989); Janice T. Gibson and Mika Haritos-Fatouros, "The Education of a Torturer," *Psychology Today* 20 (1986): 50–56.

18. Steven Poe, "The Decision to Repress: An Integrative Theoretical Approach to the Research on Human Rights and Repression" (Dept. of Political Science, University of North Texas, manuscript, 1997).

19. Alison Des Forges, *Leave None to Tell the Story: Genocide in Rwanda* (New York: Human Rights Watch, 1999).

20. Poe, "Decision."

21. Thomas Risse, Stephen C. Ropp, and Kathryn Sikkink, eds., *The Power of Human Rights: International Norms and Domestic Change* (Cambridge: Cambridge University Press, 1999).

22. Karl E. Weick, *Sensemaking in Organizations* (Thousand Oaks, Calif.: Sage, 1995).

23. Perelli, "Military's Perception," pp. 100–101; see also Alfred Stepan, "The New Professionalism of Internal Warfare and Military Role Expansion," in *Authoritarian Brazil,* ed. Alfred Stepan (New Haven: Yale University Press, 1973), pp. 47–65.

24. Perelli, "Military's Perception," p. 101.

25. See Michael Klare and Cynthia Arnson, "Exporting Repression: U.S. Support for Authoritarianism in Latin America," in *Capitalism and the State in U.S.–Latin American Relations,* ed. Richard Fagen (Stanford: Stanford University Press, 1979), pp. 138–168.

26. Steven C. Poe and Rangsima Sirigangsi, "Human Rights and U.S. Economic Aid during the Reagan Years," *Social Science Quarterly* 75 (September 1994): 494; David Cigranelli and Thomas Pasquarello, "Human Rights Practices and Distribution of U.S. Foreign Aid to Latin American Countries," *American Journal of Political Science* 29 (1985): 561.

27. There are two key exceptions to this general statement. In El Salvador, government violence against a peasant uprising in 1932, referred to as *la matanza* (the slaughter), left over 30,000 peasants dead. John Booth and Thomas W. Walker, *Understanding Central America* (Boulder, Colo.: Westview, 1989), p. 33. In Colombia, a period of civil war and rural violence called *la violencia* left over 126,000 dead between 1947 and 1950. Medofilo Medina, "Violence and Economic Development: 1945–1950 and 1985–1988," in *Violence in Colombia: The Contemporary Crisis in Historical Perspective,* ed.

Charles Bergquist, Ricardo Penaranda, and Gonzalo Sanchez (Wilmington: Scholarly Resources, 1992), pp. x, 15, 157.

28. Arzobispado de Guatemala, Oficina de Derechos Humanos, *Guatemala Nunca Más,* 3:119.

29. Steven C. Poe et al., "The Calculus of Human Suffering: Threats to Regimes' Rule and the Abuse of Human Rights" (Dept. of Political Science, University of North Texas, manuscript), p. 3.

30. Stanley has critiqued the rational actor model of repression for these faults. See William Stanley, *The Protection-Racket State: Elite Politics, Military Extortion, and Civil War in El Salvador* (Philadelphia: Temple University Press, 1996).

31. Stanley, *Protection-Racket State,* p. 4.

32. See, for example, Brian Loveman, *For la Patria: Politics and the Armed Forces in Latin America* (Wilmington: Scholarly Resources, 1999).

33. Philip Tetlock and Aaron Belkin, "Counterfactual Thought Experiments in World Politics: Logical, Methodological and Psychological Perspectives," in *Counterfactual Thought Experiments in World Politics* (Princeton: Princeton University Press, 1996), pp. 5—6.

34. National Commission on Disappeared Persons, *Nunca más: Informe de la Comisión Nacional sobre la Desaparición de Personas* (Buenos Aires: Editorial Universitaria de Buenos Aires, 1984); Truth and National Reconciliation Commission, *Informe Rettig: Informe de la Comisión de Verdad y Reconciliación* (Santiago: Talleres de La Nación, 1991); Commission for Historical Clarification, *Guatemala: Memory of Silence: Report of the Commission for Historical Clarification,* 2d ed. (Guatemala: CEH, 1998); United Nations, *From Madness to Hope: The Twelve-Year War in El Salvador,* Report for the Commission for the Truth for El Salvador, UN doc. s/25500, April 1, 1993.

35. Some of these documents are available on the website of the National Security Archive at http://nsarchive.chadwyck.com; others can be consulted at the National Security Archives at the George Washington University Library.

36. Archdiocese of Sao Paulo, *Torture in Brazil: A Shocking Report on the Pervasive Use of Torture by Brazilian Military Governments, 1964–1979* (New York: Vintage Books, 1986), pp. 79—80.

37. Ibid., pp. 235—238, 192—203.

38. Martin Weinstein, *Uruguay: Democracy at the Crossroads* (Boulder, Colo.: Westview, 1988), p. 53; Servicio Paz y Justicia Uruguay, *Uruguay nunca más: Informe sobre la violación a los derechos humanos (1972–1985)* (Montevideo: Altamira, 1989), pp. 417—430.

39. Servicio Paz y Justicia Uruguay, *Uruguay nunca más,* pp. 417—430.

40. Truth and National Reconciliation Commission, *Informe Rettig.*

41. Jose, Luis Simon G., *La dictadura de Stroessner y los derechos humanos,* Serie Nunca Más, vol. 1 (Asunción: Comite de Iglesias, 1990), p. 128.

42. Rene Antonio Mayorga, "Democracy Dignified and an End to Impunity: Bolivia's Military Dictatorship on Trial," in *Transitional Justice and the Rule of Law in New Democracies,* ed. A. James McAdams (Notre Dame, Ind.: University of Notre Dame Press, 1997), p. 63.

43. Federico Auilo, *Nunca más para Bolivia* (Cochabamba: IESE-UMSS, 1993), cited in Mayorga, "Democracy Dignified," p. 88.

44. United Nations, Working Group on Enforced or Involuntary Disappearances, *Report of the United Nations Working Group on Enforced or Involuntary Disappearances*, UN doc. E/CN.4/1435, January 1991.

45. Barbara Crossette, "U.N. Reports Latin America Suffers Fewer 'Disappearances,'" *New York Times*, May 25, 1997, p. 4.

46. Amnesty International, *Annual Report 1997* (London: International Secretariat, 1997).

47. David Scott Palmer, "Collectively Defending Democracy in the Western Hemisphere," in *Beyond Sovereignty: Collectively Defending Democracy in the Americas*, ed. by Tom Farer (Baltimore: Johns Hopkins University Press, 1996), pp. 257—258.

48. From 1950 to 1980, 3,360 Guatemalan military officers were trained by the United States as a part of the International Education and Training Program (IMET). United States Department of Defense, *Foreign Military Sales, Foreign Military Construction Sales and Military Assistance Facts as of September 30, 1984* (Washington, D.C., 1984). A great number of police officers were also trained in the Office for Public Safety Program, under the aegis of AID.

49. Weick, *Sensemaking in Organizations*, p. 8.

5. U.S. Human Rights Policy during the Nixon and Ford Administrations

1. Lawrence Pezzullo, interview by author, Baltimore, Md., August 29, 1991.

2. Lars Schoultz, *Human Rights and United States Policy toward Latin America* (Princeton: Princeton University Press, 1981), pp. 198—201.

3. Darren Hawkins, "The International and Domestic Struggle for Legitimacy in Authoritarian Chile" (Ph.D. diss., University of Wisconsin, 1996), pp. 63—64.

4. Manuel Antonio Garretón, *The Chilean Political Process* (London: Unwin Hyman, 1989), p. 3.

5. Truth and National Reconciliation Commission, *Informe Rettig: Informe de la Comisión de Verdad y Reconciliación* (Santiago: Talleres de La Nación, 1991), pp. 47, 43, 45.

6. See Pamela Lowden, *Moral Opposition to Authoritarian Rule in Chile, 1973—1990* (London: Macmillan, 1996); Patricio Orellana and Elizabeth Quay Hutchinson, *El movimiento de derechos humanos en Chile, 1973—1990* (Santiago: Centro de Estudios Políticos Latinoamericanos Simón Bolivar, 1991).

7. Roberto Garreton, interview by author, Santiago, November 1993; José Zalaquett, interview by author, Santiago, November 1993.

8. "Kissinger Said to Rebuke U.S. Ambassador to Chile," *New York Times*, September 27, 1974.

9. "Kissinger is Challenged on Chile Policy," *New York Times*, September 28, 1974.

10. House Subcommittee on International Organizations and Movements and on

Inter-American Affairs, "Human Rights in Chile," 93d Cong., 2d sess., pt. 2, November 19, 1974, app. 3 and 4, pp. 21–27.

11. Jim Lobe, "Kissinger OK'ed Argentina 'Dirty War' Document," *Imágen Latinoamericana,* January 1, 2002.

12. Senate, *Staff Report of the Select Committee of Intelligence Activities: Covert Action in Chile, 1963–1973,* 92d Cong., 1st sess. (Washington, D.C.: GPO, 1976); Peter Kornbluh, ed., *The Pinochet File: A Declassified Dossier of Atrocity and Accountability* (New York: New Press, 2003); see also Paul Sigmund, *The United States and Democracy in Chile* (Baltimore: Johns Hopkins University Press, 1993).

13. Kornbluh, *Pinochet File.*

14. Ian Guest, *Behind the Disappearances: Argentina's Dirty War against Human Rights and the United Nations* (Philadelphia: University of Pennsylvania Press, 1990), p. 19.

15. *Nunca Más: The Report of the Argentine National Commission on the Disappeared* (New York: Farrar, Straus and Giroux, 1986), pp. 209–234.

16. This conclusion is from Martin Anderson and John Dinges, "Kissinger Had a Hand in the Dirty War," *Insight on the News,* January 7, 2002, pp. 3, 6. Anderson and Dinges are critical of U.S. policy toward Argentina in other respects.

17. Ibid., p. 25.

18. U.S. Embassy (Buenos Aires), "Conversation with Undersecretary of the Presidency," telegram, document no. 1976Buenos03460, May 25, 1976.

19. U.S. Embassy (Buenos Aires), "Demarche to Foreign Minister on Human Rights," document no. 1976Buenos03462, May 28, 1976.

20. Walter Isaacson, *Kissinger: A Biography* (New York: Simon and Schuster, 1992).

21. Henry Kissinger, *Years of Renewal* (New York: Simon and Schuster, 1999), p. 753.

22. U.S. Department of State, "Sixth General Assembly of the Organization of American States," Santiago, June 1976 (Washington, Department of State).

23. U.S. Embassy (Buenos Aires), "Other Aspects of September 17 Conversation with Foreign Minister," document no. 1976Buenos06130, September 20, 1976.

24. U.S. Embassy (Buenos Aires), "Abduction of Refugees in Argentina," document no. 1976Buenos03985, June 16, 1976.

25. U.S. Embassy (Buenos Aires), "Ambassador Discusses U.S.-Argentine Relations with President Videla," document no. 1976Buenos06276, September 24, 1976.

26. U.S. Department of State, "U.S. Argentine Relations," memorandum of conversation, October 6, 1976, p. 2.

27. Ibid., p. 3.

28. U.S. Department of State, "Secretary's Meeting with Argentine Foreign Minister Guzzetti," memorandum of conversation, October 7, 1976, New York.

29. U.S. Embassy (Buenos Aires), "Other Aspects of September 17 Conversation with Foreign Minister," document no. 1976Buenos06130, September 20, 1976.

30. U.S. Department of State, "Meeting with Guzzetti."

31. State Department to U.S. embassy in Buenos Aires, "Guzzetti's visit to the U.S," cable, October 20, 1976.

32. U.S. Department of State, "U.S.–Argentine Relations," document no. 3281, February 2, 1977.

33. From "The Papers of Robert C. Hill at Dartmouth College," Digital Library, http://olympia.dartmouth.edu/library/ead/html/ml38.html#seriesd1.

6. The Carter Administration and Human Rights Policy toward Latin America

1. Patricia Derian, interview by author, telephone, July 23, 2002.

2. Ibid.

3. Ibid.; F. Allan "Tex" Harris, interview by author, Washington, D.C., March 5, 2003.

4. Ibid.

5. Harris, interview.

6. See, for example, Michael Stohl, David Carleton, and Steven E. Johnson, "Human Rights and U.S. Foreign Assistance from Nixon to Carter," *Journal of Peace Research* 21, 2 (1984); Carlos Escudé, "Argentina: The Costs of Contradiction," in *Exporting Democracy: The United States and Latin America: Case Studies,* ed. Abraham F. Lowenthal (Baltimore: Johns Hopkins University Press, 1991); Jeane Kirkpatrick, "Dictatorships and Double Standards," *Commentary* 68, 5 (November 1979).

7. *Washington Post,* May 22, 1981.

8. For example, Lars Schoultz published his excellent study of the Carter administration human rights policy in 1981: *Human Rights and United States Policy toward Latin America* (Princeton: Princeton University Press, 1981).

9. This chapter does not attempt to fully describe or document the adoption or implementation of Carter human rights policy toward Latin America, which has already been done elsewhere. See Schoultz, *Human Rights;* Jo Marie Griesgraber, "Implementation by the Carter Administration of Human Rights Legislation Affecting Latin America" (Ph.D. diss., Georgetown University, 1983).

10. These phases come from Griesgraber, "Implementation," pp. 55–70, though she speaks of three phases in congressional-executive relations over human rights. I use the phases to characterize the administration human rights policy more generally and compress her first two phases into a single "active" phase.

11. See House Subcommittee on International Organizations, *Human Rights and the Phenomenon of Disappearances: Hearings before the Subcommittee on International Organizations of the Committee on Foreign Affairs,* 96th Cong., 1st sess., October 18, 1979 (Washington, D.C.: U.S. GPO, 1980), p. 331.

12. Griesgraber, "Implementation," pp. 69, 262.

13. Derian, interview.

14. On two-level games see: *Double-Edged Diplomacy: International Bargaining and Domestic Politics,* ed. Peter B. Evans, Harold K. Jacobson, and Robert D. Putnam (Berkeley: University of California Press, 1993); and Lisa L. Martin and Kathryn Sikkink, "U.S. Policy and Human Rights in Argentina and Guatemala, 1973–1980," in *Double-*

Edged Diplomacy: International Bargaining and Domestic Politics, ed. Peter B. Evans, Harold K. Jacobson and Robert D. Putnam (Berkeley, University of California Press, 1993).

15. House Committee on House Administration, *The Presidential Campaign 1976,* vol. 3, *The Debates* (Washington, D.C.: GPO, 1979), pp. 97−98, 112.

16. Paul Sigmund, *The United States and Democracy in Chile* (Baltimore: Johns Hopkins University Press, 1993), p. 108.

17. Truth and National Reconciliation Commission, *Informe Rettig: Informe de la Comisión Nacional de Verdad y Reconciliación* (Santiago, Chile: Talleres de la Nación, 1991), annex 2, table 8, p. 886.

18. "Reagan's Latin Policy," *Washington Post,* April 15, 1981, pp. A25−A26.

19. Darren G. Hawkins, *International Human Rights and Authoritarian Rule in Chile* (Lincoln: University of Nebraska Press, 2002), pp. 93−100.

20. Roberta Cohen, "Human Rights Diplomacy: The Carter Administration and the Southern Cone," *Human Rights Quarterly,* 4, 2 (1982): 228.

21. House Committee on International Relations, Study Mission to Colombia, Ecuador, Peru, Chile, Argentina, and Brazil, *United States in the Western Hemisphere: Report of a Study Mission to Colombia, Ecuador, Peru, Chile, Argentina, and Brazil, August 9 to 23, 1977 to the Committee on International Relations,* 95th Cong., 2d sess., February 21, 1978 (Washington, D.C.: GPO, 1978), p. 19.

22. Americas Watch, *Chile: Human Rights and the Plebiscite* (New York: Americas Watch, July 1988), pp. 23−27.

23. Darren Hawkins, "The International and Domestic Struggle for Legitimacy in Authoritarian Chile" (Ph.D. diss., University of Wisconsin, 1996), pp. 83−84.

24. Cited in Hawkins, "International," p. 62.

25. *Latin American Regional Report: Southern Cone* 11, 18 (May 13, 1977); and *Latin America* 10, 41 (October 22, 1976).

26. Schoultz, *Human Rights,* p. 295.

27. *Latin American Political Report* 12, 6 (February 10, 1978).

28. Derian, interview.

29. *Latin American Political Report* 11, 5 (February 4, 1977); 11, 23 (June 17, 1977).

30. *Latin American Political Report* 11, 23 (June 17, 1977); Lawrence Pezzullo, interview by author, Baltimore, August 29, 1991.

31. *Latin America* 11, 6 (February 11, 1977); Schoultz, *Human Rights,* p. 350.

32. Alejandro Vegh Villegas, interview by author, Washington, D.C., August 29, 1991.

33. *Latin American Political Report* 12, 6 (February 10, 1978).

34. Lawrence Weschler, *A Miracle, a Universe: Settling Accounts with Torturers* (New York: Pantheon Books, 1990); Charles Gillespie, "From Suspended Animation to Animated Suspension: Political Parties and the Reconstruction of Democracy in Uruguay" (unpublished), p. 32. Other authors minimize the role of external pressures in the process of redemocratization, stressing instead the pressure of internal political groups, especially political parties, and the democratic tradition within the Uruguayan armed forces. See, for example, German Rama, *La democracia en Uruguay* (Buenos

Aires: Grupo Editor Latinoamericano, 1987), p. 200. Rama argues in passing that diplomatic pressures from the United States and Europe were not significant in the process of redemocratization, but he does not present any material to back up this argument.

35. Gillespie, "From Suspended Animation," p. 32.

36. *Latin American Political Report* 11, 37–38 (September 23 and 30, 1977).

37. U.S. Department of State, *Human Rights and U.S. Policy: Argentina, Haiti, Indonesia, Iran, Peru, and the Philippines, December 31, 1976,* U.S. House Committee on International Relations (Washington, D.C.: GPO, 1977), p. 6.

38. Patrick J. Flood, "U.S. Human Rights Initiatives concerning Argentina," in *The Diplomacy of Human Rights,* ed. David D. Newsom (New York: University Press of America, 1986), p. 129.

39. Derian, interview; testimony given by Patricia Derian to the National Criminal Appeals Court in Buenos Aires during the trials of Junta members, as cited in *Diario del Juicio,* no. 18 (June 1985): 3; Iain Guest, *Behind the Disappearances: Argentina's Dirty War against Human Rights and the United Nations* (Philadelphia: University of Pennsylvania Press, 1990), pp. 161–163. Later it was confirmed that the Navy Mechanical School was one of the most notorious secret torture and detention centers. Argentine National Commission on the Disappeared, *Nunca Más: The Report of the Argentine National Commission on the Disappeared* (New York: Farrar, Straus and Giroux, 1986), pp. 79–84.

40. Derian, interview.

41. "Security Links Cited Assistance is Reduced Argentina, Uruguay and Ethiopia, Vance Says," *New York Times,* February 25, 1977, p. A1; "Argentina and Uruguay Reject U.S. Assistance Linked to Human Rights," *New York Times,* March 2, 1977, p. A10.

42. In addition, in two years, the U.S. embassy made more than twelve hundred representations to the Argentine government on cases of human rights abuse. Americas Watch, *With Friends like These: The Americas Watch Report on Human Rights and U.S. Policy in Latin America* (New York: Pantheon Books, 1985), pp. 99–100.

43. "House Bars U.S. Aid to Seven Countries in Rebuff to Carter," *New York Times,* June 24, 1977, p. A1.

44. Congressional Research Service, *Human Rights and U.S. Foreign Assistance: Experiences and Issues in Policy Implementation (1977–1978),* report prepared for U.S. Senate Committee on Foreign Relations (Washington: GPO, 1979), p. 106.

45. Harris, interview.

46. Schoultz, *Human Rights,* pp. 331–332.

47. House Subcommittee on International Organizations, *Human Rights and the Phenomenon of Disappearances,* p. 331.

48. Walter Mondale, interview by author, Minneapolis, June 20, 1989; Robert Pastor, interview by author, Wianno, Mass., June 28, 1990.

49. Organization of American States, Inter-American Commission on Human Rights, *Report on the Situation of Human Rights in Argentina* (Washington, D.C.: OAS General Secretariat, 1980), p. 134.

50. House Committee on International Relations, *United States in the Western Hemisphere*, p. 29.

51. José A. Martinez de Hoz, interview, Buenos Aires, August 6, 1990. Martinez de Hoz was minister of economics during the Videla administration.

52. Jacobo Timerman, *Prisoner without a Name, Cell without a Number* (New York: Random House, 1981).

53. See Asamblea Permanente por los Derechos Humanos, *Las cifras de la guerra sucia*, pp. 26–31.

54. This interpretation differs from that of Carlos Escudé, who claims that U.S. human rights policy was unsuccessful in Argentina. Escudé does not discuss the granting of blocked Eximbank credits in exchange for the Argentine invitation of the IACHR, which is key to the argument here, and underestimates the importance of diplomatic pressures on the Argentine military government. Escudé, "Argentina."

55. See for example, *Washington Post*, May 22, 1981; anonymous interview by author, Buenos Aires, July 31, 1990; Arnoldo Listre, interview by author, Buenos Aires, July 20, 1990; Ricardo Yofre, interview by author, Buenos Aires, August 1, 1990.

56. David Rock, *Argentina, 1516–1987: From Spanish Colonization to Alfonsin* (Berkeley: University of California Press, 1985), pp. 370–371; Timerman, *Prisoner without a Name*, p. 163.

57. Anonymous interview, Buenos Aires, July 31, 1990.

58. Martinez de Hoz, interview.

59. *Carta Política,* no. 59 (October 1978).

60. Tom J. Farer, interview by author, Washington, D.C., May 13, 1990; Arnoldo Listre, interview by author, Buenos Aires, July 20, 1990. Farer was a member of the IACHR and conducted on-site observations in Argentina in September 1979. Listre was U.S. ambassador to Argentina at the time.

61. Listre, interview.

62. Guest, *Behind the Disappearances,* p. xiii.

63. Patrick Bell, Paul Kobrak, and Herbert F. Spirer, *State Violence in Guatemala, 1960–1996: A Quantitative Reflection* (Washington, D.C.: American Association for the Advancement of Science, 1999), p. 39.

64. Peiro Gleijeses, "Guatemala: Crisis and Response," in *Report on Guatemala: Findings of the Study Group on United States-Guatemalan Relations* (Boulder, Colo.: Westview, 1985), pp. 51–74.

65. Although the ban on U.S. military assistance to Guatemala was in effect until 1983, commercial military sales and economic assistance continued throughout the 1978–83 period. General Accounting Office, *Military Sales: The United States Continuing Munitions Supply Relationship with Guatemala,* report to the chairman, House Subcommittee on Western Hemisphere Affairs (Washington, D.C.: GPO, 1986).

66. Amnesty International, *Guatemala: The Human Rights Record* (London: Amnesty International, 1987), p. 7. See also Amnesty International, *Guatemala: A Government Program of Political Murder* (London: Amnesty International, 1981); Americas Watch, *Human Rights in Guatemala: No Neutrals Allowed* (New York: Americas Watch, 1982).

67. Amnesty International, *Annual Report* (London: Amnesty International Publications, 1980), pp. 139–144.

68. Amnesty International, *Guatemala: A Government Program of Murder,* p. 7.

69. See: Americas Watch, *Persecuting Human Rights Monitors: The CERJ in Guatemala* (New York: Americas Watch, 1989), p. 43.

70. Rachel Garst, interview by author, Guatemala City, May 3, 1998.

71. "Navy Ship's Visit to Guatemala Reveals U.S. Split on Policy," *Washington Post,* April 21, 1980, p. A14.

72. Gabriel Aguilera Peralta, "El proceso de militarización en el Estado Guatemalteco," *Polémica* 1 (September–October 1981), p. 35.

73. Thomas Buergenthal et al., *Protecting Human Rights in the Americas: Selected Problems* (Strasbourg: N. P. Engel, 1986), pp. 157–162.

74. Testimony by Lars Schoultz, "Human Rights in Guatemala," in House Subcommittees on Human Rights and International Organizations, *Human Rights in Guatemala: Hearings,* 97th Cong., 1st sess., July 30, 1981 (Washington: Government Printing Office), p. 98.

75. General Accounting Office, *Military Sales,* pp. 4, 21.

76. "Guatemala: A Sharp Twist to the Right," *Latin American Regional Report: Mexico and Central America,* November 28, 1980, RM-80-10, p. 3.

77. Enrique Baloyra, *El Salvador in Transition* (Chapel Hill: University of North Carolina Press, 1982), pp. 1–3; William Stanley, *The Protection Racket State: Elite Politics, Military Extortion, and Civil War in El Salvador* (Philadelphia: Temple University Press, 1996), pp. 67–68.

78. Baloyra, *El Salvador in Transition,* pp. 3, 54.

79. Stanley, *Protection Racket State,* p. 109.

80. Derian, interview.

81. Stanley, *Protection Racket State,* pp. 109; 111–112.

82. Ibid., p. 112.

83. Baloyra, *El Salvador in Transition,* p. 66.

84. Stanley, *Protection Racket State,* p. 115.

85. Baloyra, *El Salvador in Transition,* table 4.1, p. 190. Reliable human rights data for the 1970s is hard to find because the best source, the UN Truth Commission, was not asked to consider the 1970s, and the major domestic human rights organizations were just being formed.

86. Cited in Bruno V. Bitker, "The United States and International Codification of Human Rights: A Case of Split Personality," in *The Dynamics of Human Rights in U.S. Foreign Policy* ed. Natalie Kaufman Hevener (New Brunswick, N.J.: Transaction Books, 1981), p. 91.

87. Harris, interview.

88. Raymond Bonner, *Weakness and Deceit: U.S. Policy and El Salvador* (New York: Times Books, 1984), p. 41.

89. U.S. Department of State, "Private Visit of Congressman Drinan," National Security Archives, January 23, 1980.

90. Harris, interview.

7. The Reagan Administration and Human Rights Policy toward Latin America

1. Richard Shifter, interview by author, Washington, D.C., August 12, 1992.

2. Elliot Abrams, interview by author, Washington, D.C., May 17, 2000.

3. Patricia Derian, interview by author, telephone, July 23, 2002.

4. Jean Kirkpatrick, "Dictatorships and Double Standards," *Commentary* 68, 5 (November, 1979): 34−35.

5. Tom Carothers, *In the Name of Democracy: U.S. Policy toward Latin America in the Reagan Years* (Berkeley: University of California Press, 1991), p. 107.

6. Rachel Neild and Katherine Roberts Hite, "Human Rights and United States Policy toward Chile" (paper presented at the Latin American Studies Association Conference, Washington, D.C., April 6, 1991).

7. Martha Lynn Doggett, "Washington's Not-So-Quiet Diplomacy," *NACLA Report on the Americas* 12, 2 (March−April 1988): 29−40.

8. Carothers, *In the Name of Democracy*, p. 142.

9. William M. Leogrande, *Our Own Backyard: The United States in Central America, 1977−1992* (Chapel Hill: University of North Carolina Press, 1998), p. 291.

10. "Excerpts from Haig's Remarks at First News Conference as Secretary of State," *New York Times,* January 29, 1981, p. A10.

11. Tamar Jacoby, "The Reagan Turnaround on Human Rights," *Foreign Affairs* 64 (summer 1986): 1068.

12. UN Commission on the Truth, *From Madness to Hope: The Twelve-Year War in El Salvador* (New York: United Nations Security Council, 1993); United Nations, *The United Nations and El Salvador, 1990−1995,* United Nations Blue Book Series, vol. 5 (New York: Department of Public Information, 1995), pp. 363, 318−322.

13. George Lister, "The Human Rights Cause: How We Can Help" (speech at Lynchburg College, Lynchburg, Va., February 20, 1990). Lister was a senior policy advisor in the Bureau of Human Rights, Department of State.

14. Richard Shifter, "Enhancing Our Human Rights Effort" (address at the annual dinner of the Journal of International Law and Politics, New York University Law School, New York, April 16, 1992).

15. Richard Shifter, "Building Firm Foundations: The Institutionalization of United States Human Rights Policy in the Reagan Years," *Harvard Human Rights Record* 2 (spring 1989): 8.

16. Iain Guest, *Behind the Disappearances: Argentina's Dirty War against Human Rights and the United Nations* (Philadelphia: University of Pennsylvania Press, 1990), p. 269.

17. As cited in ibid., p. 277.

18. Carothers, *In the Name of Democracy*, p. 106.

19. Leogrande, *Our Own Backyard*, p. 293.

20. Carothers, *In the Name of Democracy*, p. 107.

21. Leogrande, *Our Own Backyard*, p. 291.

22. Robert Kagen, interview by author, Washington, D.C., May 18, 2000.

23. *New York Times,* Nov. 5, 1981.

24. Elliot Abrams, interview by author, Washington, D.C., May 19, 2000.

25. Jacoby, "Reagan Turnaround," p. 1071.

26. Thomas Enders, "El Salvador: The Search for Peace," *U.S. Department of State Bulletin,* September 1981, p. 73, as cited in Leogrande, *Our Own Backyard,* p. 127.

27. Abrams, interview, May 17, 2000.

28. The period from 1978 to 1983 is part of the much longer period of civil war (1962–96). Susanne Jonas has used the phrase "total war" to distinguish this particularly harsh period of repression from other cycles of repression during the Cold War years in *The Battle for Guatemala: Rebels, Death Squads, and U.S. Power* (Boulder, Colo.: Westview, 1991), p. 148.

29. Ibid.

30. *Wall Street Journal,* December 23, 1980, as quoted in Leogrande, *Our Own Backyard,* p. 57.

31. Arzobispado de Guatemala, Oficina de Derechos Humanos, *Guatemala: Nunca Más,* 3:106.

32. As cited in Leogrande, *Our Own Backyard,* p. 57.

33. Paul Albert, "The Undermining of Legal Standards for HR Violations in US Foreign Policy: The Case of Improvement in Guatemala," in *Columbia Human Rights Law Review* 14 (1982–83): 251.

34. Jonas, *Battle for Guatemala,* p. 200.

35. U.S. Department of State, "President Lucas Comments on the Current Situation," National Security Archives, January 1980.

36. Arzobispado de Guatemala, *Guatemala: Nunca Más,* 3:96, 106.

37. Ibid., p. 119.

38. UN Commission for Historical Clarification, *Guatemala: Memory of Silence: Report of the Commission for Historical Clarification,* http://hrdata.aaas.org/ceh/report/english/toc.html.

39. U.S. Department of State, "Initiative on Guatemala," cable to embassy from Latin America Bureau, National Security Archive, April 4, 1981.

40. U.S. Department of State, "Guatemalan Foreign Minister Calls upon Deputy Secretary Clark," memorandum of conversation, National Security Archives, May 8, 1981, pp. 1–3.

41. U.S. Department of State, "Initiative on Guatemala."

42. U.S. Department of State, "Guatemala and El Salvador," briefing memorandum to the secretary of state from Vernon Walters, May 27, 1981.

43. U.S. Department of State, "Violence and Human Rights Report for January 1981," National Security Archives, July 21, 1981.

44. House Subcommittee on Human Rights and International Organizations, *Human Rights in Guatemala: Hearing before the Subcommittees on Human Rights and on International Organizations and Inter-American Affairs of the Committee on Foreign Affairs,* 97th Cong., 1st sess., July 30, 1981 (Washington, D.C.: GPO, 1981), pp. 5–6.

45. Ibid., p. 6.

46. Ibid. pp. 21–23.

47. U.S. Department of State, "Guatemala: What Next," memorandum to Mr. Einaudi from Robert Jacobs, National Security Archives, October 5, 1981.

48. U.S. Embassy (Guatemala City), "GOG Officials Implicated in Arrests of Priests and Nuns and Murder of Sexton," document no. Guatem 00285. National Security Archives, January 13, 1982.

49. Abrams, interview, May 19, 2000.

50. F. Allan "Tex" Harris, Interview by author, March 5, 2003, Washington, D.C.

51. Central Intelligence Agency, "Guatemalan Army Conducts Sweep through Ixil Region," National Security Archives, February 1982.

52. "Lucas Criticizes Carter at Rally after Bombing," *Foreign Broadcast Information Service (Latin America)*, September 8, 1980, p. 9.

53. Arzobispado de Guatemala, *Guatemala: Nunca Más*, 3:107.

54. Jim Handy, *Gift of the Devil: A History of Guatemala* (Toronto: South End, 1984), p. 182.

55. *Latin American Weekly Report*, August 27, 1982.

56. Jonas, *Battle for Guatemala*, p. 148.

57. Americas Watch, *With Friends like These: The Americas Watch Report on Human Rights and U.S. Policy in Latin America* (New York: Pantheon Books, 1985), pp. 17–18.

58. "Remarks in San Pedro Sula, Honduras, Following a Meeting with President José Efrain Ríos Montt of Guatemala," December 4, 1982, and "Question and Answer Session with Reporters on the President's Trip to Latin America," December 4, 1982," in *Public Papers of the Presidents of the United States: Ronald Reagan, 1982*, bk. 2 (Washington, D.C.: GPO, 1983), pp. 1562–1563.

59. This figure is based on a list of named victims. Most estimates of the total number of deaths in this period suggest that the total number of victims is much higher.

60. Arzobispado de Guatemala, *Guatemala: Nunca Más*, 2:3.

61. Ibid.

62. Guest, *Behind the Disappearances*, p. 375.

63. Jorge Arturo Roche Tobar, interview by author, Minneapolis, March 15, 1990; Ana Carolina Reyes Riveiro, interview by author, Minneapolis, March 15, 1990. Tobar worked in the Human Rights Attorney's Office; Riveiro was an assistant to the Congressional Commission on Human Rights.

64. UN Commission on the Truth, *From Madness to Hope;* United Nations, *The United Nations and El Salvador, 1990–1995*, United Nations Blue Book Series, vol. 4 (New York: Department of Public Information, 1995), pp. 301–304.

65. United Nations, Commission on the Truth, *From Madness to Hope*, p. 311.

66. Leogrande, *Our Own Backyard*, p. 163.

67. Ibid., pp. 163–164.

68. Ibid., pp. 164, 170.

69. Carothers, *In the Name of Democracy*, p. 34.

70. Ibid., p. 35.

71. Leogrande, *Our Own Backyard*, p. 179.

72. Ibid.

73. Ibid., p. 230.

74. Cynthia J. Arnson, "Window on the Past: A Declassified History of Death Squads in El Salvador," in *Death Squads in Global Perspective: Murder with Deniability,* ed. Arthur Brenner and Bruce B. Campbell (New York: St. Martin's, 2000).

75. William Stanley, *The Protection-Racket State: Elite Politics, Military Extortion, and Civil War in El Salvador* (Philadelphia: Temple University Press, 1996).

76. Cited in Paul Heath Hoeffel and Peter Kornbluh, "The War at Home: Chile's Legacy in the United States," *NACLA Report on the Americas* 17, 5 (September–October 1983): 37.

77. Neild and Roberts Hite, "Human Rights"; Paul Sigmund, *The United States and Democracy in Chile* (Baltimore: Johns Hopkins University Press, 1993), p. 147.

78. Sigmund, *United States,* p. 149.

79. Abrams, interview, May 19, 2000.

80. Sigmund, *United States,* p. 157.

81. Neild and Roberts Hite, "Human Rights," p. 17.

82. Ibid., p. 19; Peter Winn, "U.S. Electoral Aid in Chile: Reflections on a Success Story" (paper presented at U.S. Electoral Assistance and Democratic Development: Chile, Nicaragua, and Panama, Washington Office on Latin America, Washington, D.C., January 19, 1990).

83. Carothers, *In the Name of Democracy,* pp. 241, 243, 244.

84. William Korey, interview by author, telephone, February 20, 1996.

8. Institutionalizing Human Rights Policy toward Latin America during the George H. W. Bush and Clinton Years

1. Commission for Historical Clarification, *Guatemala: Memory of Silence: Report of the Commission for Historical Clarification,* 2d ed. (Guatemala: CEH, 1998).

2. *Presidential Papers of the Presidents of the United States: William J. Clinton, 1999,* bk. 1 (Washington, D.C.: GPO, 2000).

3. Mark Peceny, *Democracy at the Point of Bayonets* (University Park: Pennsylvania State University Press, 1999), p. 158.

4. Human Rights Watch, "Human Rights in Post-Invasion Panama: Justice Delayed Is Justice Denied," April 7, 1991. www.hrw.org/reports/1991/panama.

5. Ibid.

6. Amnesty International, *Annual Report* (London: Amnesty International, 1986, 1988, 1989, 1990). There is no mention of Panama in the annual reports for 1985 and 1987.

7. Anthony P. Maingot, "Haiti: Sovereign Consent versus State-Centric Sovereignty," in *Beyond Sovereignty: Collectively Defending Democracy in the Americas,* ed. Tom Farer (Baltimore: Johns Hopkins University Press, 1996), pp. 189–212.

8. Fernando R. Tesón, "Changing Perceptions of Domestic Jurisdiction and Intervention," in Farer, *Beyond Sovereignty,* pp. 29–51.

9. Peceny, *Democracy,* p. 152.

10. *Public Papers of the Presidents of the United States: George Bush* (Washington, D.C.: GPO, 1989–92).

11. Richard Shifter, interview by author, Washington, D.C., August 12, 1992.

12. Dean Welty, interview by author, Washington, D.C., August 10, 1992.

13. Richard Shifter, "Enhancing Our Human Rights Effort" (address at the annual dinner of the *Journal of International Law and Politics,* New York University Law School, New York, April 16, 1992).

14. "As Diplomacy Loses Luster, Stars Flee State Department," *New York Times,* September 5, 2000, p. A12.

15. See for example, Human Rights Watch and the Lawyers Committee for Human Rights, *Critique: Review of the Department of State's Country Reports on Human Rights Practices for 1987* (New York: self-published, 1988).

16. Natalie Hevener Kaufman and David Whitehead, "Opposition to Human Rights Treaties in the U.S. Senate: The Legacy of the Bricker Amendment," *Human Rights Quarterly* 10 (1988): 330–331.

17. Senate Committee on Foreign Relations, *International Covenant on Civil and Political Rights, Report* (Washington, D.C.: GPO, 1992).

18. Hevener Kaufman and Whitehead, "Opposition to Human Rights Treaties," p. 334.

19. Senate Committee on Foreign Relations, *International Covenant,* pp. 16, 19–20.

20. Shifter, interview.

21. Heraldo Muñoz, "The Right to Democracy in the Americas," *Journal of Interamerican Studies and World Affairs* 40, 1 (spring 1998).

22. "New Rules Seen for U.S. Friendship: As Democracy Comes to Moscow, Foreign Nations Will Need More Credentials Than Just Anti-Communism," *Los Angeles Times,* September 8, 1991.

23. William Leogrande, *Our Own Backyard: The United States in Central America, 1977–1992* (Chapel Hill: University of North Carolina Press, 1998); Cynthia Arnson, *Crossroads: Congress, the President, and Central America, 1976–1993,* 2d ed. (University Park: Pennsylvania State University Press, 1993); William Stanley, *The Protection Racket State: Elite Politics, Military Extortion, and Civil War in El Salvador* (Philadelphia: Temple University Press, 1996); Robert Kagan, *A Twilight Struggle: American Power and Nicaragua, 1988–1990* (New York: Free Press, 1996).

24. Arnson, *Crossroads,* p. 232; Kagan, *Twilight Struggle,* p. 634.

25. Leogrande, *Our Own Backyard,* p. 569–570.

26. Arnson, *Crossroads.*

27. Jorge Mario García Laguardia, *Política y Constitución en Guatemala: la Constitución de 1985* (Guatemala City: Procurador de los Derechos Humanos, 1996), pp. 73–86, 167–168.

28. Americas Watch, *Persecuting Human Rights Monitors: The CERJ in Guatemala* (New York: Americas Watch, 1989), p. 54.

29. "Guatemala Rejects U.S. Aid," *Washington Post,* February 9, 1991, p. A12.

30. This summary is drawn from testimony in Senate Select Committee on Intelligence, *Hearing on Guatemala,* 104th Cong., 1st sess., April 5, 1995 (Washington, D.C.: GPO, 1995).

31. Ibid.; Jennifer Harbury, *Searching for Everardo: A Story of Love, War, and the CIA in Guatemala* (New York: Warner Books, 2000).

32. "White House Press Release Establishing Parameters of the Guatemala Investigation for the President's Intelligence Oversight Board and Noting the PIOB's Preliminary Findings in the Guatemala Matter," July 26, 1995, in House Permanent Select Committee on Intelligence, *Report on the Guatemala Review,* 105th Cong., 1st sess. (Washington, D.C.: GPO, 1997), app. E, pp. 14–15.

33. In a 2001 talk on the successes and failures of the Clinton human rights policy, Bennett Freeman, a top official from the Human Rights Bureau mentioned briefly only one Latin American country, Colombia, and then only in passing. Bennett Freeman, address at University of Minnesota, March 13, 2001. When the assistant secretary of state, John Shattuck, presented the 1996 country reports on human rights practices on January 30, 1997, he mentioned four Latin American countries—Haiti, Guatemala, Nicaragua, and El Salvador—as examples of progress in the human rights area, and singled out only one case, Cuba, as an example of ongoing repression. During the lengthy and animated question period, reporters raised questions about only two Latin American countries: Cuba and Mexico.

34. Bill Clinton, speech at the Institute of World Affairs, University of Wisconsin, Madison, October 1, 1992.

35. Ibid.

36. The two networks included a network of European Guatemalan solidarity organizations and a network of fifteen larger European NGOs working on Central America called the Copenhagen Initiative for Central America (CIFCA). Eric Oostrijk, interview by author, The Hague, November 4, 1993.

37. "White House Statement on Situation in Guatemala," Office of the Federal Register, National Archives; and Records Administration (May 25, 1993); and United States, President, *Public Papers of the Presidents: William J. Clinton, 1993,* bk. 1 (Washington, D.C.: GPO, 1993), p. 739.

38. Rachel McCleary, *Dictating Democracy: Guatemala and the End of Violent Revolution* (Gainesville: University Press of Florida, 1999).

39. On this point see Susan Burgerman, *Moral Victories: How Activists Provoke Multilateral Action* (Ithaca, N.Y.: Cornell University Press, 2001).

40. McCleary, *Dictating Democracy,* p. 135.

41. UN General Assembly, "The Situation in Central America: Procedures for the Establishment of a Firm and Lasting Peace and Progress in Fashioning a Region of Peace, Freedom, Democracy and Development," annex: *Seventh Report on Human Rights of the United Nations Verification Mission in Guatemala,* September 1997, UN doc. A/52/330 10, pp. 16–17.

42. Guatemala Human Rights Commission (United States), *Guatemala Human Rights Update,* nos. 1–20, January–October 1997.

43. David Sanger, "Economic Engine for Foreign Policy," *New York Times,* December 28, 2000, p. A1.

44. *Public Papers of the Presidents: William J. Clinton.*

45. "It's an Easy Shot to Take," interview with Madeleine Albright, *Newsweek,* July 10, 2000, p. 35.

46. Michael Dobbs, *Madeleine Albright: A Twentieth Century Odyssey* (New York: Henry Holt, 1999).

47. Ibid., p. 351.

48. Ibid., p. 372.

49. Harold Hongju Koh, "Democracy and Human Rights in the United States Foreign Policy? Lessons from the Haitian Crisis," *SMU Law Review* 48, 1 (September–October 1994): 192.

50. Harold Hongju Koh, "A United States Human Rights Policy for the 21st Century," 2001 Richard Chidress Lecture, *St. Louis Law Journal,* forthcoming.

51. Harold Hongju Koh, interview by author, telephone, December 11, 2001.

52. Koh, "United States Human Rights Policy."

53. Koh, interview.

54. Americas Watch, *Political Murder and Reform in Colombia: The Violence Continues* (New York: Human Rights Watch, 1992).

55. Human Rights Watch, *The "Sixth Division": Military-Paramilitary Ties and U.S. Policy in Colombia* (New York: Human Rights Watch, September 2001), p. 82.

56. *Cross Currents* (Washington Office on Latin America), November 1999, p. 3.

57. Human Rights Watch, *"Sixth Division,"* p. 80.

58. George Lopez, "An Anomaly Plagued by Analogies: Colombian Realities Confront U.S. Policy," in *Democracy, Human Rights, and Peace in Colombia: Presentations from a Roundtable* (University of Notre Dame, 1999).

59. Koh, interview.

60. Vicky A. Imerman, "SOA: School of Assassins," *Covert Action,* no. 46 (fall 1993): 15.

61. Kenneth Cooper, "Taking Aim at 'School of Assassins': Measure Would Strip Funds from Ga. Training Facility," *Washington Post,* May 19, 1994.

62. U.S. Department of Defense, "Improper Material in Spanish Language Intelligence Training Manuals," memorandum for the Secretary of Defense, March 10, 1992.

63. Department of Defense, "Fact Sheet concerning Training Manuals Inconsistent with U.S. Policy," n.d.

64. *Washington Post,* September 21, 1996.

65. Russell W. Ramsey and Antonio Raimondo, "Human Rights Instruction at the U.S. School of the Americas," *Human Rights Review,* April–June 2001, p. 97.

66. Carina Perelli, "The Military's Perception of Threat in the Southern Cone of South America," in *The Military and Democracy: The Future of Civil-Military Relations in South America,* ed. Louis W. Goodman, Johanna S. R. Mendelson, and Juan Rial (Lexington, Mass.: Lexington Press, 1990), p. 99.

67. Lisa Haugaard, "Declassified Army and CIA Manuals Used in Latin America: An Analysis of Their Content," Latin American Working Group, http://www.lawg.org/manuals.htm.

68. Ibid.

69. Amnesty International, "Unmatched Power, Unmet Principles: The Human Rights Dimensions of US Training of Foreign Military and Police Forces," http://www.amnestyusa.org/stoptorture/msp.pdf.

70. Ibid.

71. Koh, "United States Human Rights Policy."

72. Welty, interview.

73. Koh, interview; Koh, "United States Human Rights Policy."

74. Marc J. Susser, interview by author, telephone, July 2001.

75. Freeman, address.

76. Koh, "United States Human Rights Policy."

9. Conclusion: The Lessons of Human Rights Policies

1. Christopher Marquis, "Bush Officials Met with Venezuelans Who Ousted Leader," *New York Times,* April 16, 2002, p. A1.

2. Christopher Marquis, "U.S. Cautioned Leader of Plot against Chávez," *New York Times,* April 17, 2002, p. A1.

3. "Venezuela Inquiry Clears U.S. Aides," *New York Times,* June 30, 2002.

4. Lisa Haugaard, "Declassified Army and CIA Manuals Used in Latin America: An Analysis of Their Content," *Latin American Working Group,* http://www.lawg.org/manuals.htm.

5. Carina Perelli, "The Military's Perception of Threat in the Southern Cone of South America," in *The Military and Democracy: The Future of Civil-Military Relations in South America,* ed. Louis W. Goodman, Johanna S. R. Mendelson, and Juan Rial (Lexington, Mass.: Lexington Press, 1990), pp. 101, 99.

6. Thomas Risse, "'Let's Argue!' Communicative Action in World Politics," *International Organization* 54, 1 (winter 2000): 1–39.

7. Karl E. Weick, *Sensemaking in Organizations* (Thousand Oaks, Calif.: Sage, 1995), p. 8.

8. Thayer, p. 254, cited in ibid., p. 10.

9. "Cuba Base Sent Its Interrogators to Iraqi Prison," *New York Times,* May 29, 2004.

10. Jacobo Timerman, interview by Bill Moyers, *Crossroads,* PBS, 1984.

Index